MUTTS

SUNDAY EVENINGS

By Patrick McDonnell

Andrews McMeel
Publishing

Kansas City

Other Books by Patrick McDonnell

Mutts

Cats and Dogs: Mutts II

More Shtuff: Mutts III

Yesh!: Mutts IV

Our Mutts: Five

A Little Look-See: Mutts VI

What Now: Mutts VII

I Want to Be the Kitty: Mutts No. Eight

Dog-Eared: Mutts IX

Who Let the Cat Out?: Mutts X

Mutts Sundays

Mutts Sunday Mornings

Mutts Sunday Afternoons

The Mutts Little Big Book

Mutts is distributed internationally by King Features Syndicate, Inc. For information, write King Features Syndicate, Inc., 888 Seventh Avenue, New York, New York 10019.
Mutts Sunday Evenings copyright © 2005 by Patrick McDonnell. All rights reserved. Printed in the United States of America. No part of this book may be used or reproduced in any manner whatsoever without written permission except in the case of reprints in the context of reviews.
For information, write Andrews McMeel Publishing, an Andrews McMeel Universal company, 4520 Main Street, Kansas City, Missouri 64111.

05 06 07 08 09 BAM 10 9 8 7 6 5 4 3 2 1

ISBN-13: 978-0-7407-5535-4
ISBN-10: 0-7407-5535-8

Library of Congress Control Number: 2005928928

Mutts Sunday Evenings is printed on recycled paper.

Mutts can be found on the Internet at
www.muttscomics.com.

www.andrewsmcmeel.com

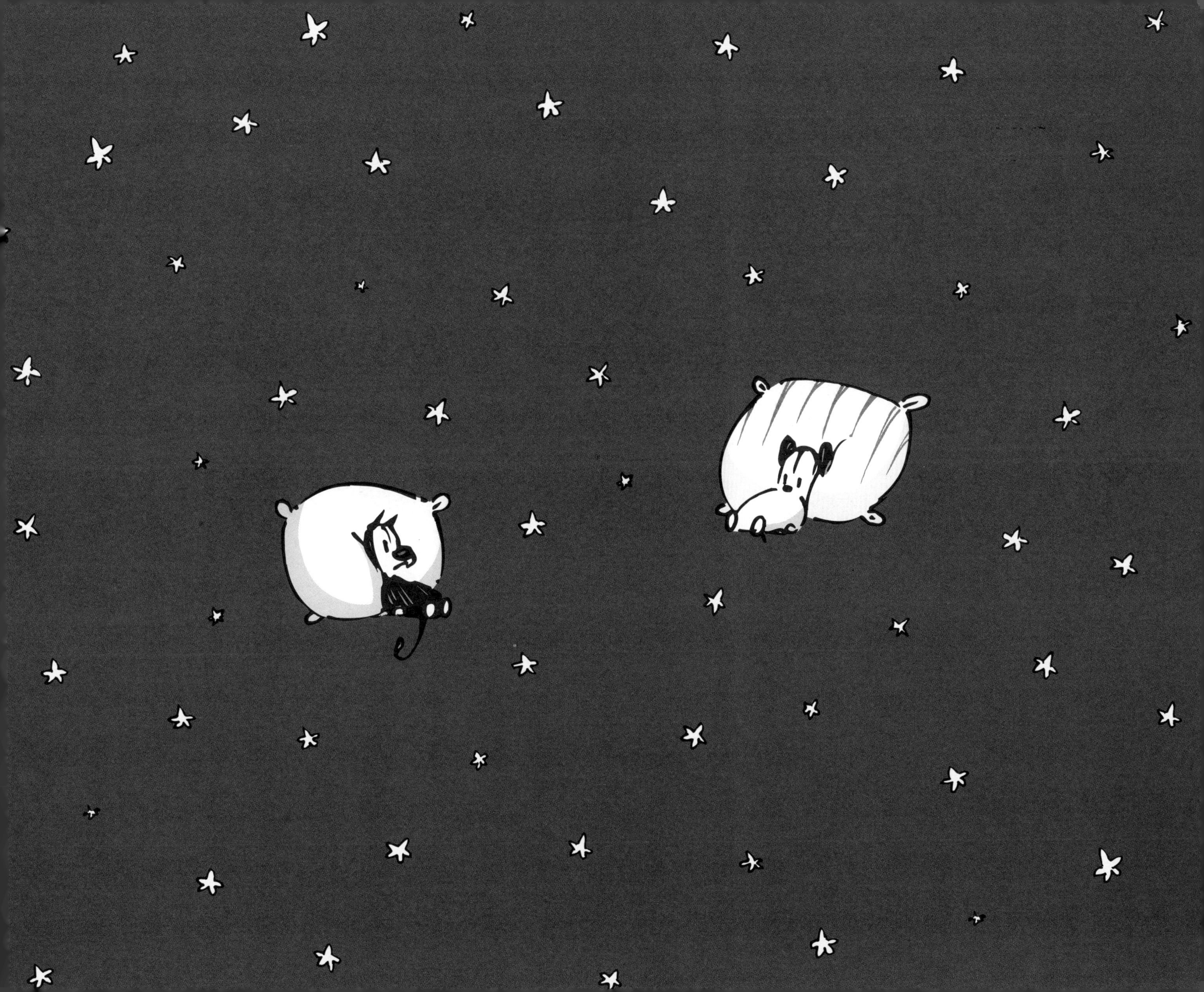

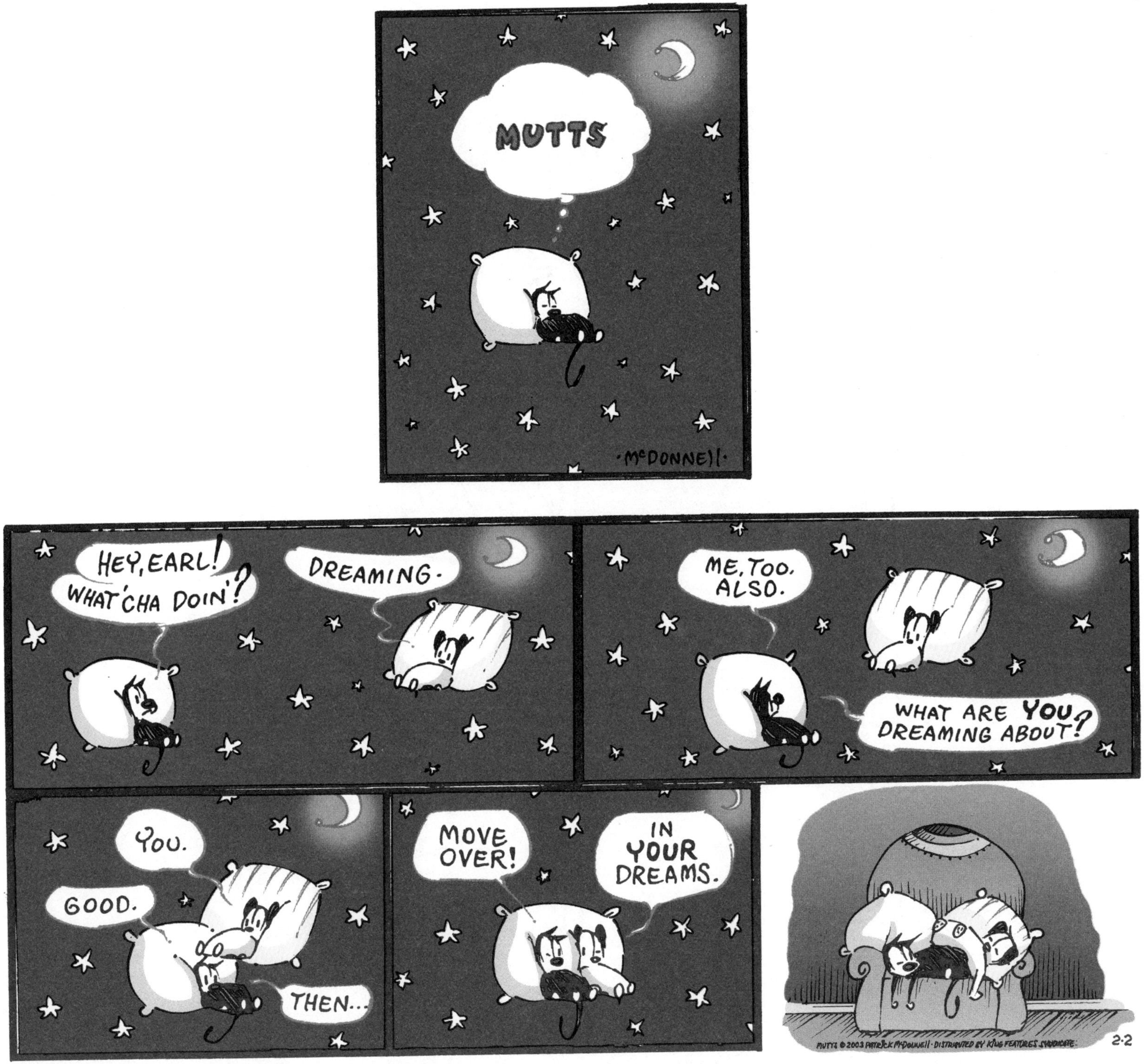
MUTTS
·McDONNELL·
HEY, EARL! WHAT'CHA DOIN'?
DREAMING.
ME, TOO, ALSO.
WHAT ARE YOU DREAMING ABOUT?
YOU.
GOOD.
THEN...
MOVE OVER!
IN YOUR DREAMS.
MUTTS © 2003 PATRICK McDONNELL · DISTRIBUTED BY KING FEATURES SYNDICATE.
2·2

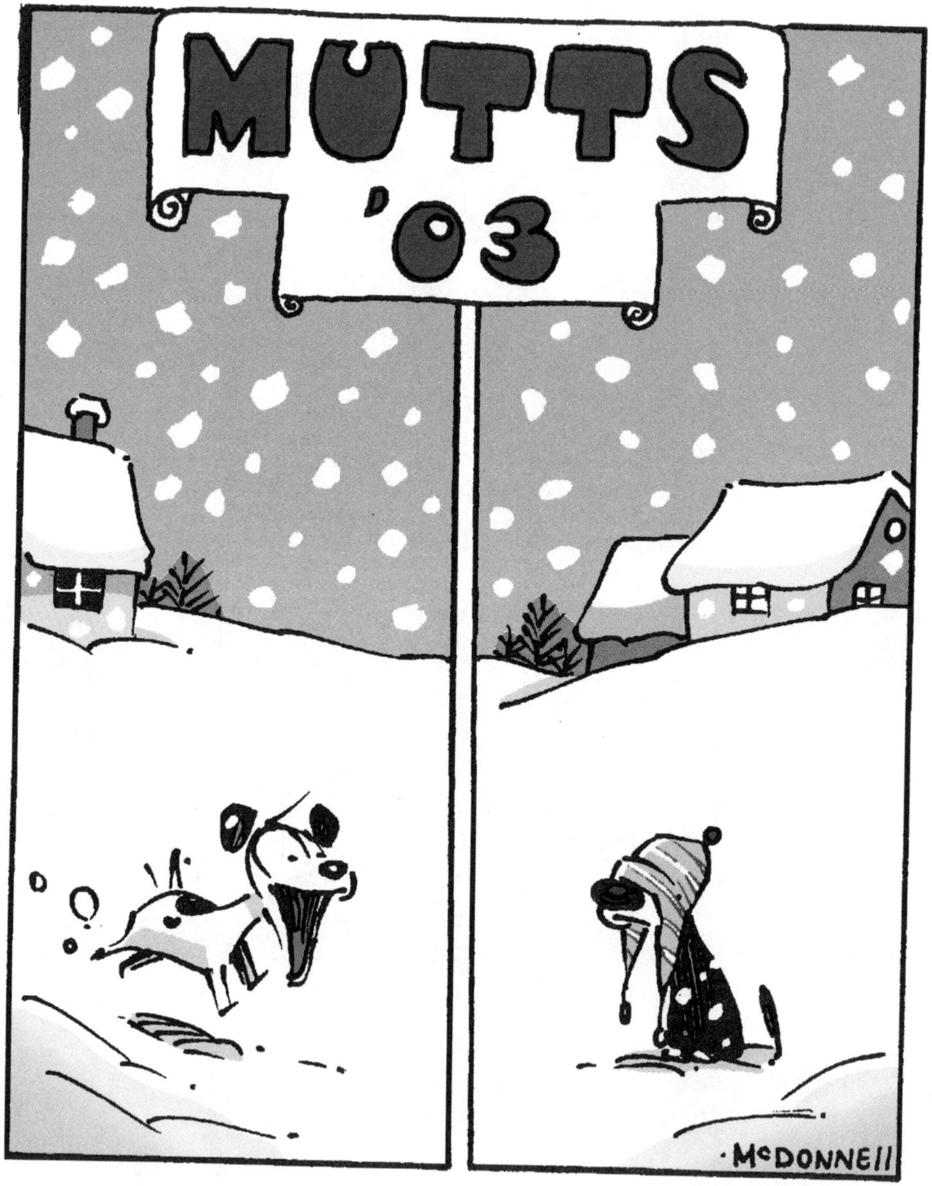
MUTTS
'03
McDONNELL

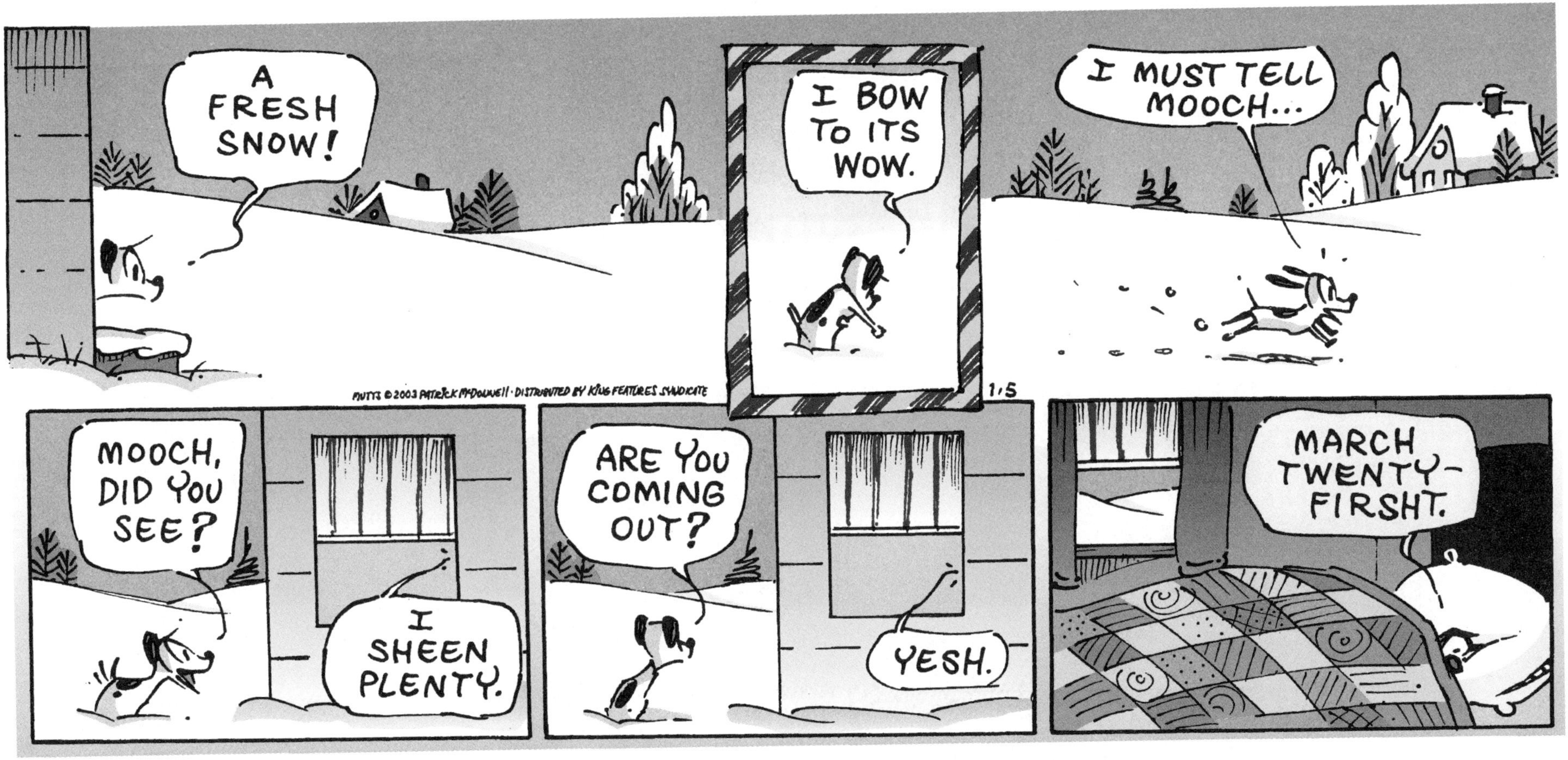
A FRESH SNOW!
I BOW TO ITS WOW.
I MUST TELL MOOCH...
MUTTS © 2003 PATRICK McDONNELL · DISTRIBUTED BY KING FEATURES SYNDICATE
1.5
MOOCH, DID YOU SEE?
I SHEEN PLENTY.
ARE YOU COMING OUT?
YESH.
MARCH TWENTY-FIRSHT.

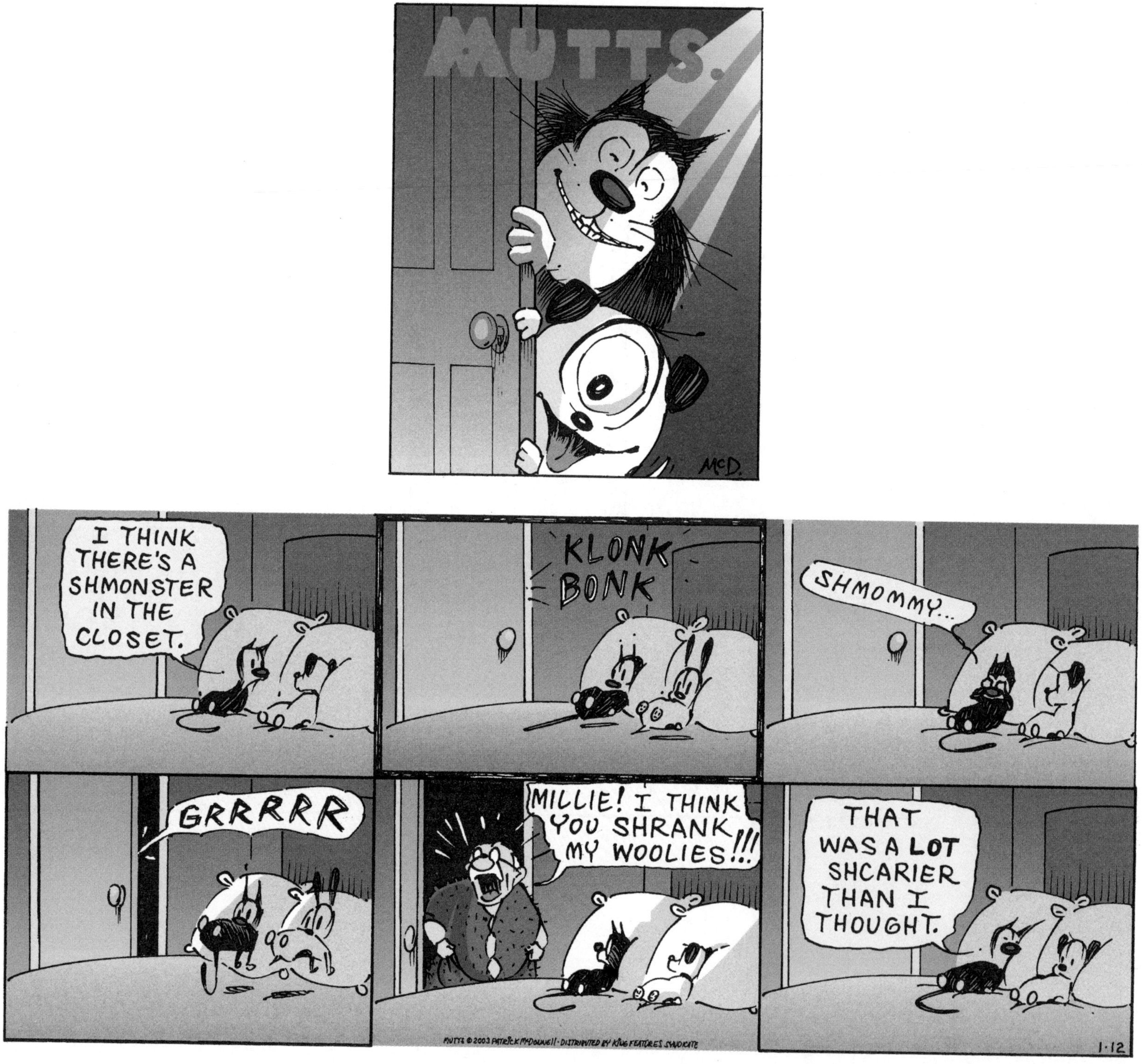
MUTTS.
McD.
I THINK THERE'S A SHMONSTER IN THE CLOSET.
KLONK BONK
SHMOMMY...
GRRRRR
MILLIE! I THINK YOU SHRANK MY WOOLIES!!!
THAT WAS A **LOT** SHCARIER THAN I THOUGHT.
MUTTS © 2003 PATRICK McDONNELL · DISTRIBUTED BY KING FEATURES SYNDICATE
1·12

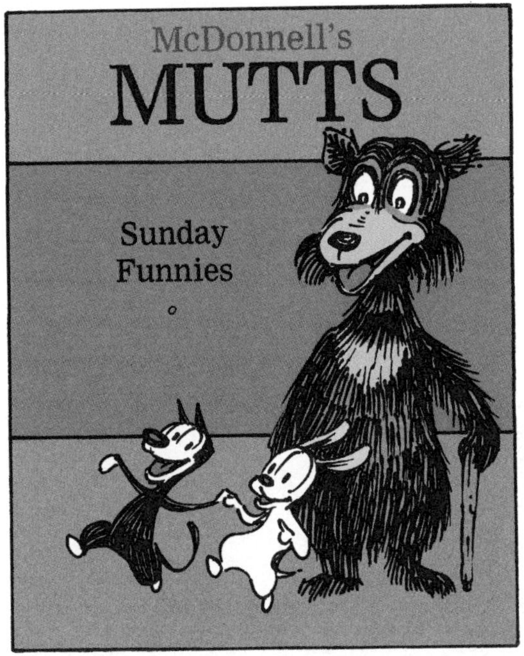
McDonnell's
MUTTS
Sunday Funnies

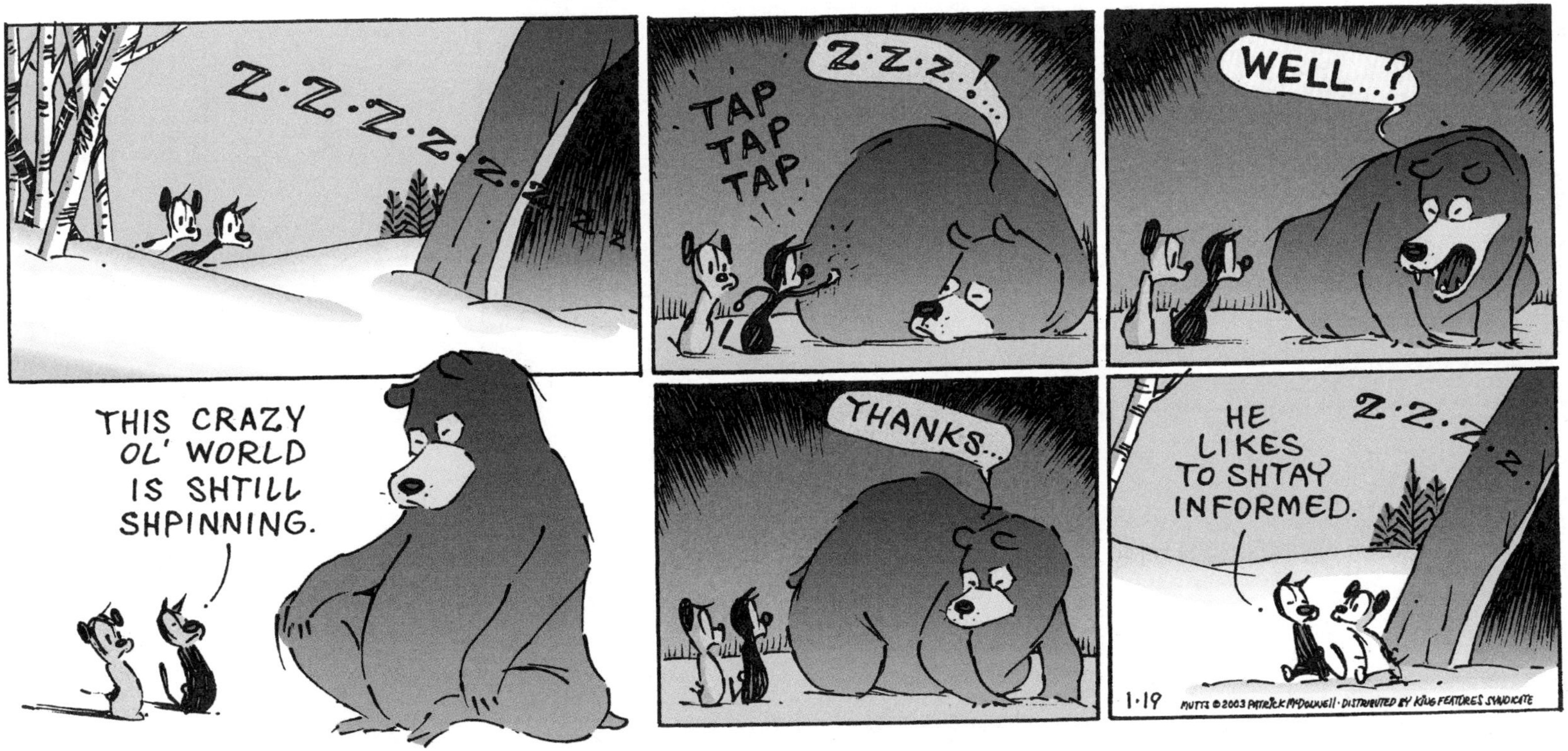
Z·Z·Z·Z·Z·Z·Z·Z
TAP TAP TAP
Z·Z·Z·!...
WELL...?
THIS CRAZY OL' WORLD IS SHTILL SHPINNING.
THANKS...
HE LIKES TO SHTAY INFORMED.
Z·Z·Z·Z
1·19
MUTTS © 2003 PATRICK McDONNELL · DISTRIBUTED BY KING FEATURES SYNDICATE

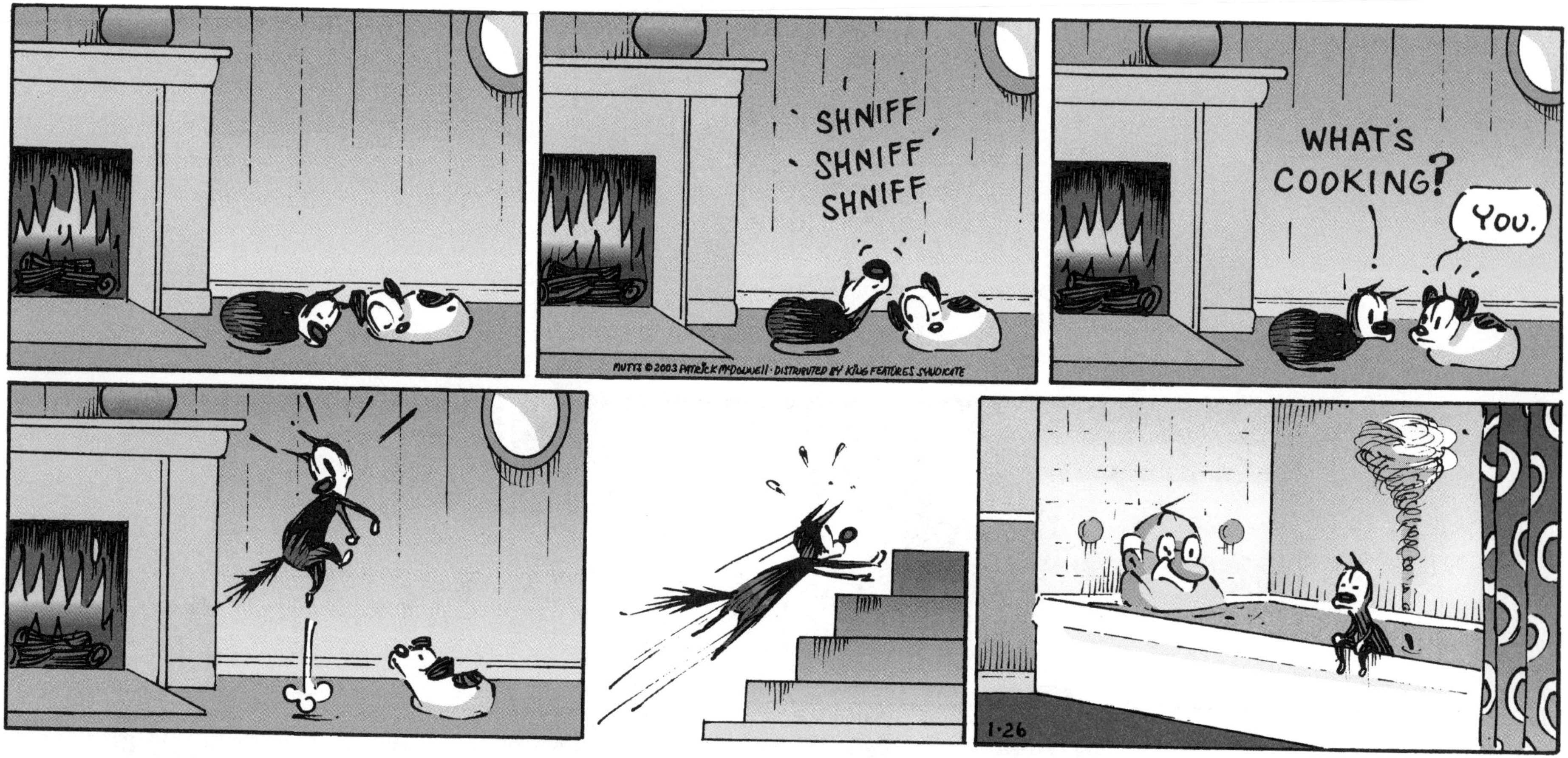
SHNIFF
SHNIFF
SHNIFF
MUTTS © 2003 PATRICK McDONNELL · DISTRIBUTED BY KING FEATURES SYNDICATE
WHAT'S COOKING?
YOU.
1·26

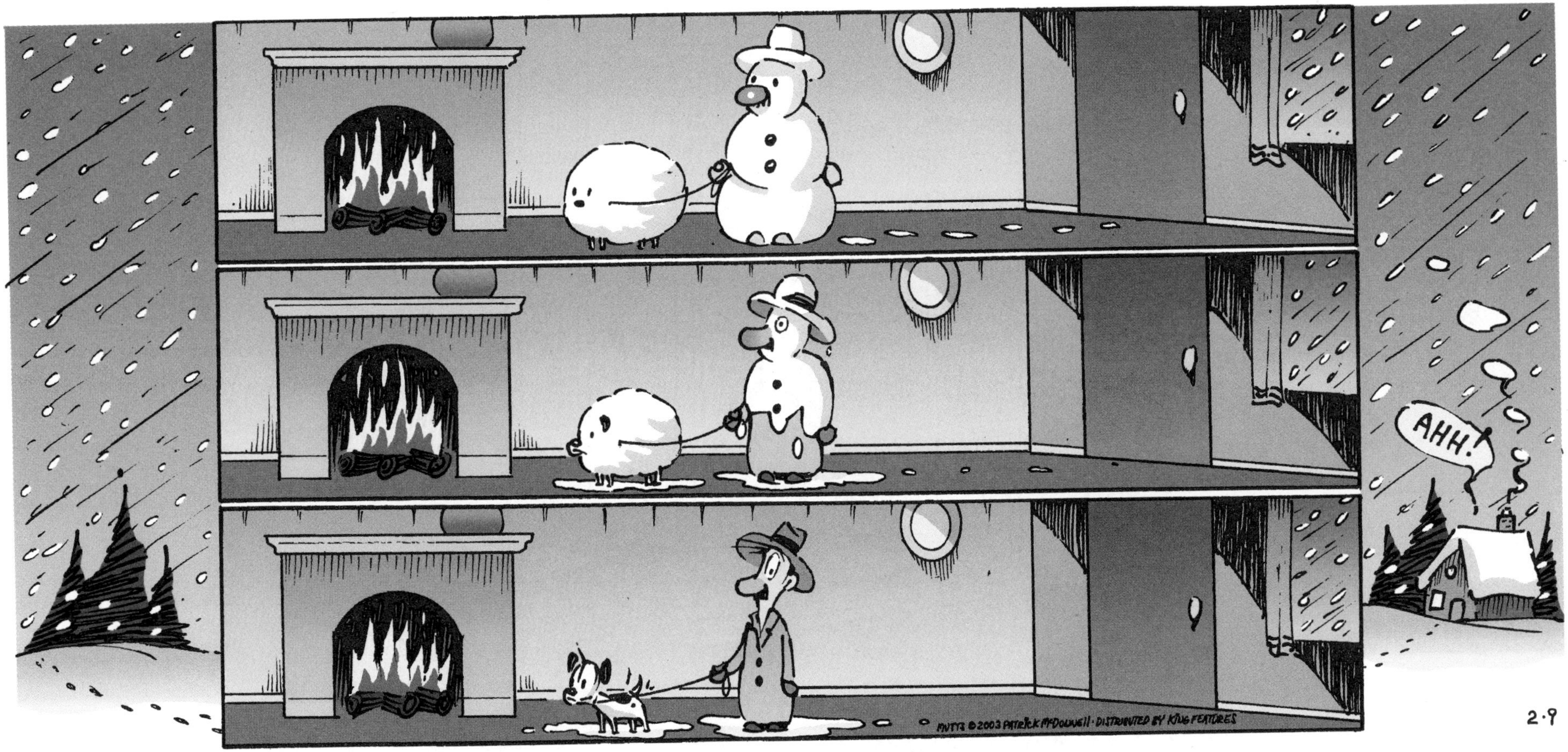
AHH!
MUTTS © 2003 PATRICK McDONNELL · DISTRIBUTED BY KING FEATURES
2·9

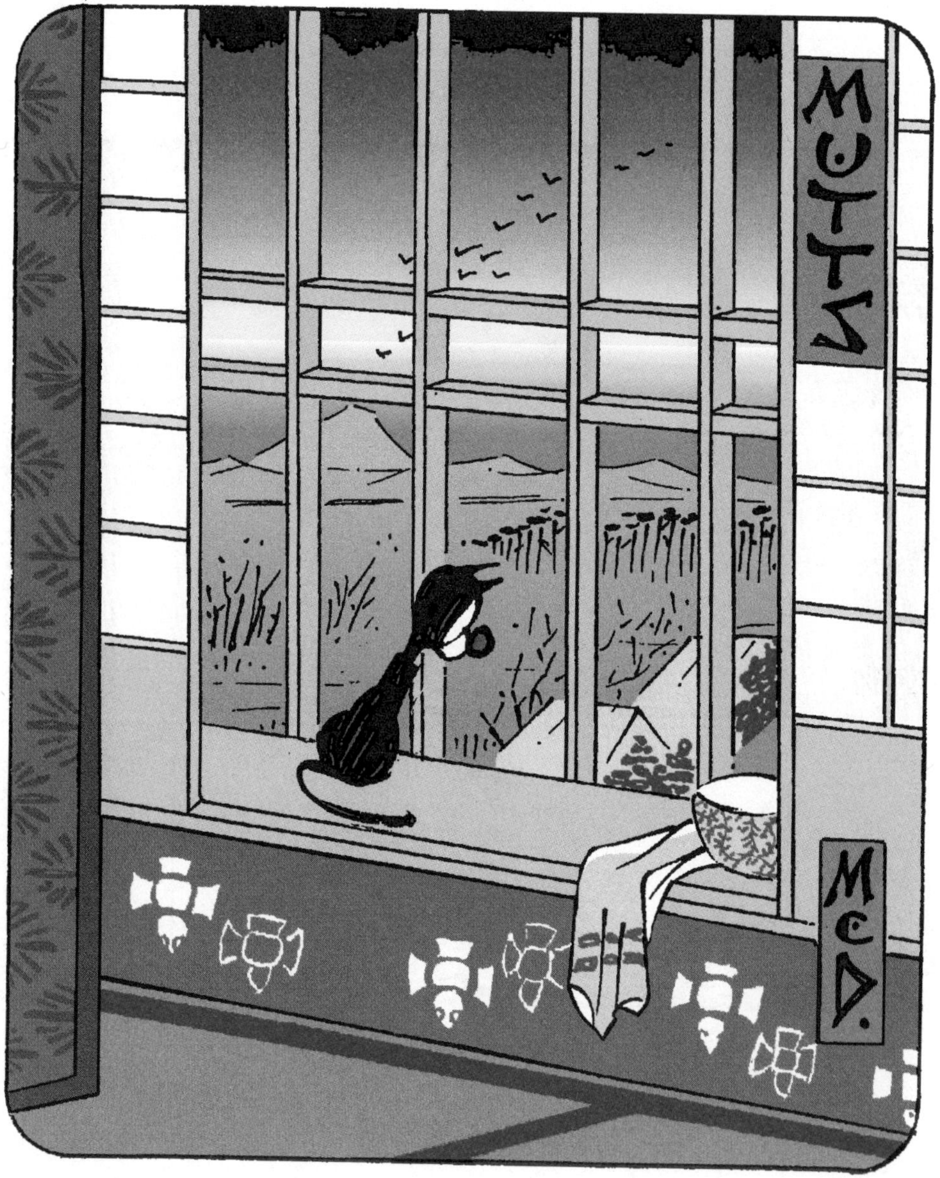
MUTTS
McD.

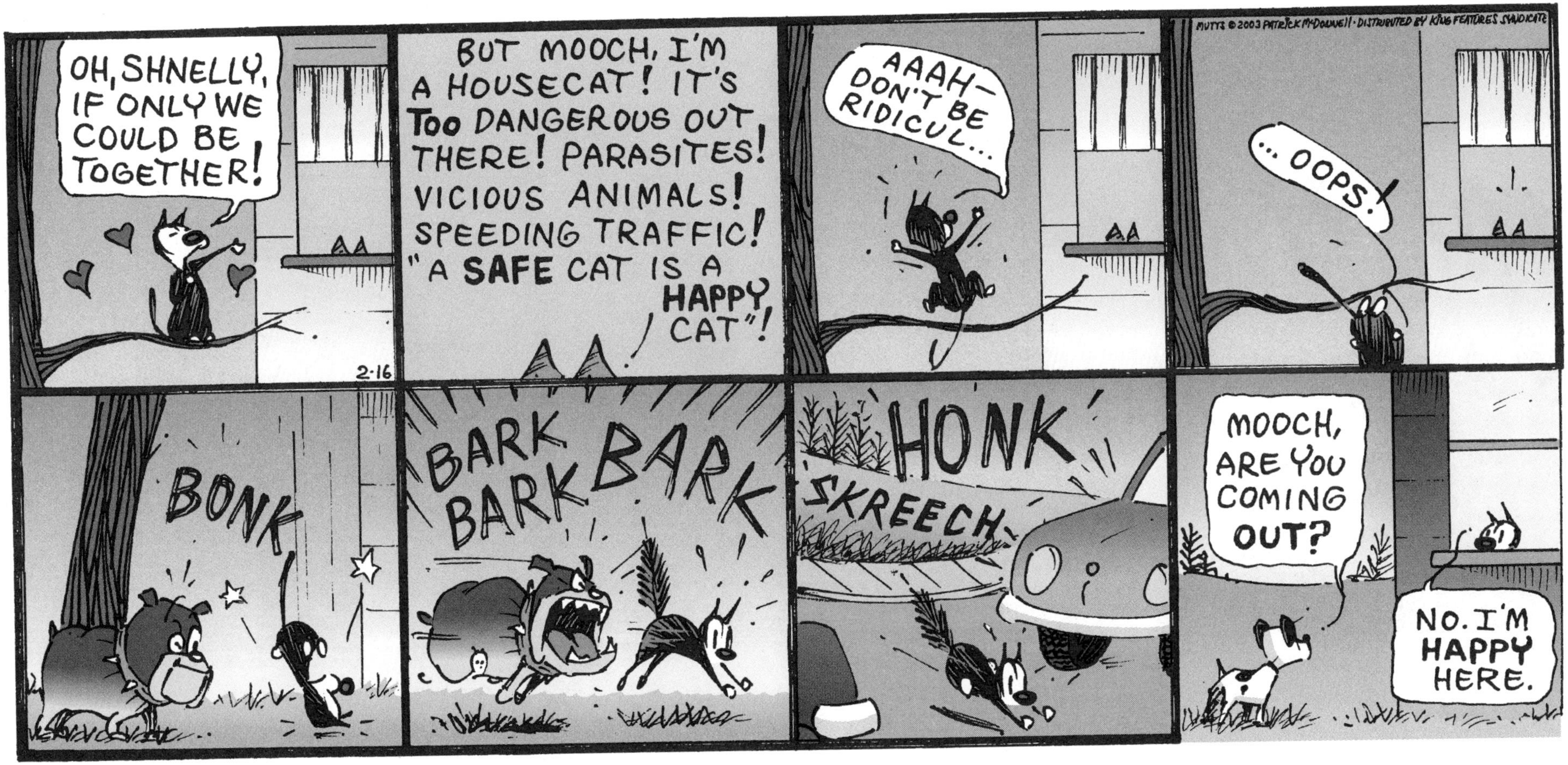
OH, SHNELLY, IF ONLY WE COULD BE TOGETHER!
2·16
BUT MOOCH, I'M A HOUSECAT! IT'S TOO DANGEROUS OUT THERE! PARASITES! VICIOUS ANIMALS! SPEEDING TRAFFIC! "A SAFE CAT IS A HAPPY CAT"!
AAAH—DON'T BE RIDICUL...
MUTTS © 2003 PATRICK McDONNELL · DISTRIBUTED BY KING FEATURES SYNDICATE
...OOPS!
BONK
BARK BARK BARK BARK
HONK
SKREECH
MOOCH, ARE YOU COMING OUT?
NO. I'M HAPPY HERE.

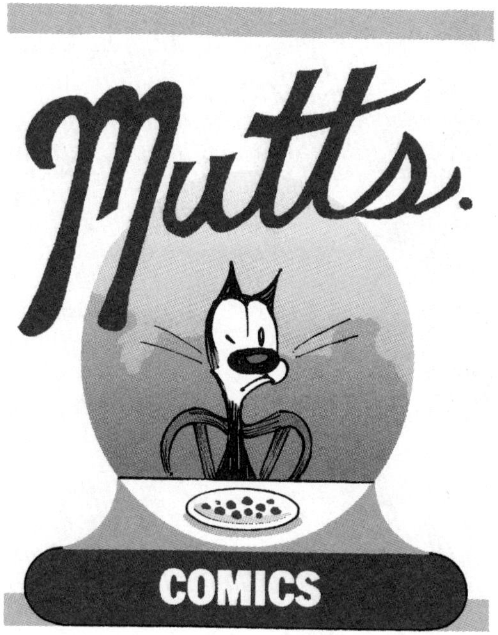
Mutts.
COMICS

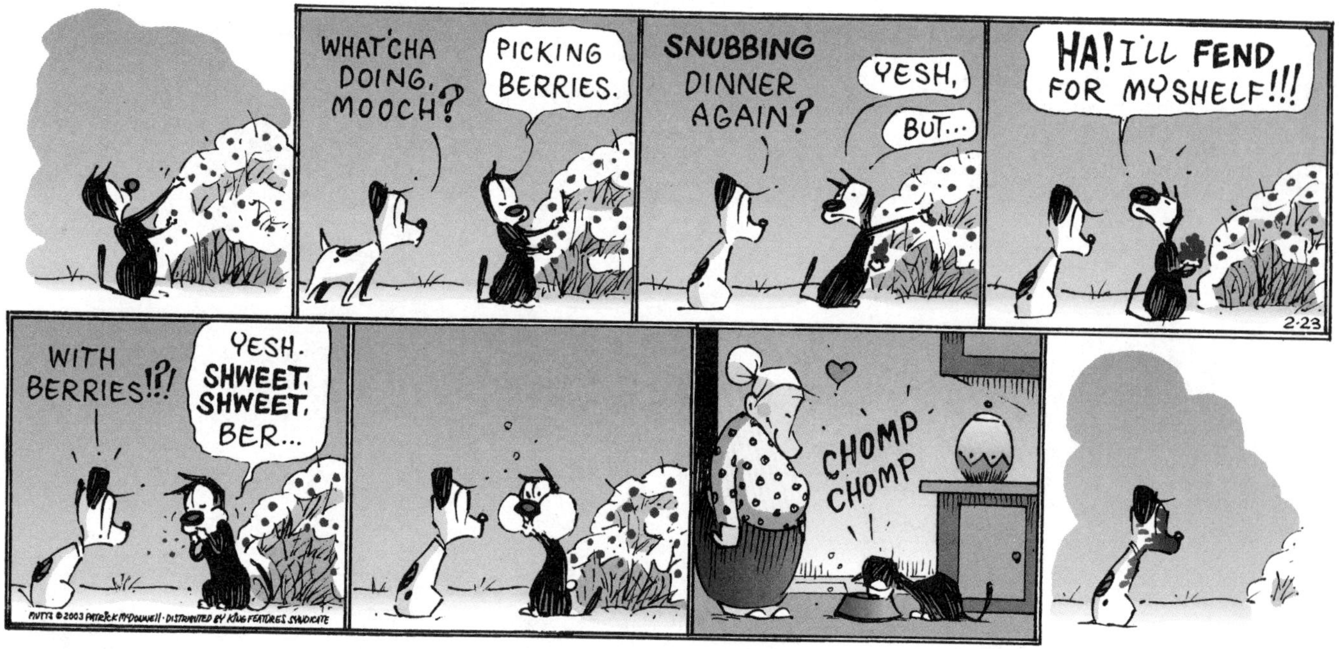
WHAT'CHA DOING, MOOCH?
PICKING BERRIES.
SNUBBING DINNER AGAIN?
YESH,
BUT...
HA! I'LL FEND FOR MYSHELF!!!
2·23
WITH BERRIES!?!
YESH. SHWEET, SHWEET, BER...
CHOMP CHOMP
MUTTS © 2003 PATRICK McDONNELL · DISTRIBUTED BY KING FEATURES SYNDICATE

MUTTS
1. SKETCH
2. INK
3. LETTER
4. COLOR

WHAT'S ON MY LIST TODAY?
EAT FOOD IN BOWL.
NAP ON FOLDED LAUNDRY.
Z Z Z
PLAY WITH LI'L PINK SOCK.
STARE AT FAUCET.
SLEEP ON BIG BED.
Z Z Z
EAT FOOD IN BOWL AGAIN.
REVIEW LIST.
AUGH! I FORGOT TO NAP ON THE SHOFA!
THERE'S NEVER ENOUGH TIME IN THE DAY!
MUTTS © 2003 PATRICK McDONNELL · DISTRIBUTED BY KING FEATURES
3/2

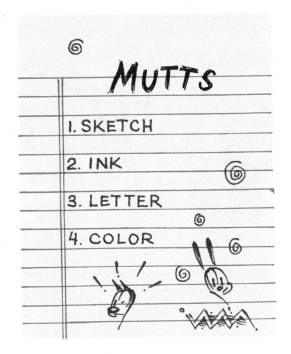

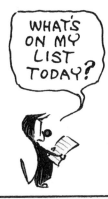

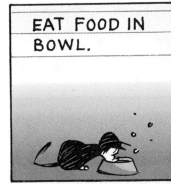

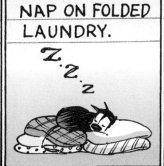

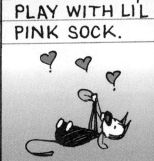

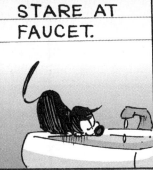

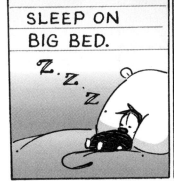

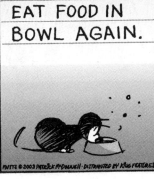

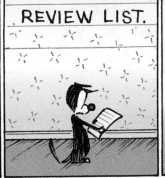

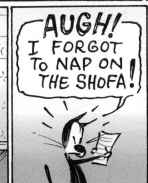

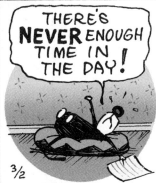

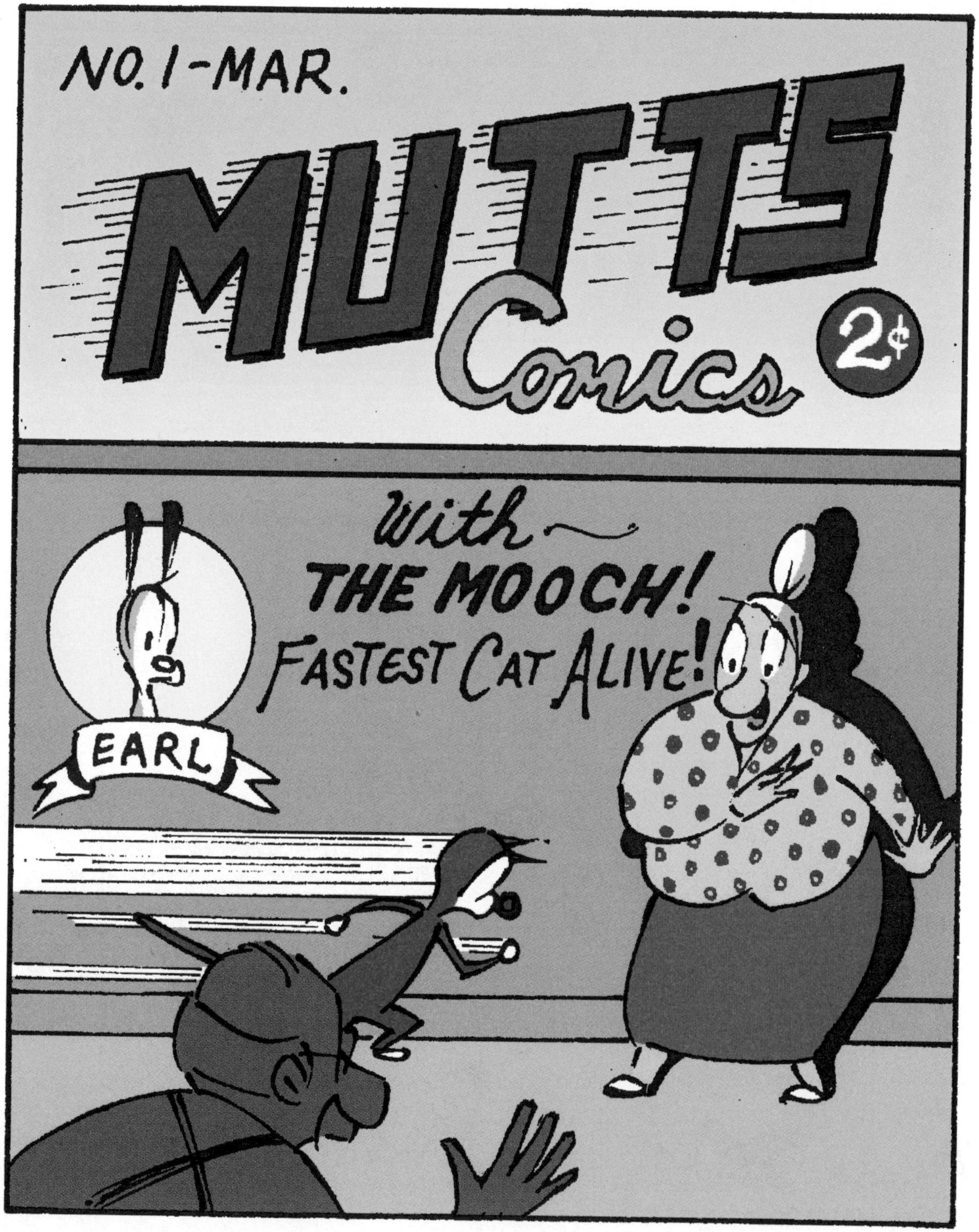
NO. 1 - MAR.
MUTTS Comics
2¢
With
THE MOOCH!
FASTEST CAT ALIVE!
EARL

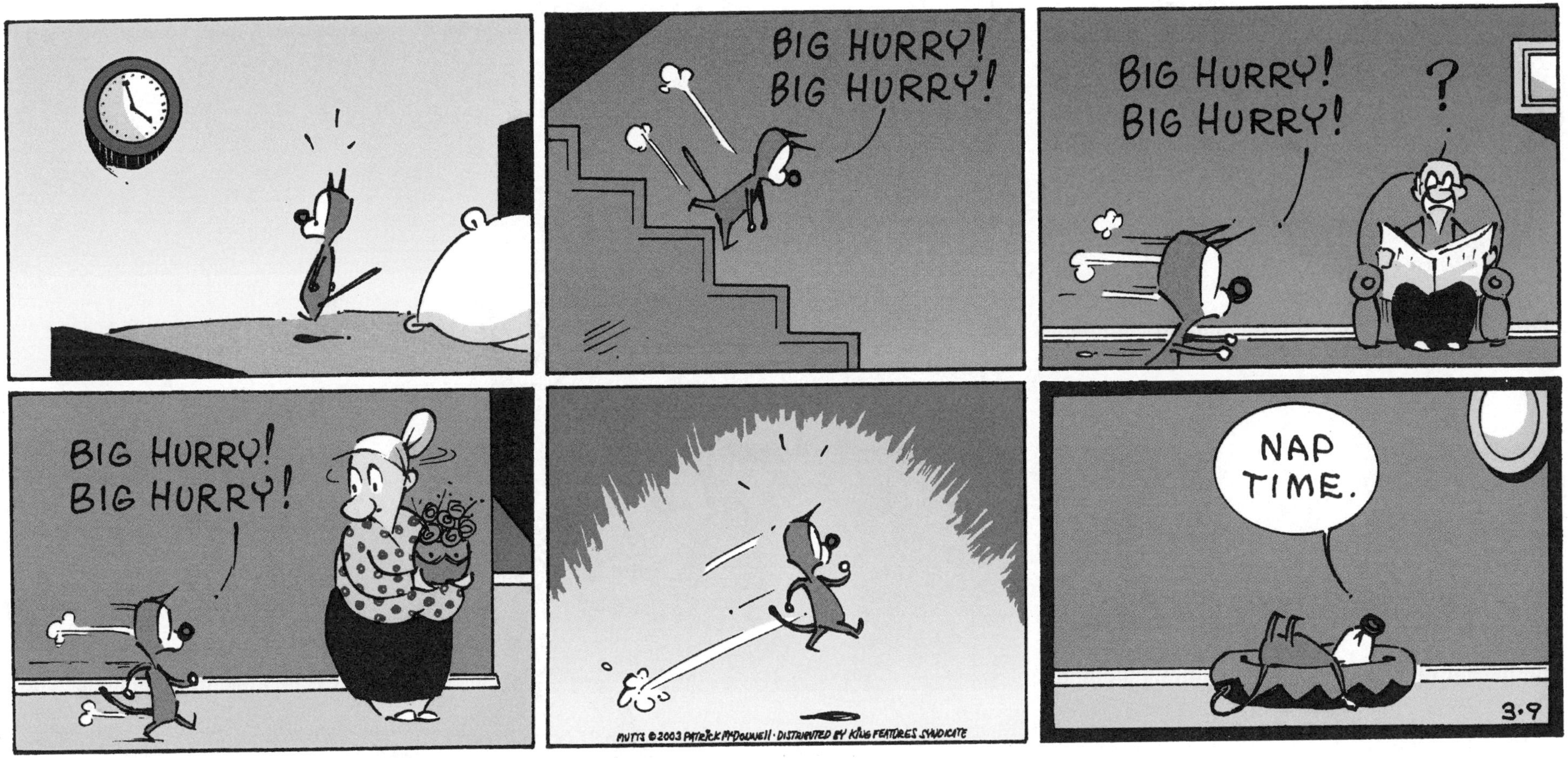
BIG HURRY! BIG HURRY!
BIG HURRY! BIG HURRY!
?
BIG HURRY! BIG HURRY!
MUTTS © 2003 PATRICK McDONNELL · DISTRIBUTED BY KING FEATURES SYNDICATE
NAP TIME.
3·9

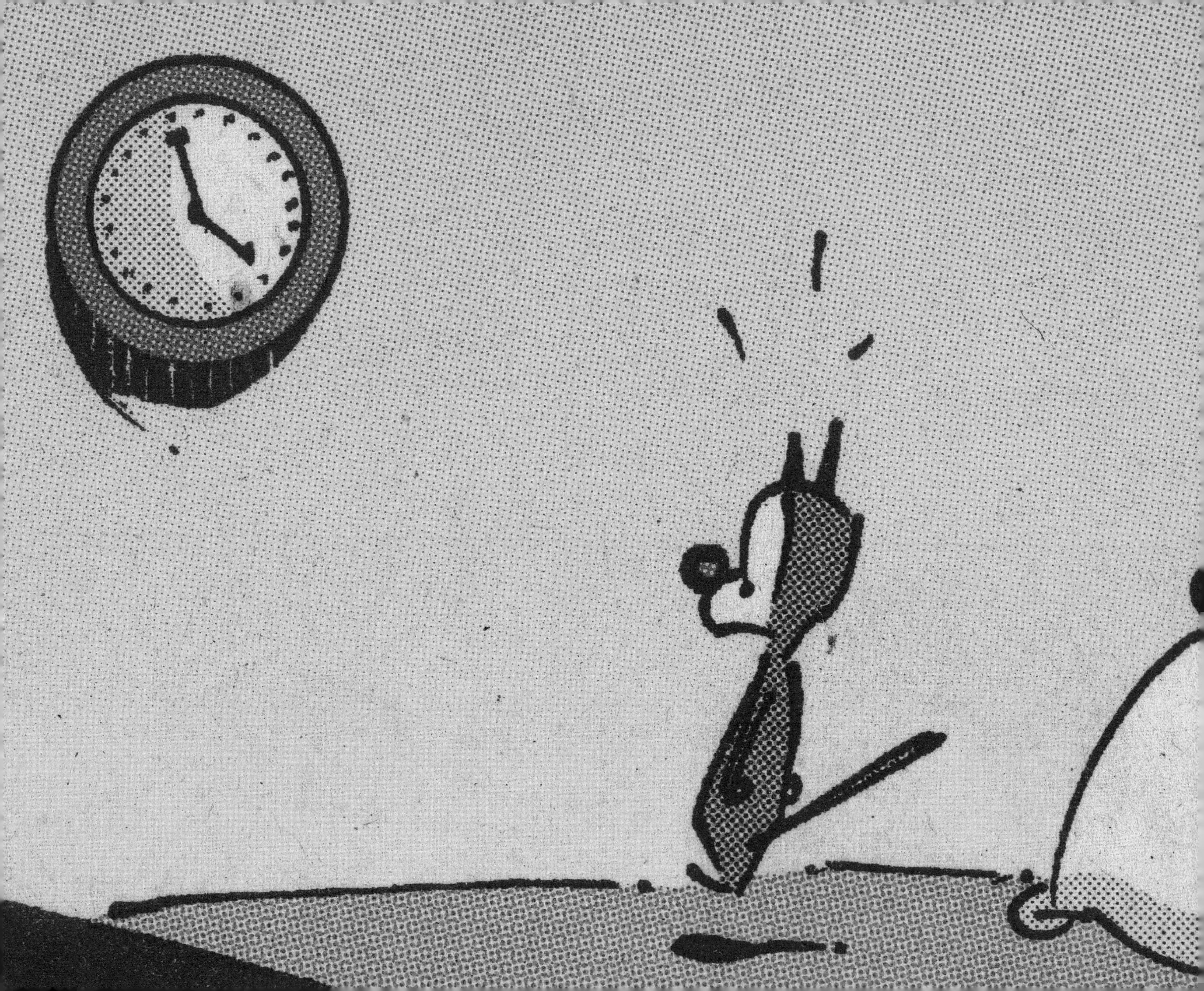

MUTTS

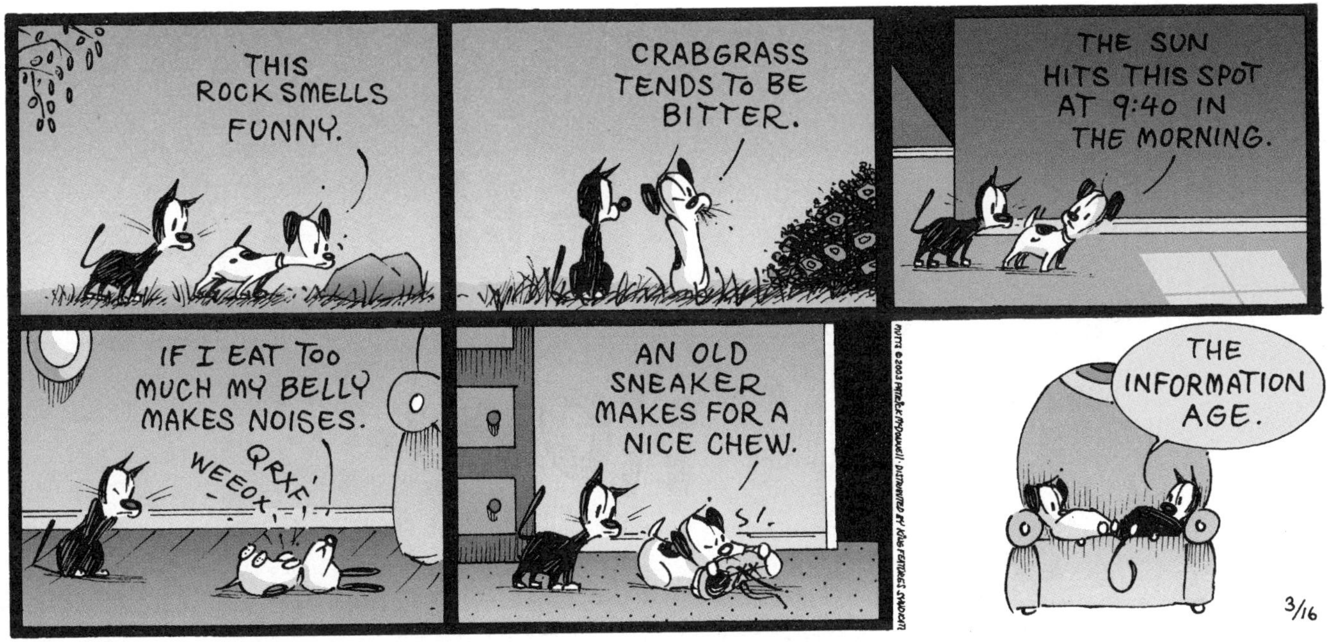
THIS ROCK SMELLS FUNNY.
CRABGRASS TENDS TO BE BITTER.
THE SUN HITS THIS SPOT AT 9:40 IN THE MORNING.
IF I EAT TOO MUCH MY BELLY MAKES NOISES.
QRXF
WEEOX
AN OLD SNEAKER MAKES FOR A NICE CHEW.
THE INFORMATION AGE.
3/16

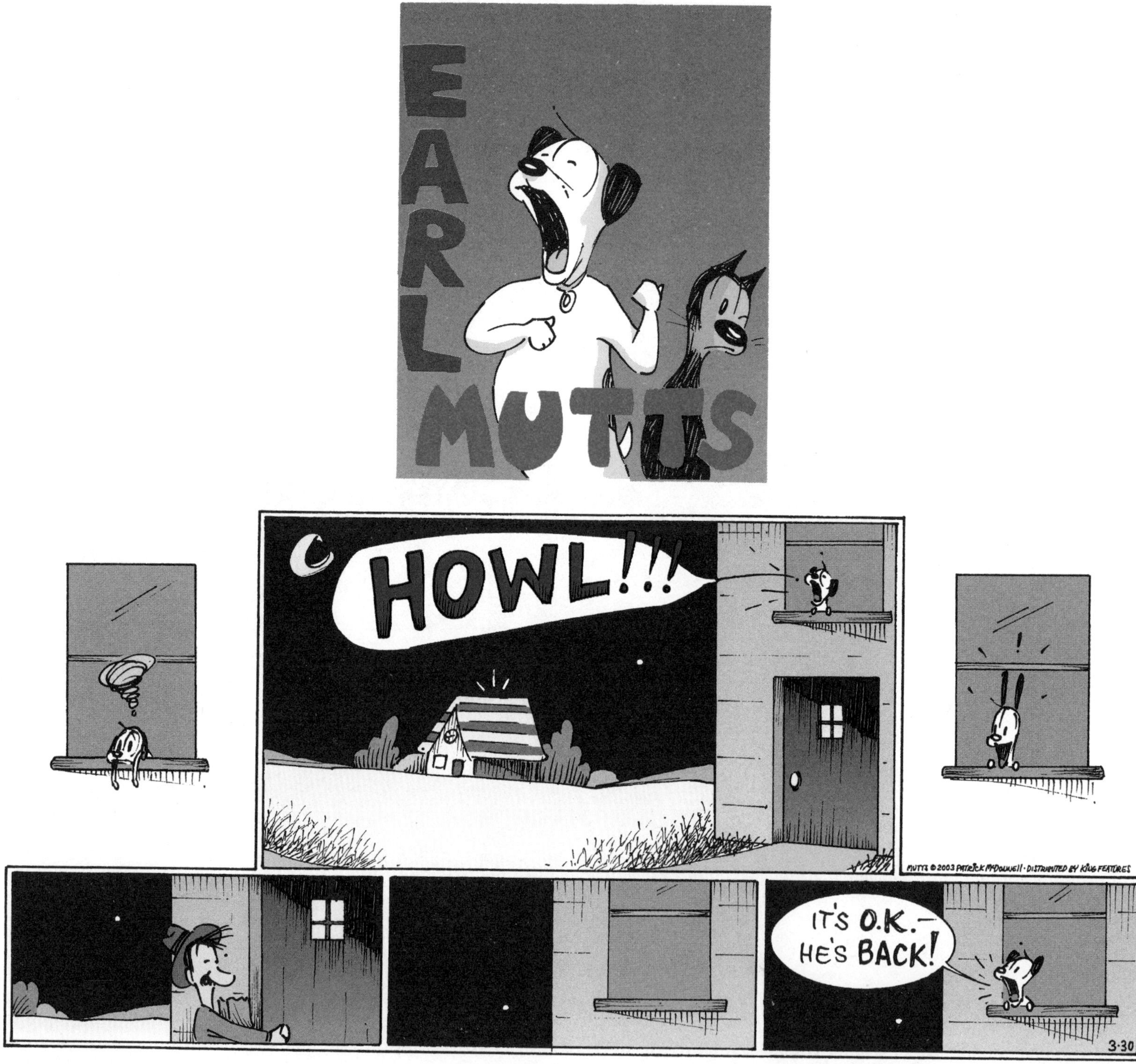
EARL
MUTTS
HOWL!!!
MUTTS © 2003 PATRICK McDONNELL · DISTRIBUTED BY KING FEATURES
IT'S O.K.— HE'S BACK!
3·30

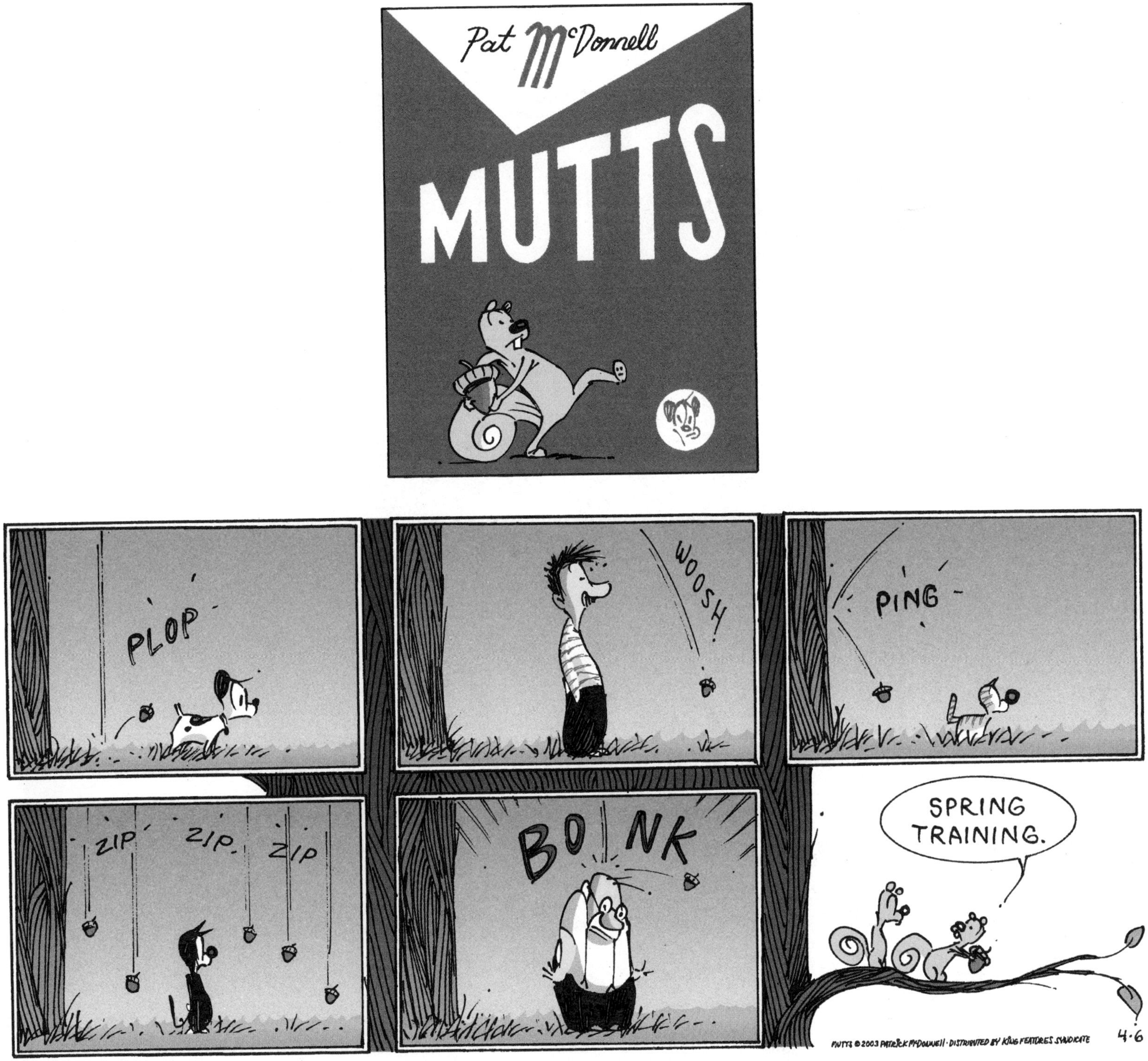

Pat McDonnell
MUTTS
PLOP
WOOSH
PING
ZIP
ZIP
ZIP
BONK
SPRING TRAINING.
MUTTS © 2003 PATRICK McDONNELL · DISTRIBUTED BY KING FEATURES SYNDICATE
4·6

MUTTS
AND THE
FATTY SNAX DELI
OF MONGO
YESH!
FROM THE FAMOUS COMIC STRIP

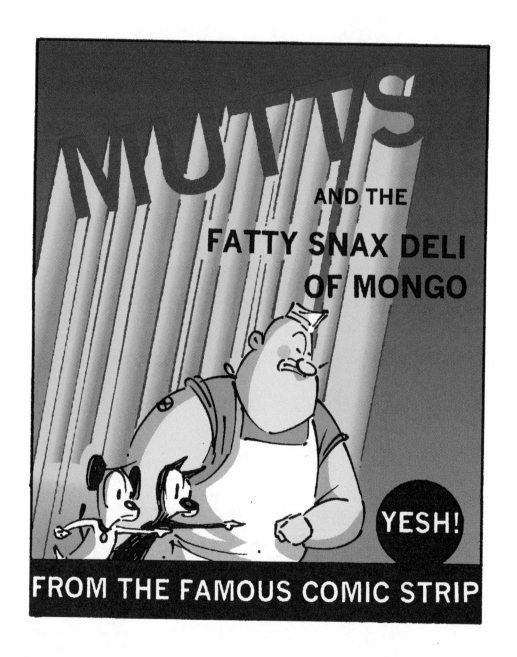

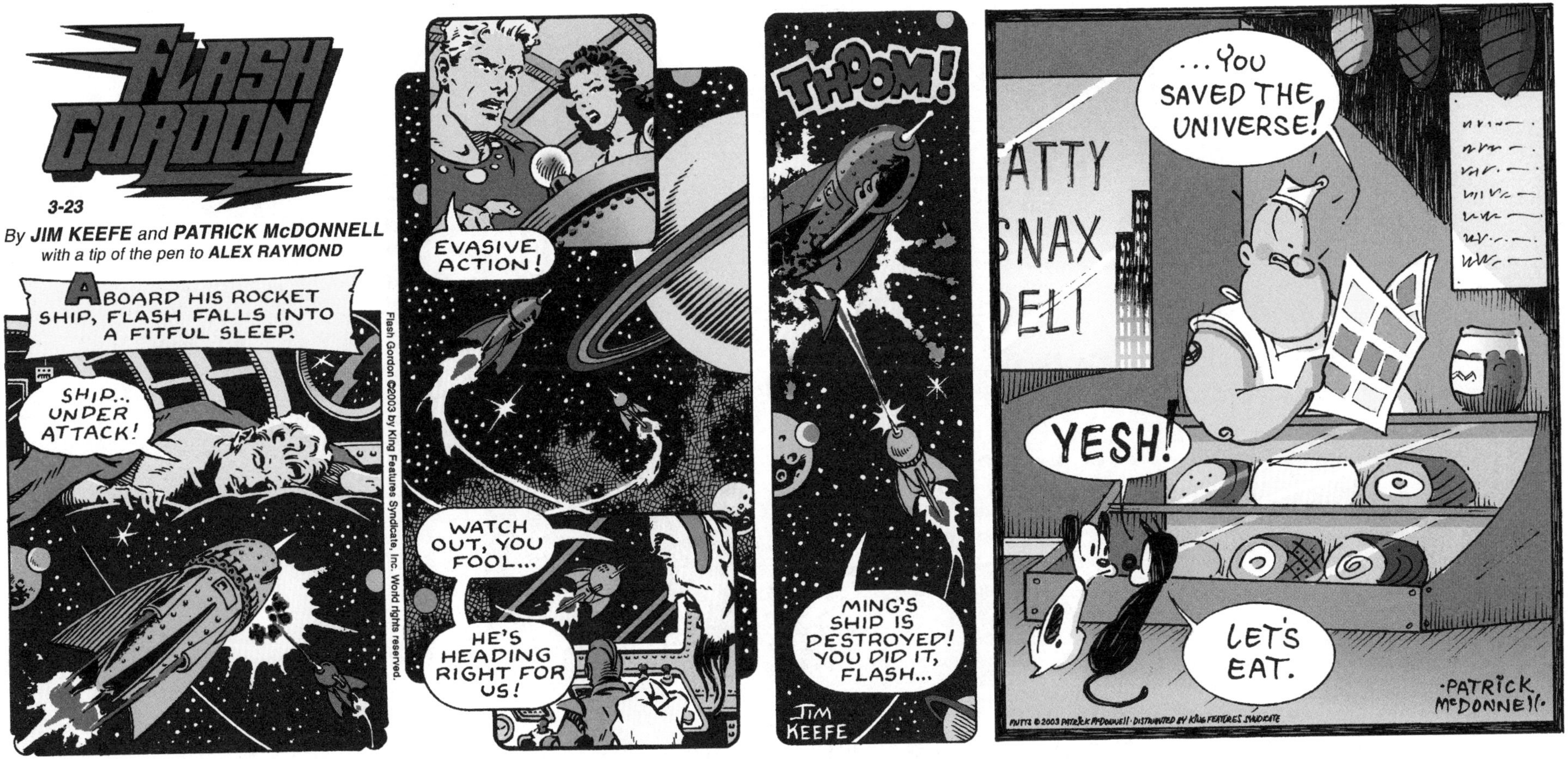
FLASH GORDON
3-23
By JIM KEEFE and PATRICK McDONNELL
with a tip of the pen to ALEX RAYMOND
ABOARD HIS ROCKET SHIP, FLASH FALLS INTO A FITFUL SLEEP.
SHIP... UNDER ATTACK!
Flash Gordon ©2003 by King Features Syndicate, Inc. World rights reserved.
EVASIVE ACTION!
WATCH OUT, YOU FOOL...
HE'S HEADING RIGHT FOR US!
THOOM!
MING'S SHIP IS DESTROYED! YOU DID IT, FLASH...
JIM KEEFE
...YOU SAVED THE UNIVERSE!
FATTY SNAX DELI
YESH!
LET'S EAT.
PATRICK McDONNELL

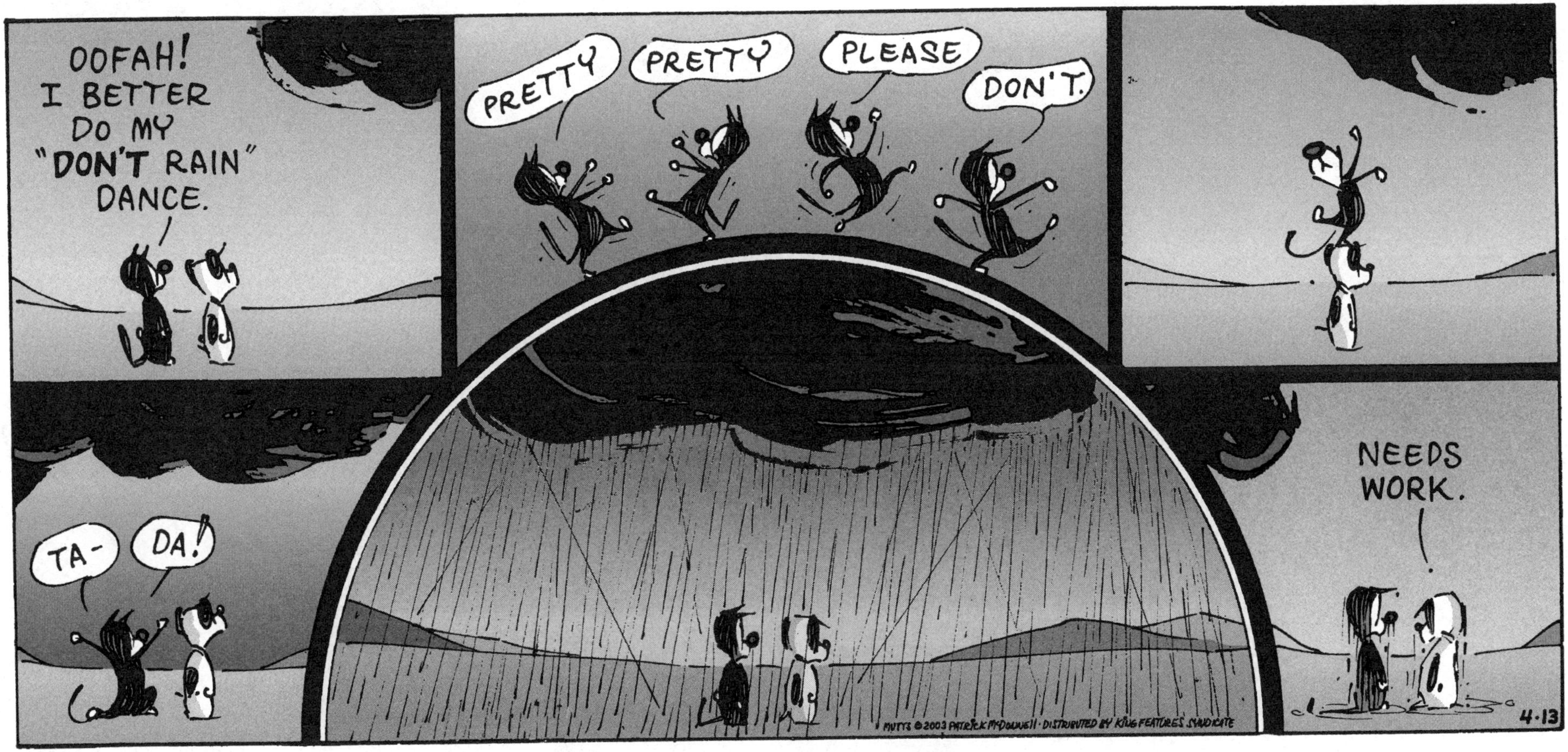
OOFAH! I BETTER DO MY "DON'T RAIN" DANCE.
PRETTY
PRETTY
PLEASE
DON'T.
TA-
DA!
NEEDS WORK.
MUTTS © 2003 PATRICK McDONNELL · DISTRIBUTED BY KING FEATURES SYNDICATE
4·13

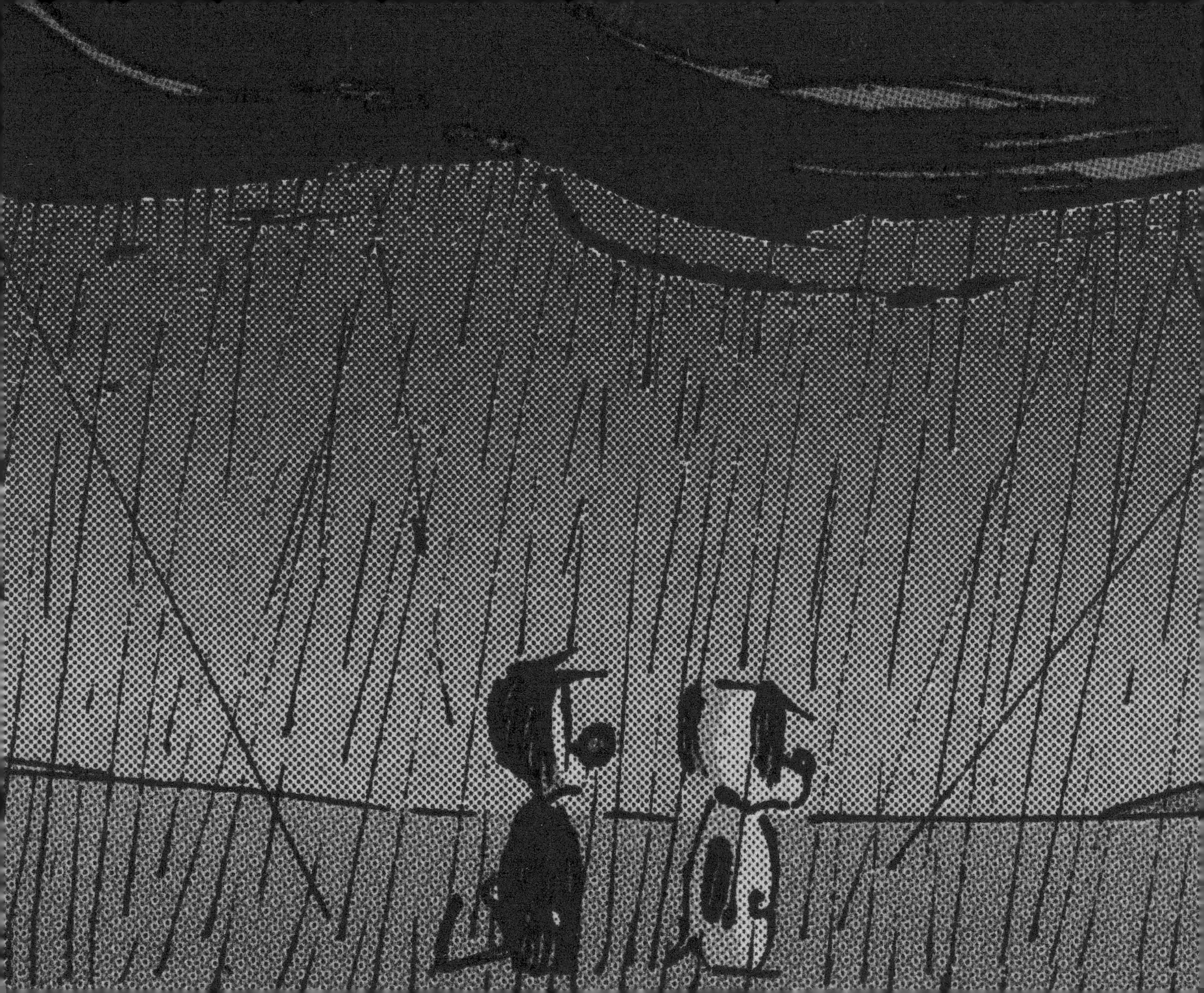

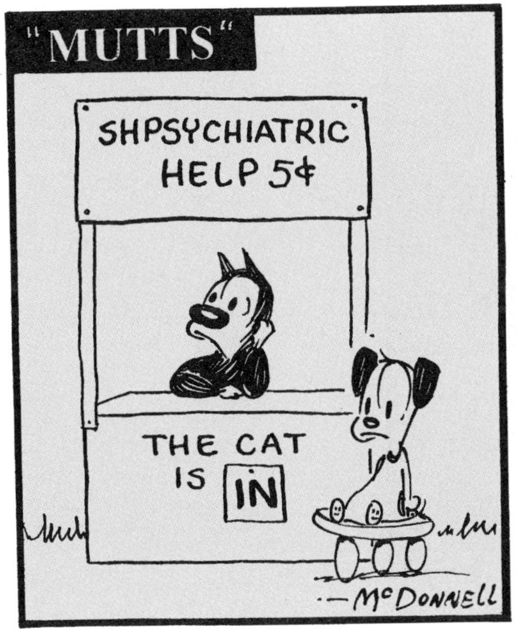
"MUTTS"
SHPSYCHIATRIC HELP 5¢
THE CAT IS IN
McDONNELL

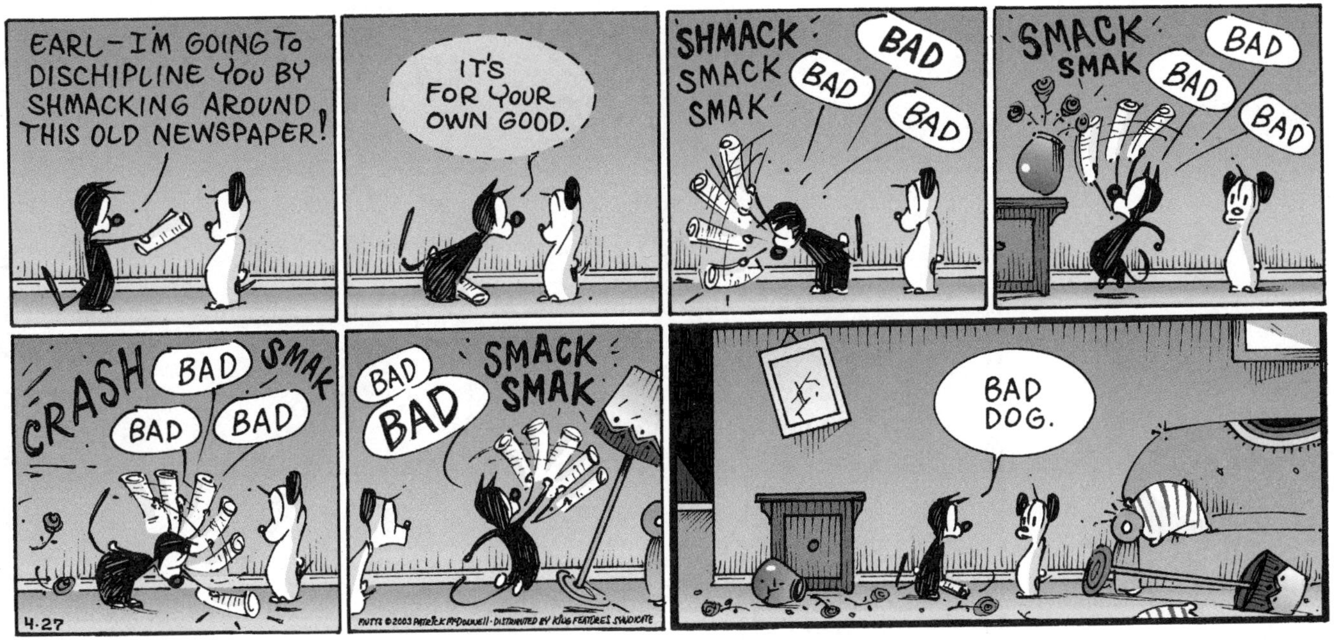
EARL – I'M GOING TO DISCHIPLINE YOU BY SHMACKING AROUND THIS OLD NEWSPAPER!
IT'S FOR YOUR OWN GOOD.
SHMACK SMACK SMAK
BAD
BAD
BAD
SMACK SMAK
BAD
BAD
BAD
CRASH
BAD
SMAK
BAD
BAD
4.27
BAD
BAD
SMACK SMAK
MUTTS ©2003 PATRICK McDONNELL · DISTRIBUTED BY KING FEATURES SYNDICATE
BAD DOG.

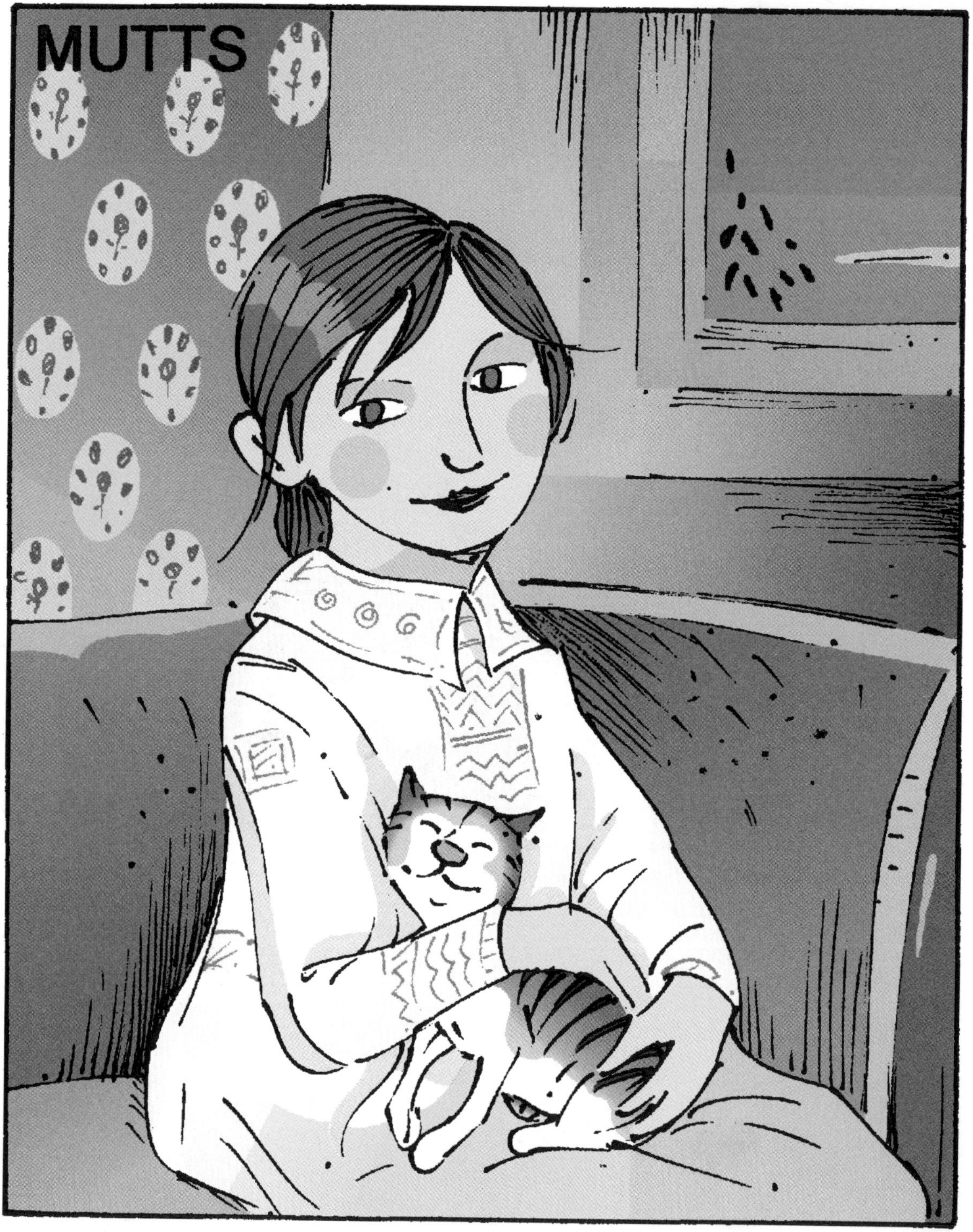
MUTTS

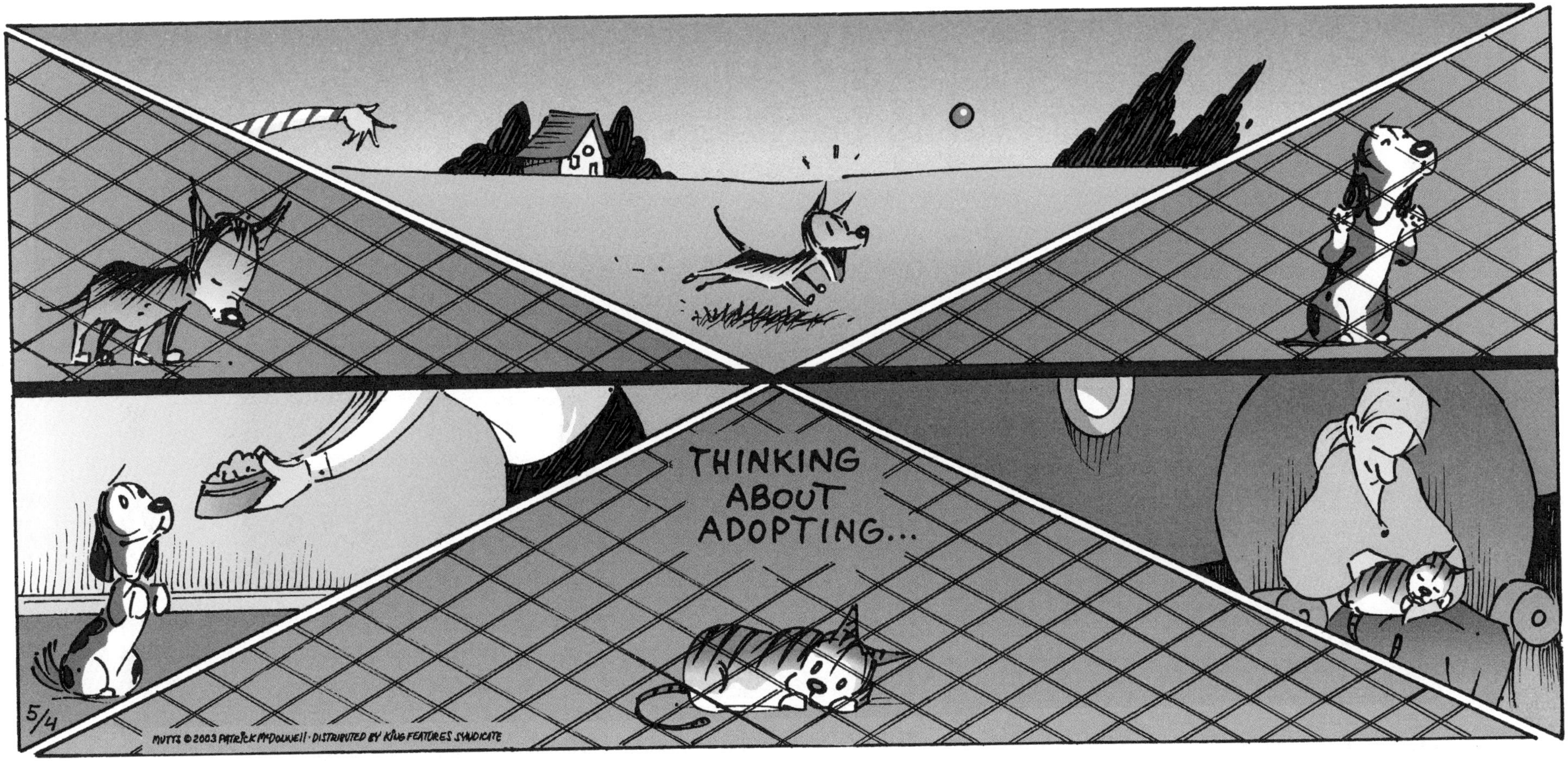
THINKING ABOUT ADOPTING...
5/4
MUTTS © 2003 PATRICK McDONNELL · DISTRIBUTED BY KING FEATURES SYNDICATE

Mutts
by P. L. McDonnell

WHO ELSE WOULD GENTLY WASH YOUR DIRTY WITTLE FACE?
WHO ELSE WOULD KEEP YOUR WITTLE FOOTSIES WARM ALL NIGHT?
WHO ELSE WOULD UNCONDITIONALLY LOVE AND PROTECT YOUR WITTLE SELF?
WHO ELSE WOULD REGURGITATE A BUGGY SNACK INTO YOUR HUNGRY WITTLE MOUTH?
SIGH...
MOM
5/11

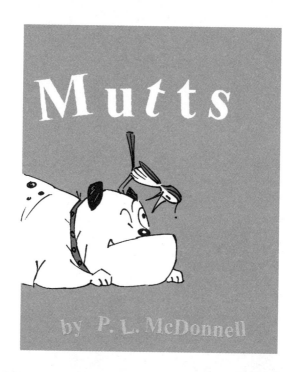

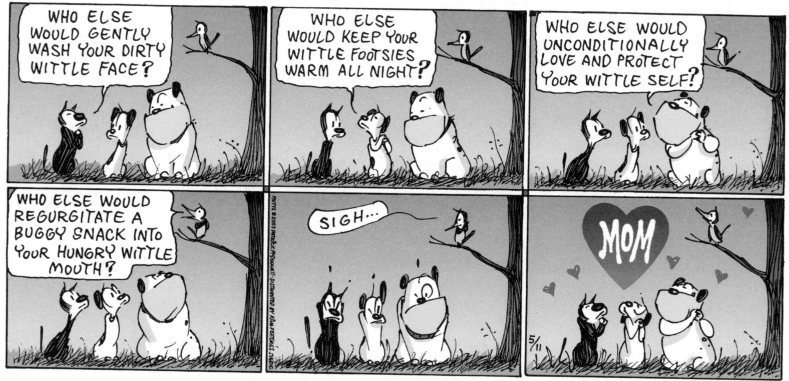

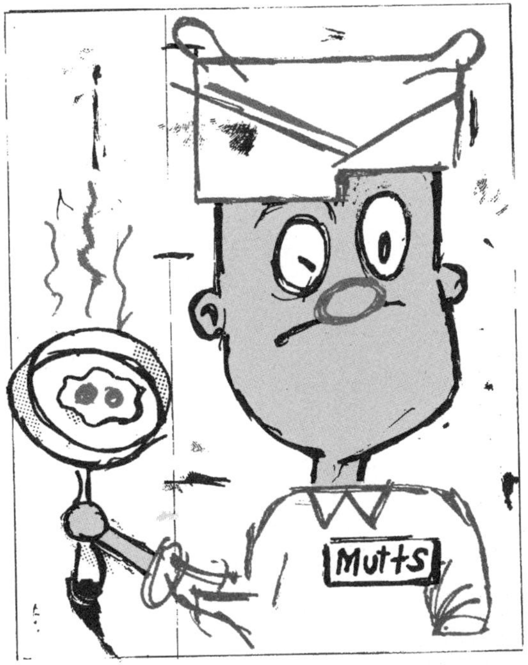
Mutts

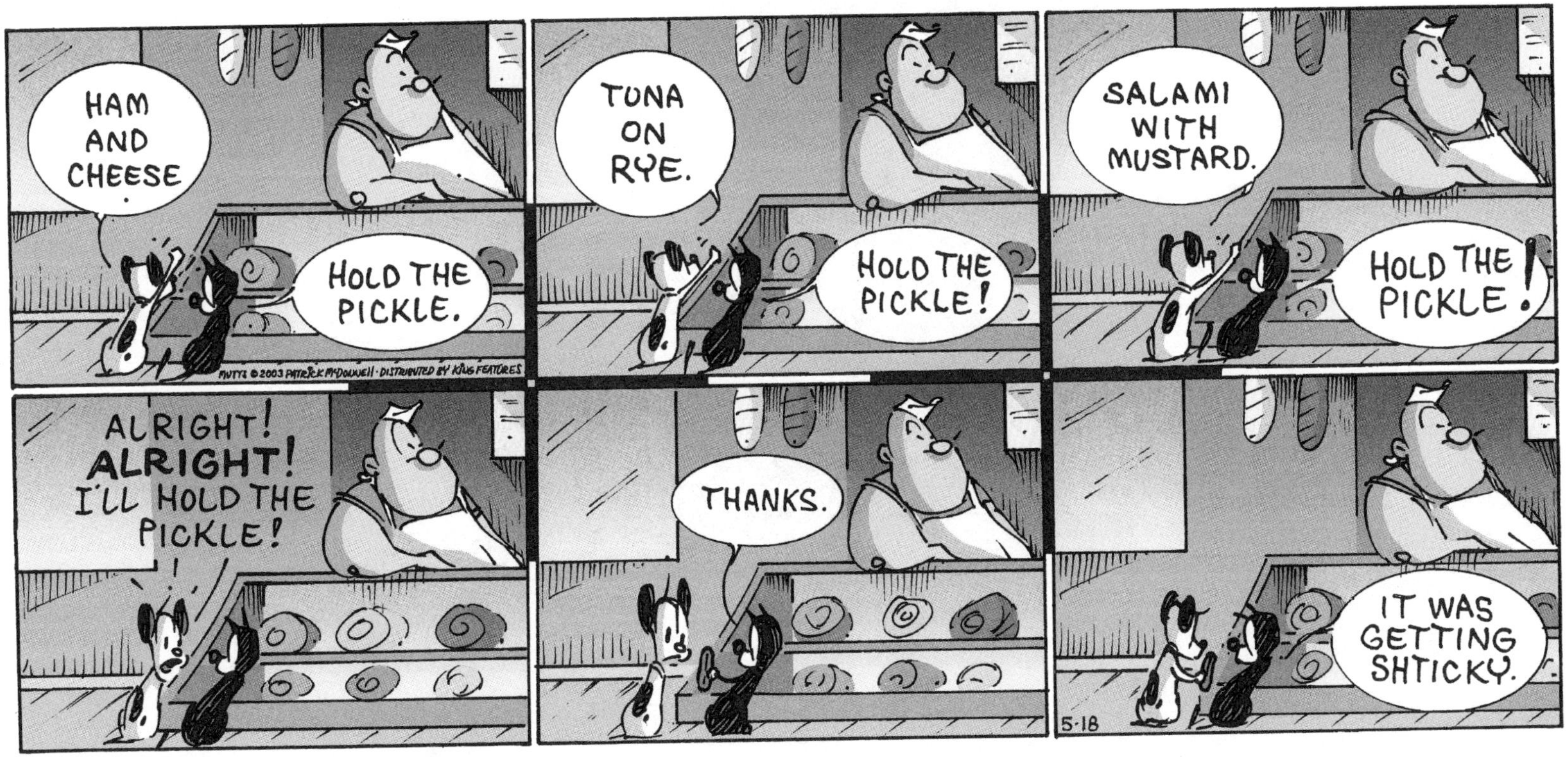
HAM AND CHEESE.
HOLD THE PICKLE.
MUTTS © 2003 PATRICK McDONNELL · DISTRIBUTED BY KING FEATURES
TUNA ON RYE.
HOLD THE PICKLE!
SALAMI WITH MUSTARD.
HOLD THE PICKLE!
ALRIGHT! ALRIGHT! I'LL HOLD THE PICKLE!
THANKS.
IT WAS GETTING SHTICKY.
5·18

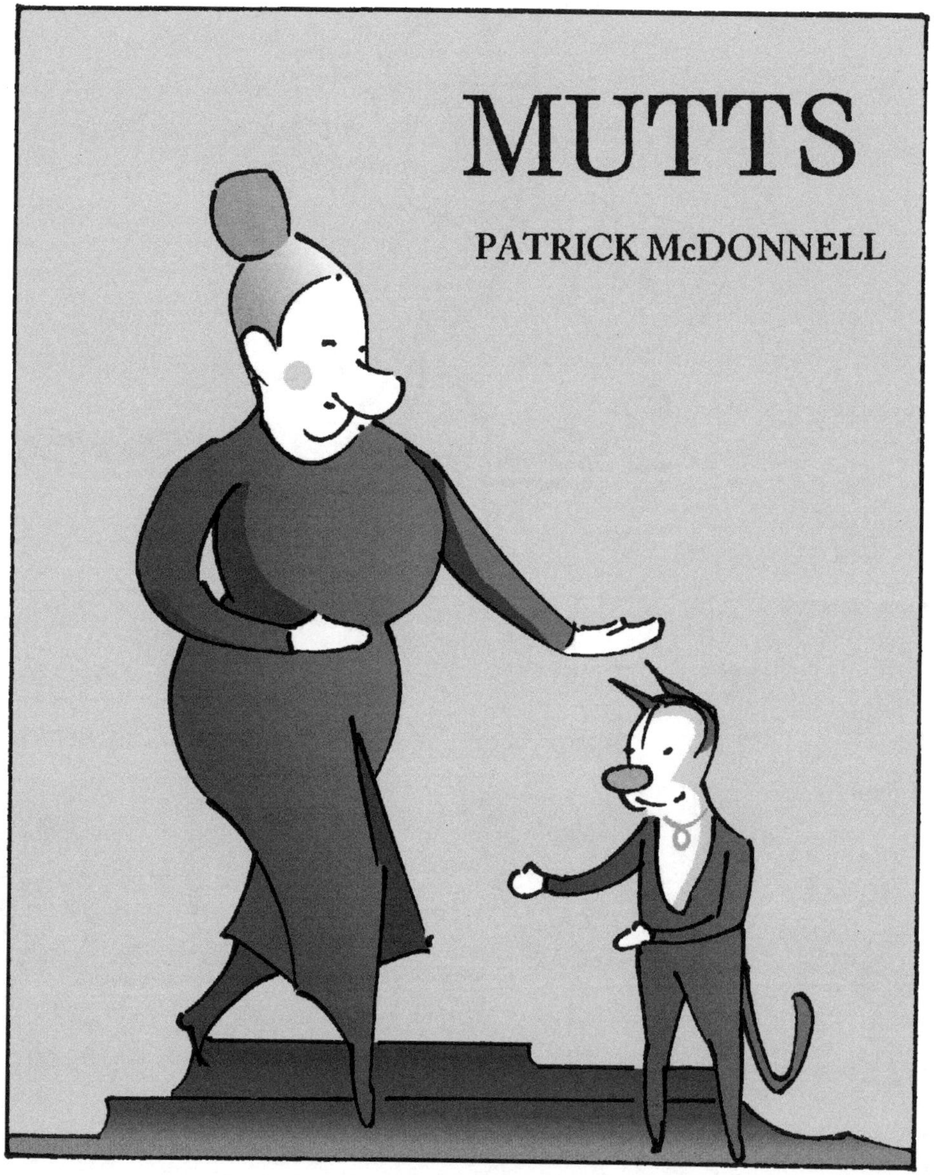
MUTTS
PATRICK McDONNELL

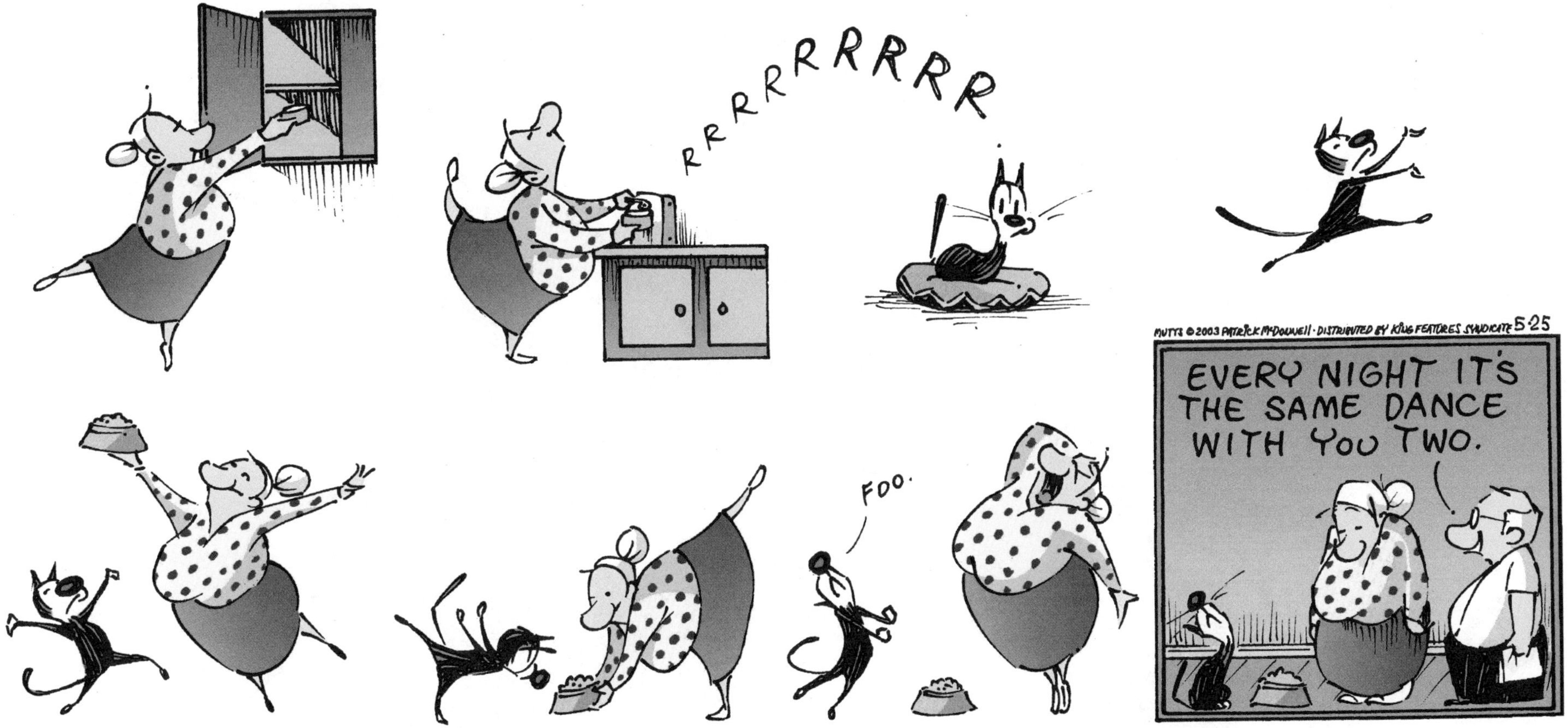
RRRRRRRRR
MUTTS © 2003 PATRICK McDONNELL · DISTRIBUTED BY KING FEATURES SYNDICATE 5·25
EVERY NIGHT IT'S THE SAME DANCE WITH YOU TWO.
FOO.

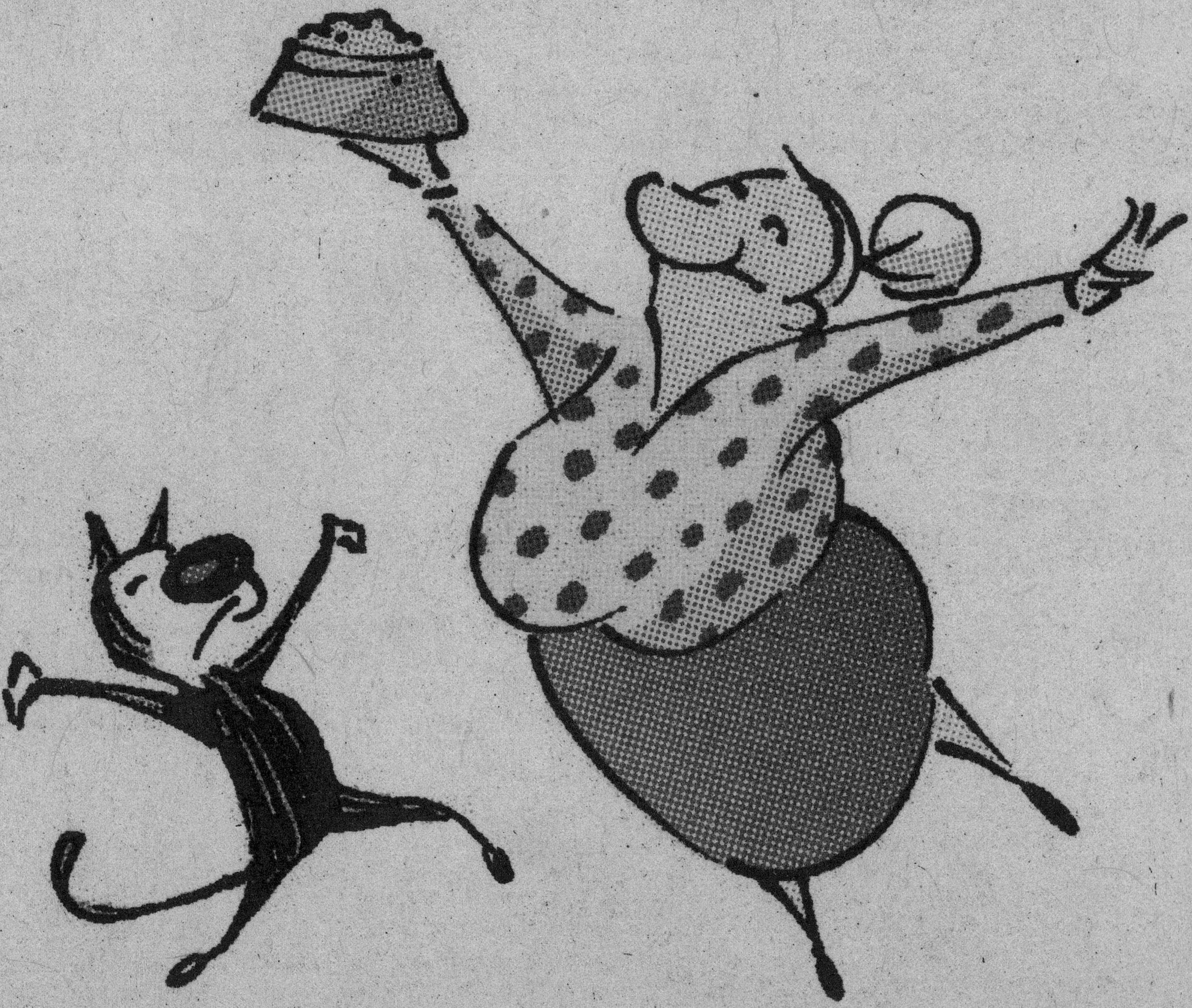

Mutts

PATRICK McDONNELL

MY HUSBAND WILL BE RIGHT WITH YOU.
MUTTS © 2003 PATRICK McDONNELL · DISTRIBUTED BY KING FEATURES SYNDICATE
HELLO, KITTY.
POOM POOM POOM
YOU'RE IN HIS CHAIR.
6·1

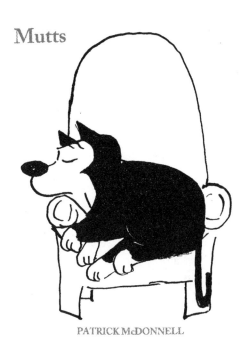

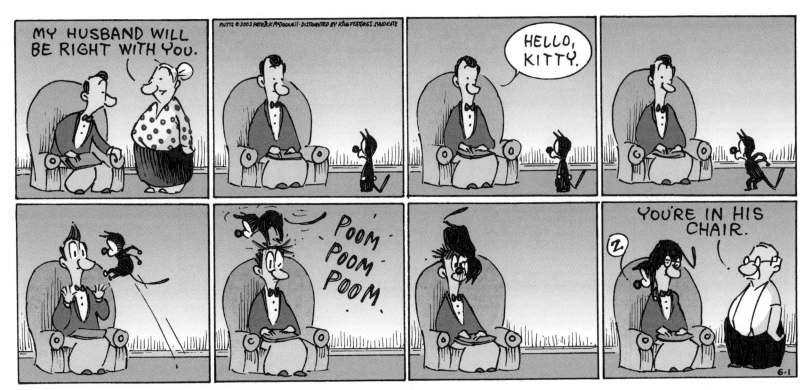

Fun *with* Mutts

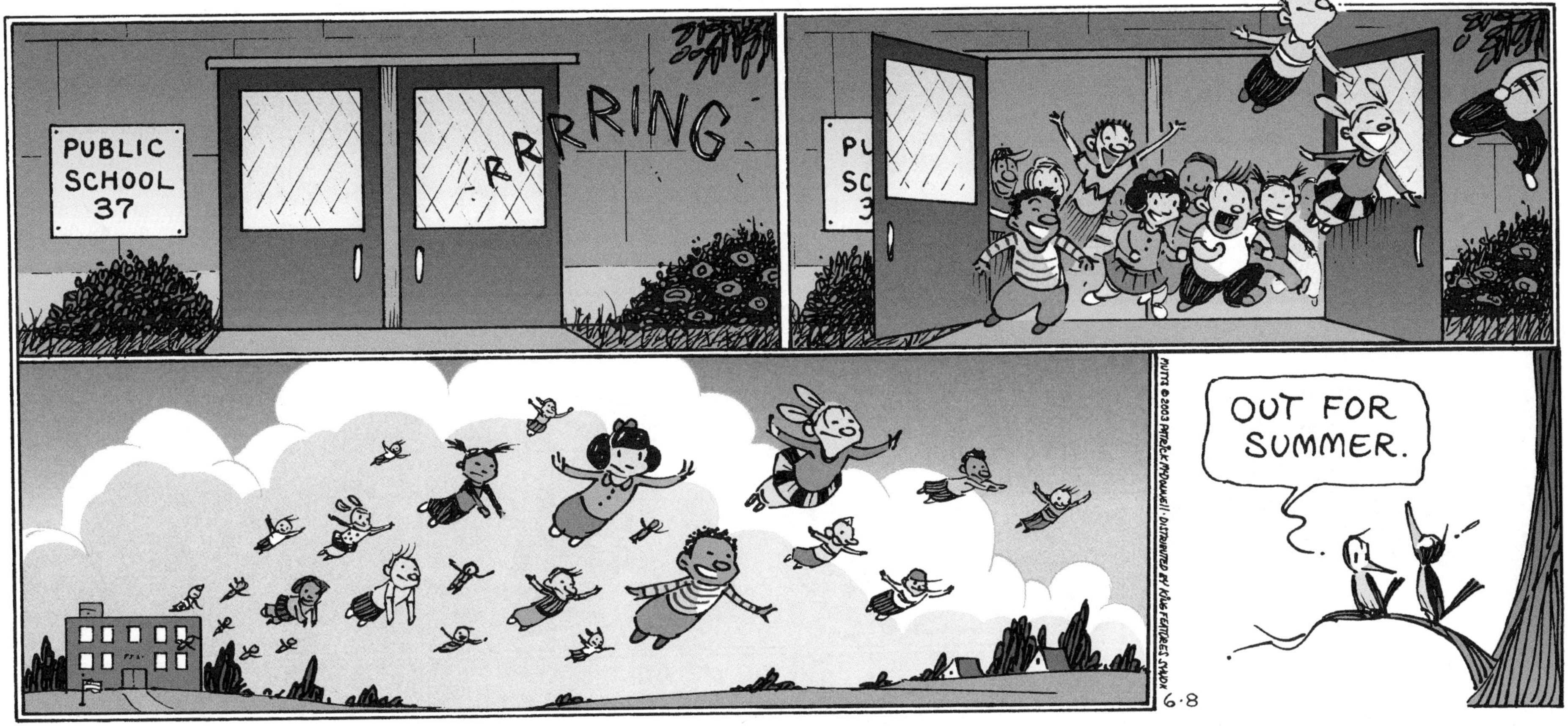
PUBLIC SCHOOL 37
RRRRING
PU SC 3
MUTTS © 2003 PATRICK McDONNELL · DISTRIBUTED BY KING FEATURES SYNDICATE
6·8
OUT FOR SUMMER.

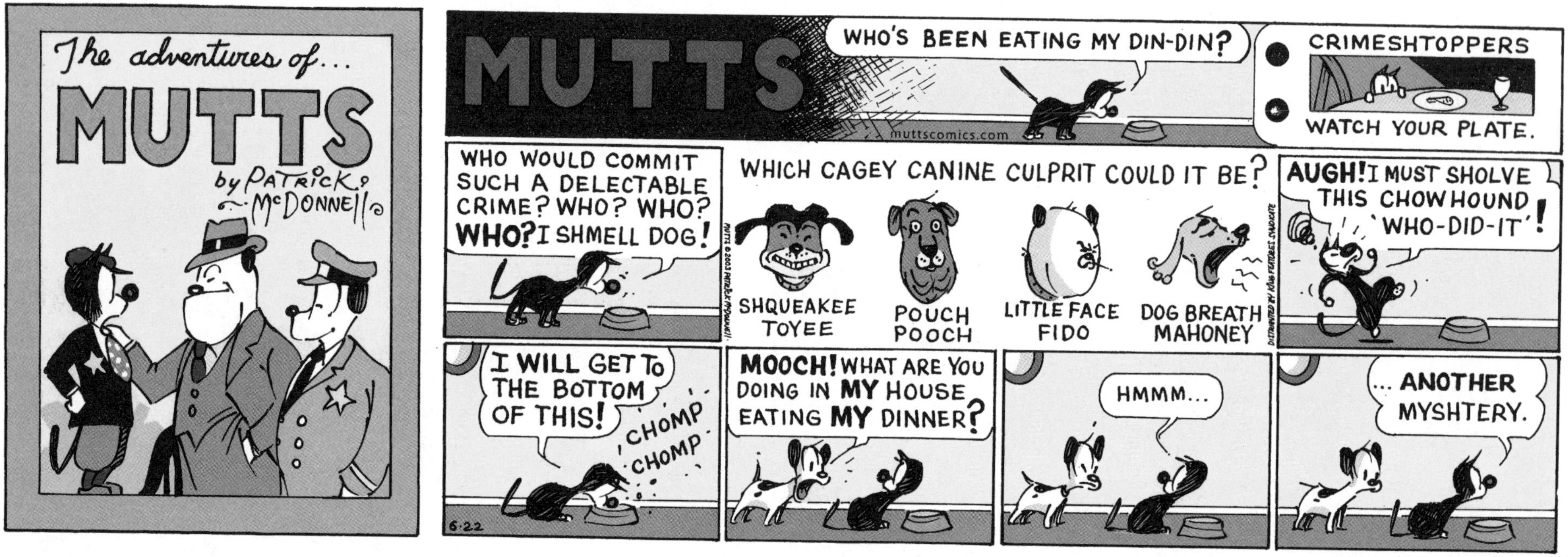
The adventures of...
MUTTS
by PATRICK McDONNELL
MUTTS
WHO'S BEEN EATING MY DIN-DIN?
muttscomics.com
CRIMESHTOPPERS
WATCH YOUR PLATE.
WHO WOULD COMMIT SUCH A DELECTABLE CRIME? WHO? WHO? WHO? I SHMELL DOG!
WHICH CAGEY CANINE CULPRIT COULD IT BE?
SHQUEAKEE TOYEE
POUCH POOCH
LITTLE FACE FIDO
DOG BREATH MAHONEY
AUGH! I MUST SHOLVE THIS CHOWHOUND 'WHO-DID-IT'!
I WILL GET TO THE BOTTOM OF THIS!
CHOMP CHOMP
6.22
MOOCH! WHAT ARE YOU DOING IN MY HOUSE EATING MY DINNER?
HMMM...
... ANOTHER MYSHTERY.

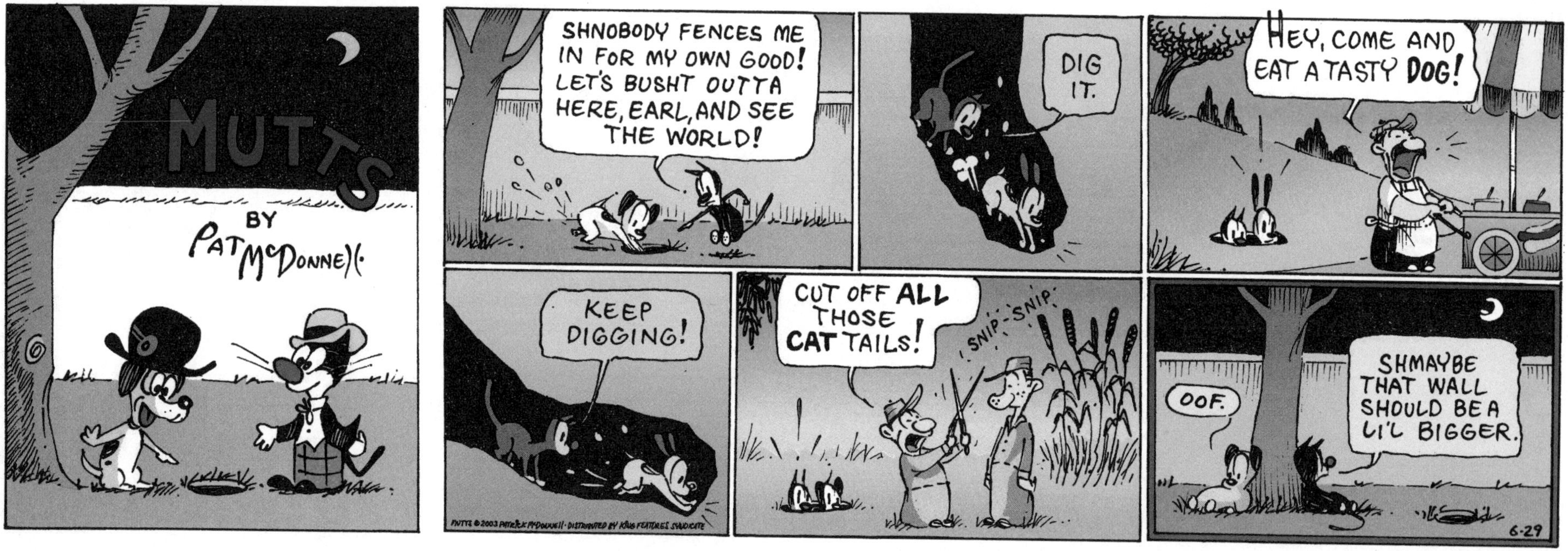
MUTTS
BY PAT McDONNELL
SHNOBODY FENCES ME IN FOR MY OWN GOOD! LET'S BUSHT OUTTA HERE, EARL, AND SEE THE WORLD!
DIG IT.
HEY, COME AND EAT A TASTY DOG!
KEEP DIGGING!
MUTTS © 2003 PATRICK McDONNELL · DISTRIBUTED BY KING FEATURES SYNDICATE
CUT OFF ALL THOSE CAT TAILS!
SNIP SNIP
OOF.
SHMAYBE THAT WALL SHOULD BE A LI'L BIGGER.
6-29

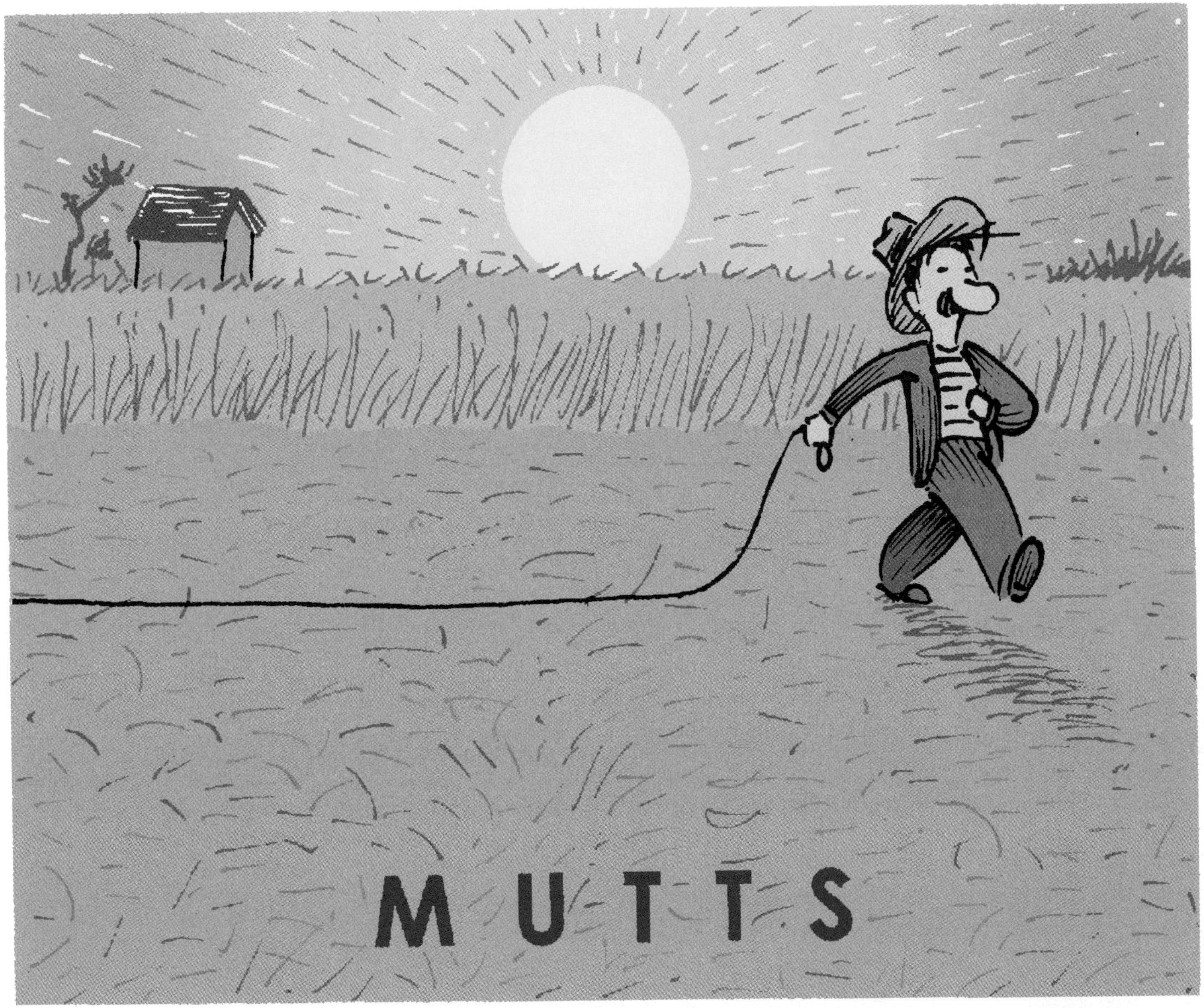
MUTTS

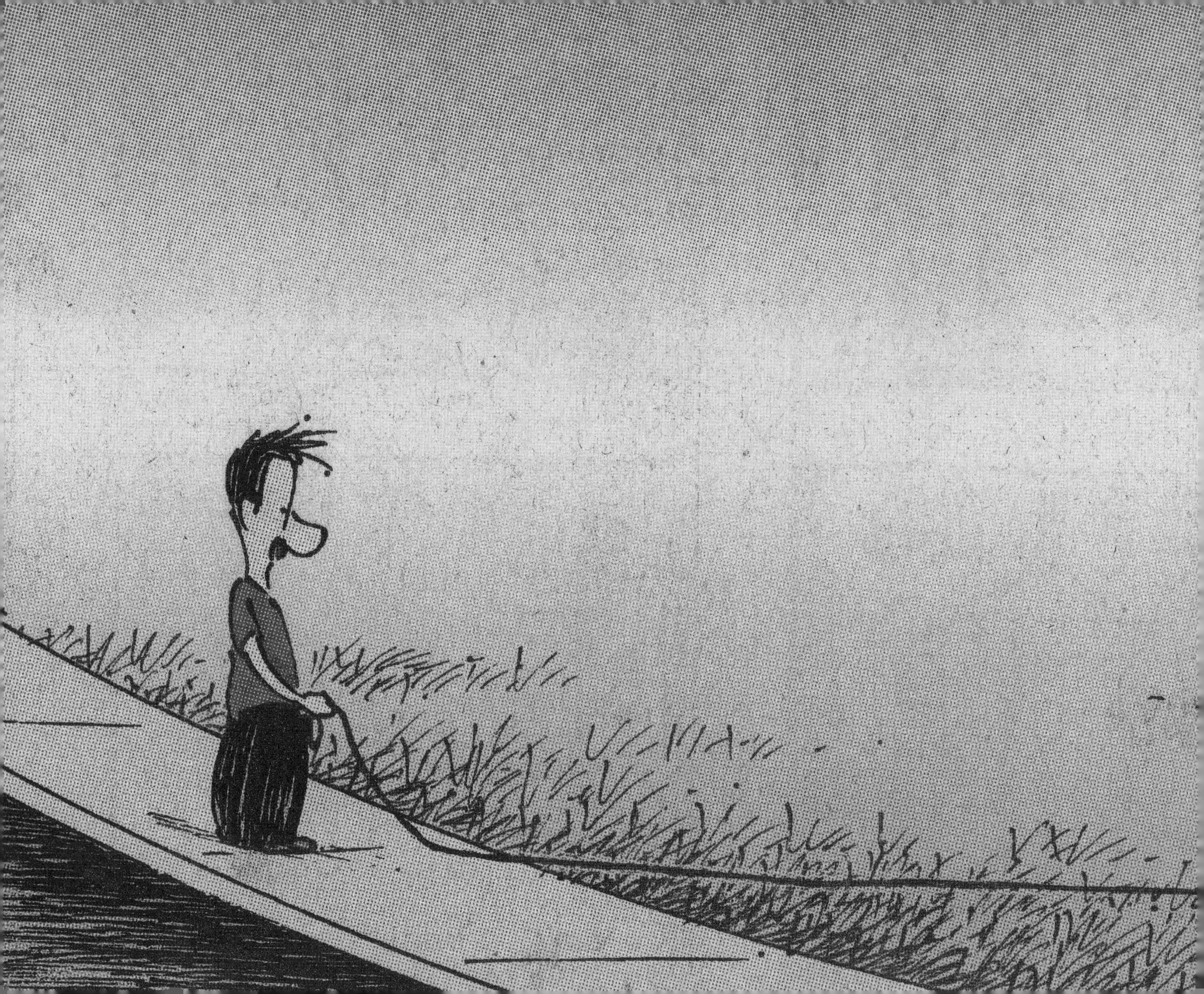

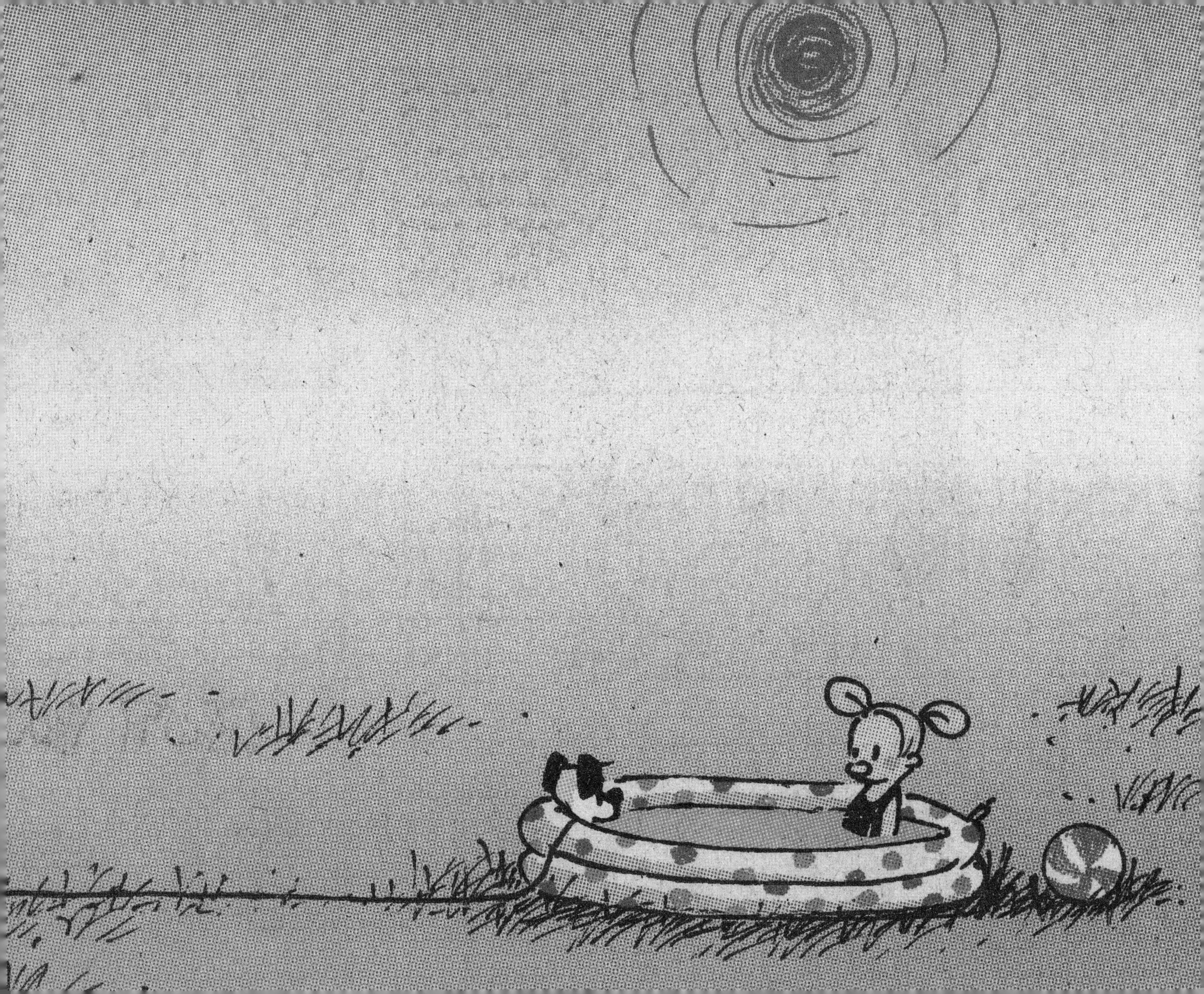

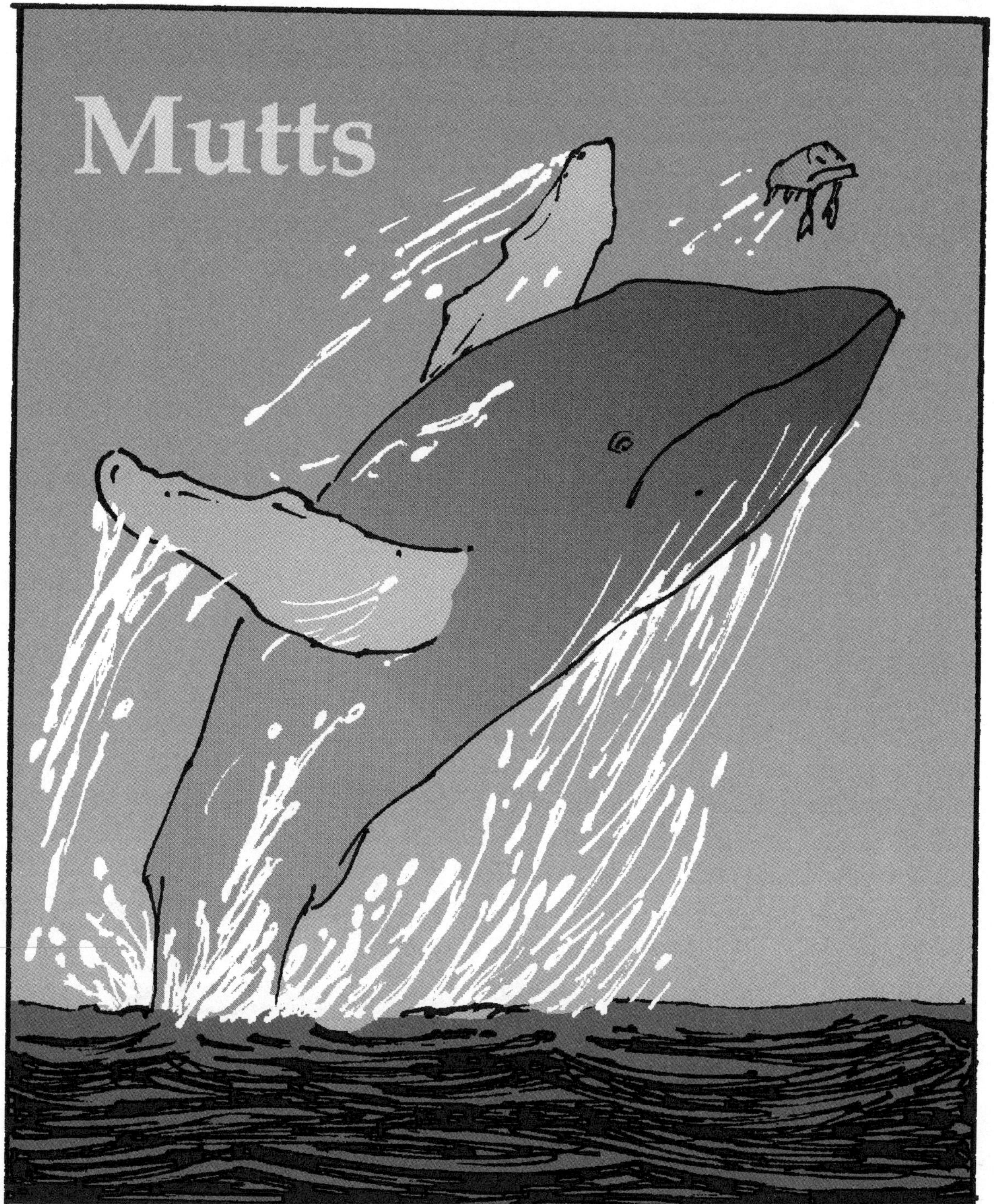
Mutts

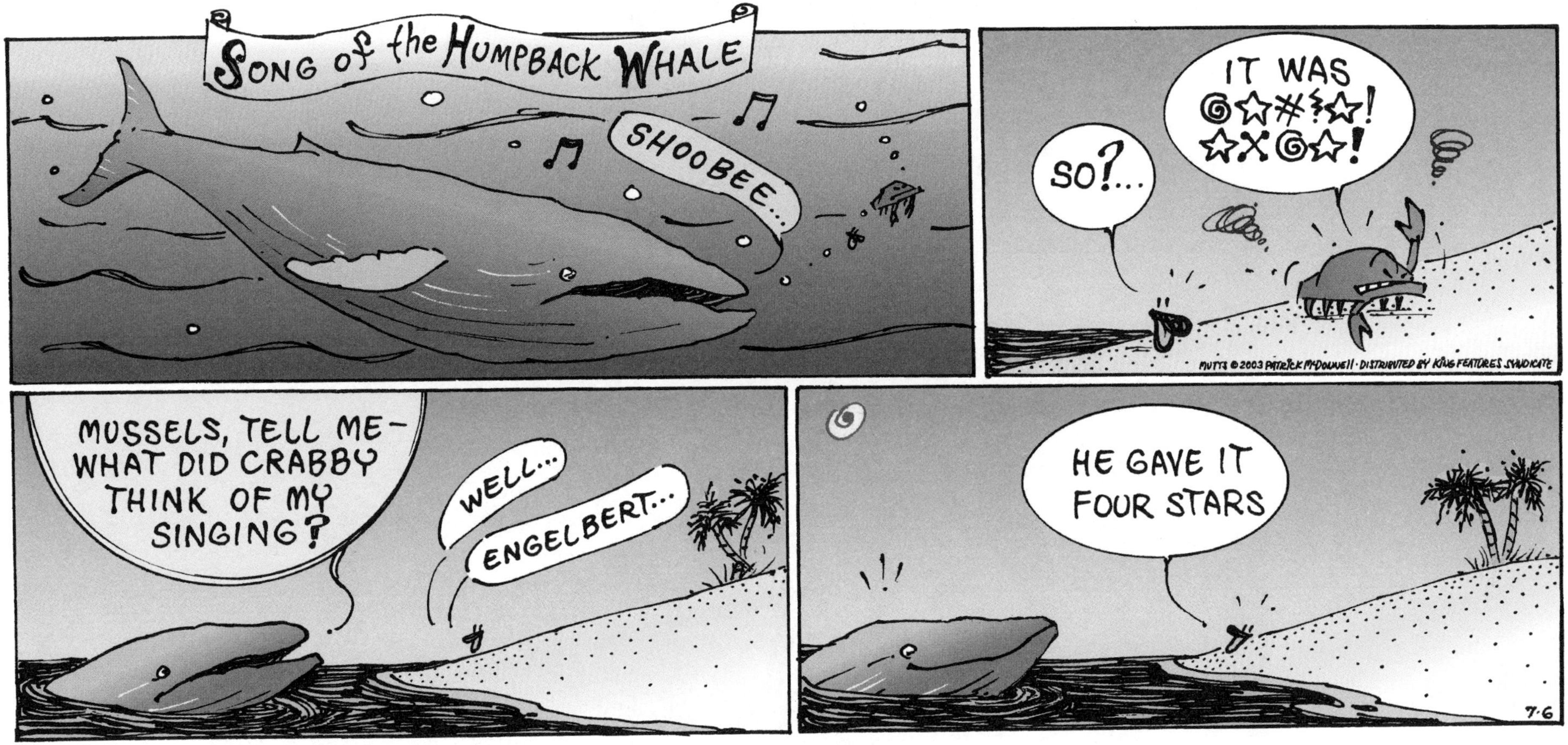
SONG of the HUMPBACK WHALE
SHOOBEE...
SO?...
IT WAS
MUSSELS, TELL ME— WHAT DID CRABBY THINK OF MY SINGING?
WELL...
ENGELBERT...
HE GAVE IT FOUR STARS
MUTTS © 2003 PATRICK McDONNELL · DISTRIBUTED BY KING FEATURES SYNDICATE
7·6

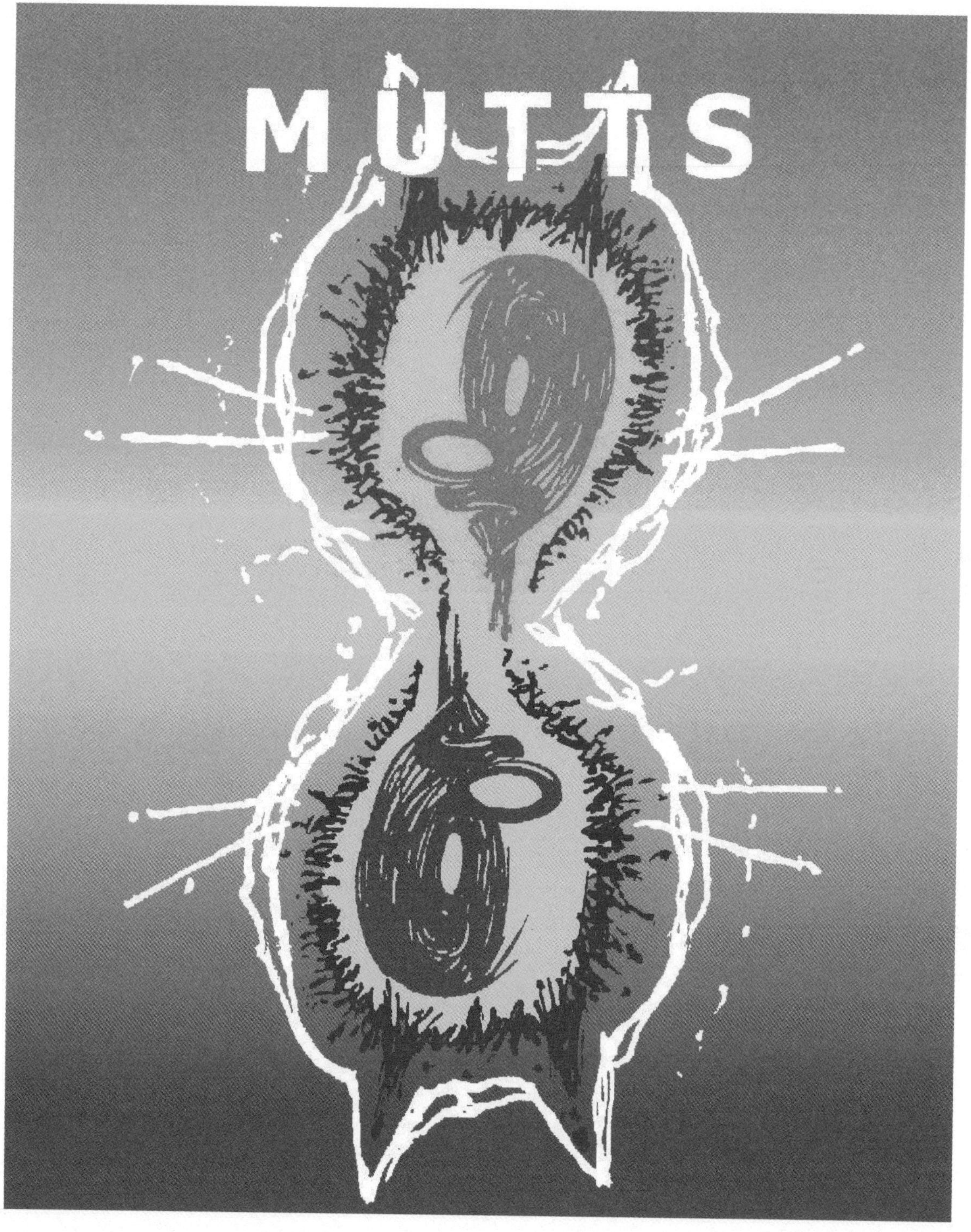
MUTTS

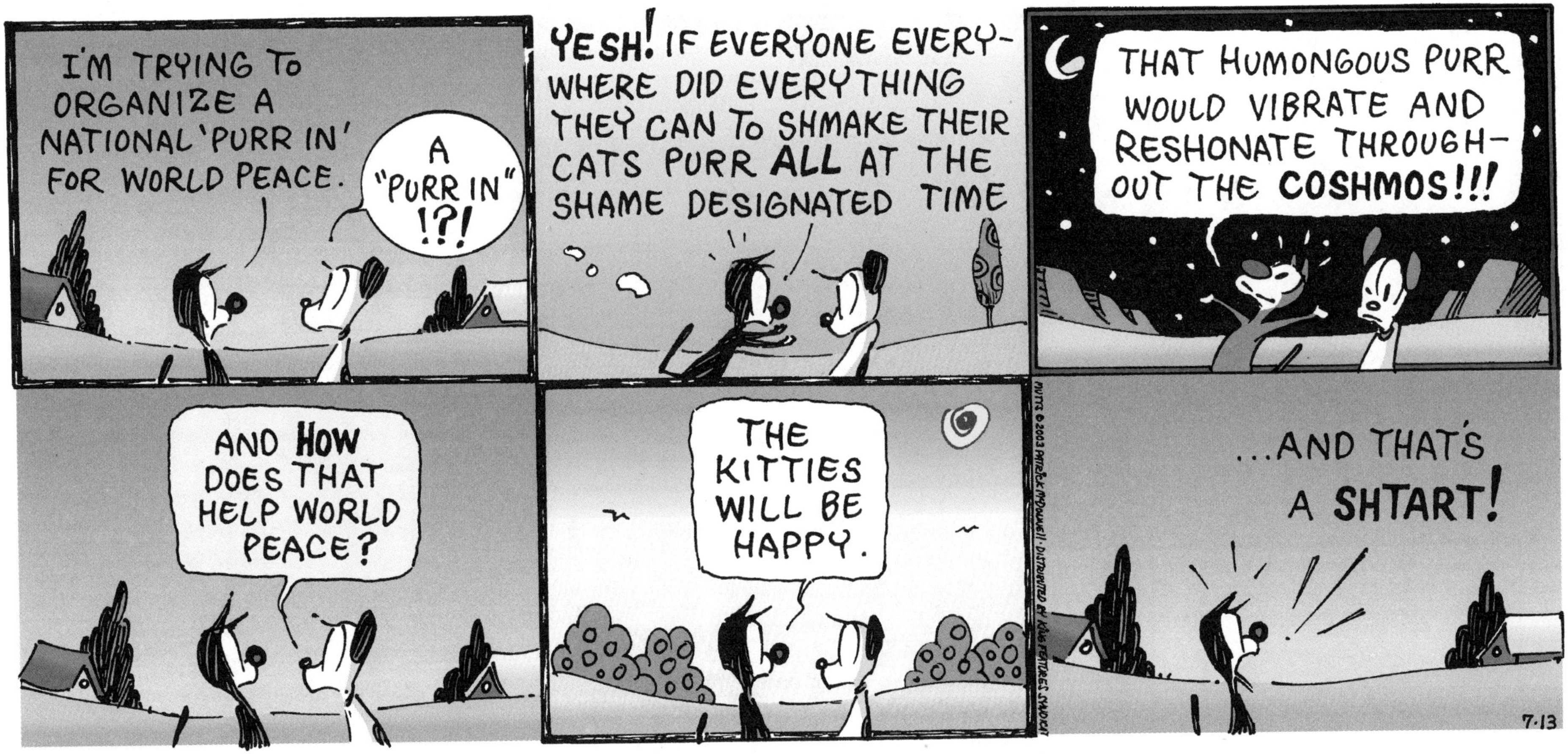
I'M TRYING TO ORGANIZE A NATIONAL 'PURR IN' FOR WORLD PEACE.
A "PURR IN" !?!
YESH! IF EVERYONE EVERY-WHERE DID EVERYTHING THEY CAN TO SHMAKE THEIR CATS PURR ALL AT THE SHAME DESIGNATED TIME
THAT HUMONGOUS PURR WOULD VIBRATE AND RESHONATE THROUGH-OUT THE COSHMOS!!!
AND HOW DOES THAT HELP WORLD PEACE?
THE KITTIES WILL BE HAPPY.
...AND THAT'S A SHTART!
MUTTS ©2003 PATRICK MCDONNELL · DISTRIBUTED BY KING FEATURES SYNDICATE
7·13

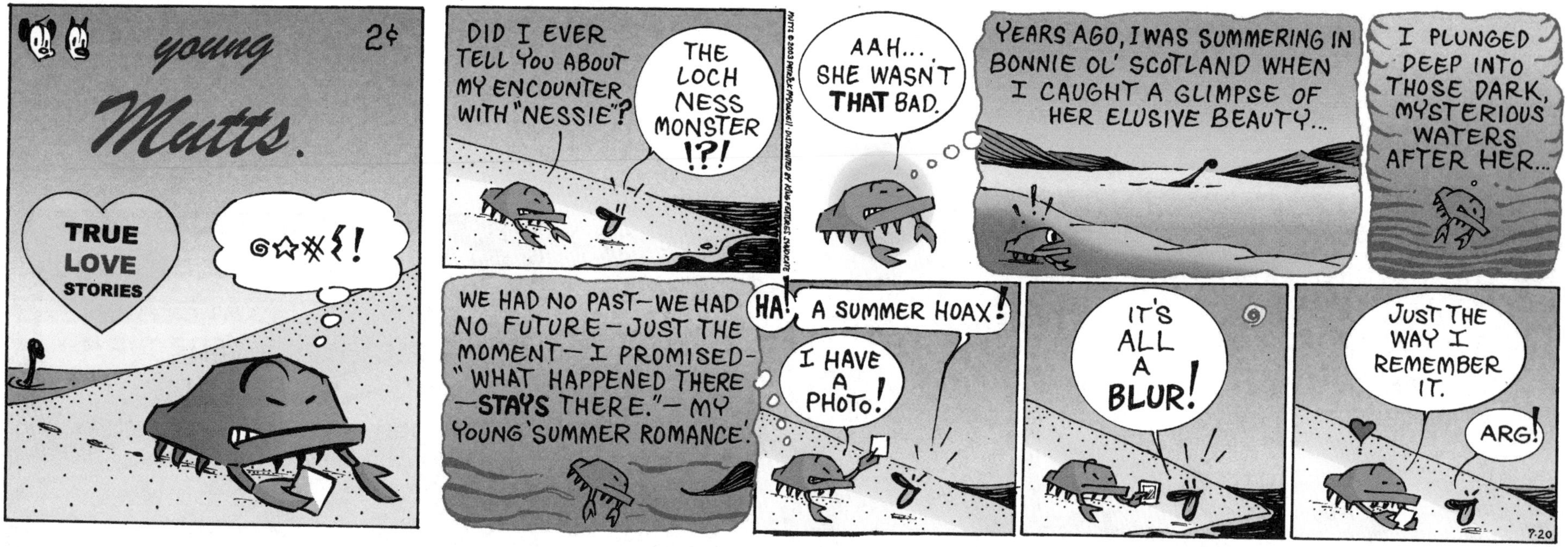
young Mutts.
2¢
TRUE LOVE STORIES
DID I EVER TELL YOU ABOUT MY ENCOUNTER WITH "NESSIE"?
THE LOCH NESS MONSTER !?!
AAH... SHE WASN'T THAT BAD.
YEARS AGO, I WAS SUMMERING IN BONNIE OL' SCOTLAND WHEN I CAUGHT A GLIMPSE OF HER ELUSIVE BEAUTY...
I PLUNGED DEEP INTO THOSE DARK, MYSTERIOUS WATERS AFTER HER...
WE HAD NO PAST—WE HAD NO FUTURE—JUST THE MOMENT—I PROMISED—"WHAT HAPPENED THERE—STAYS THERE."—MY YOUNG 'SUMMER ROMANCE'.
HA! A SUMMER HOAX!
I HAVE A PHOTO!
IT'S ALL A BLUR!
JUST THE WAY I REMEMBER IT.
ARG!
7·20

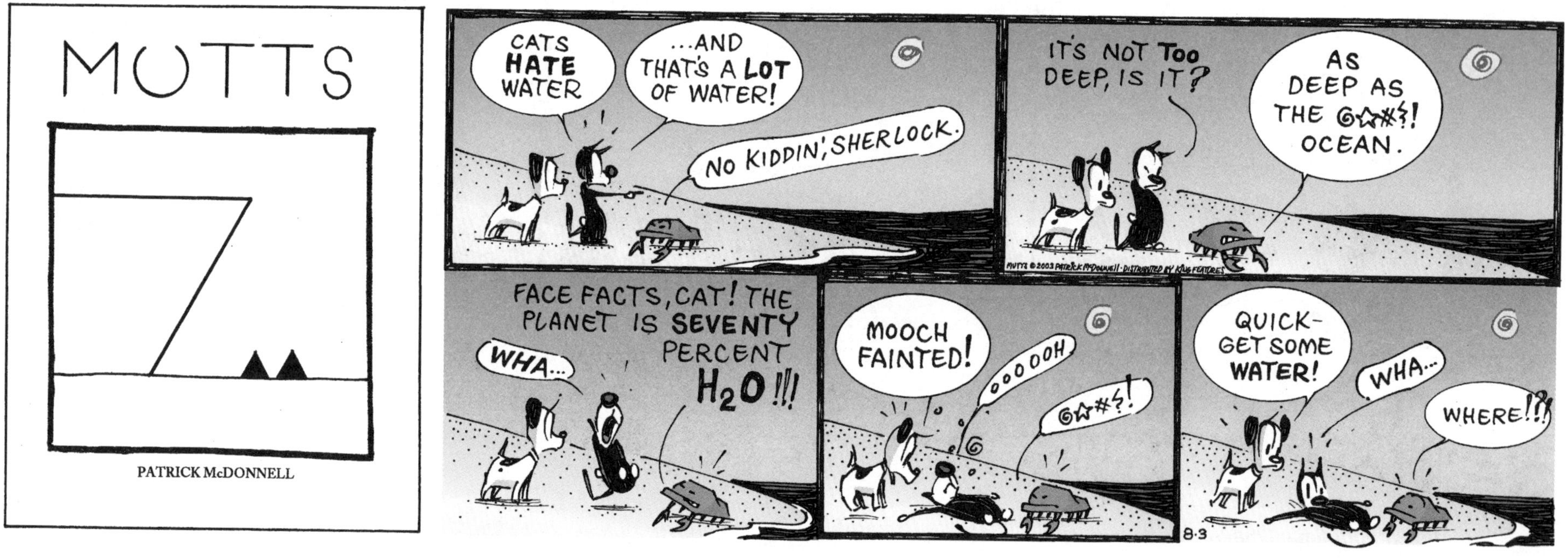
MUTTS
PATRICK McDONNELL
CATS HATE WATER
...AND THAT'S A LOT OF WATER!
NO KIDDIN', SHERLOCK.
IT'S NOT TOO DEEP, IS IT?
AS DEEP AS THE @☆#$! OCEAN.
FACE FACTS, CAT! THE PLANET IS SEVENTY PERCENT H2O!!!
WHA...
MOOCH FAINTED!
OOOOOH
QUICK-GET SOME WATER!
WHA...
WHERE!?!
8·3

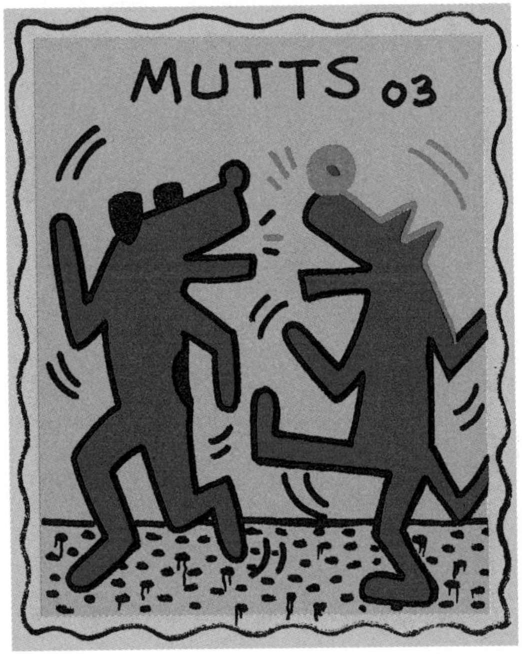
MUTTS 03

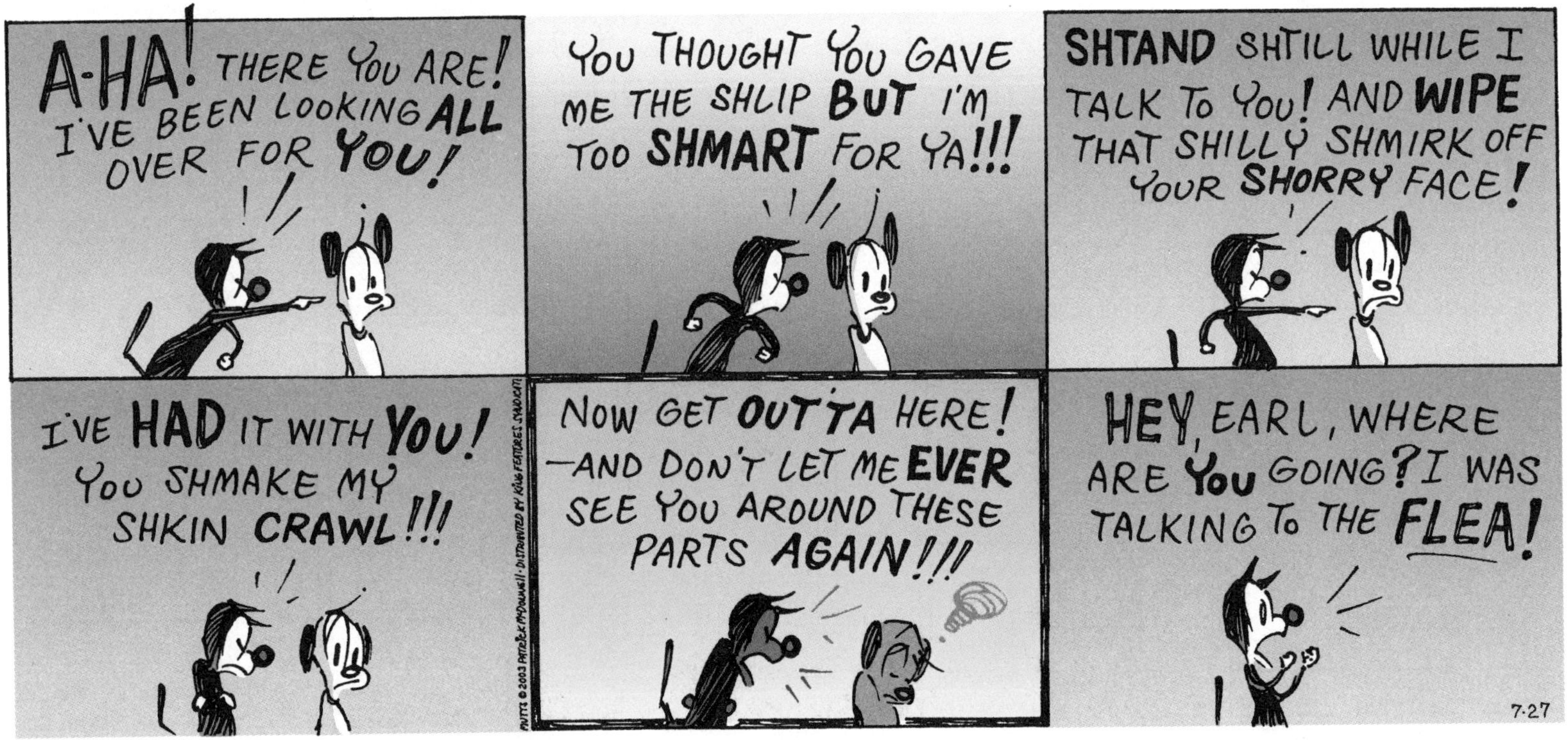
A-HA! THERE YOU ARE! I'VE BEEN LOOKING ALL OVER FOR YOU!
YOU THOUGHT YOU GAVE ME THE SHLIP BUT I'M TOO SHMART FOR YA!!!
SHTAND SHTILL WHILE I TALK TO YOU! AND WIPE THAT SHILLY SHMIRK OFF YOUR SHORRY FACE!
I'VE HAD IT WITH YOU! YOU SHMAKE MY SHKIN CRAWL!!!
MUTTS © 2003 PATRICK McDONNELL · DISTRIBUTED BY KING FEATURES SYNDICATE
NOW GET OUTTA HERE! —AND DON'T LET ME EVER SEE YOU AROUND THESE PARTS AGAIN!!!
HEY, EARL, WHERE ARE YOU GOING? I WAS TALKING TO THE FLEA!
7·27

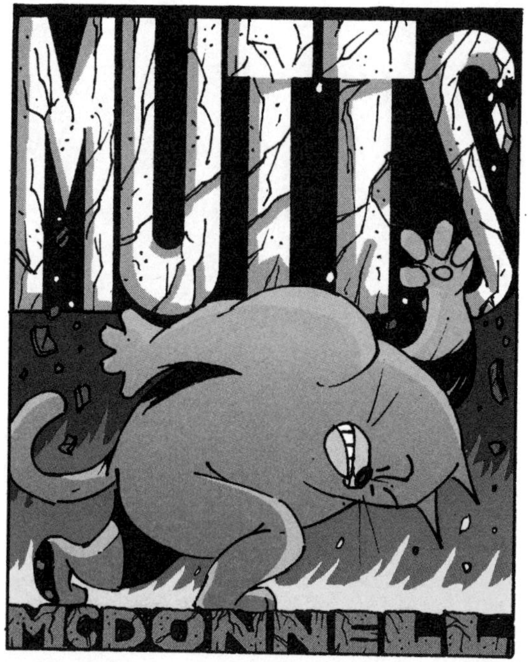

MUTTS
McDONNELL

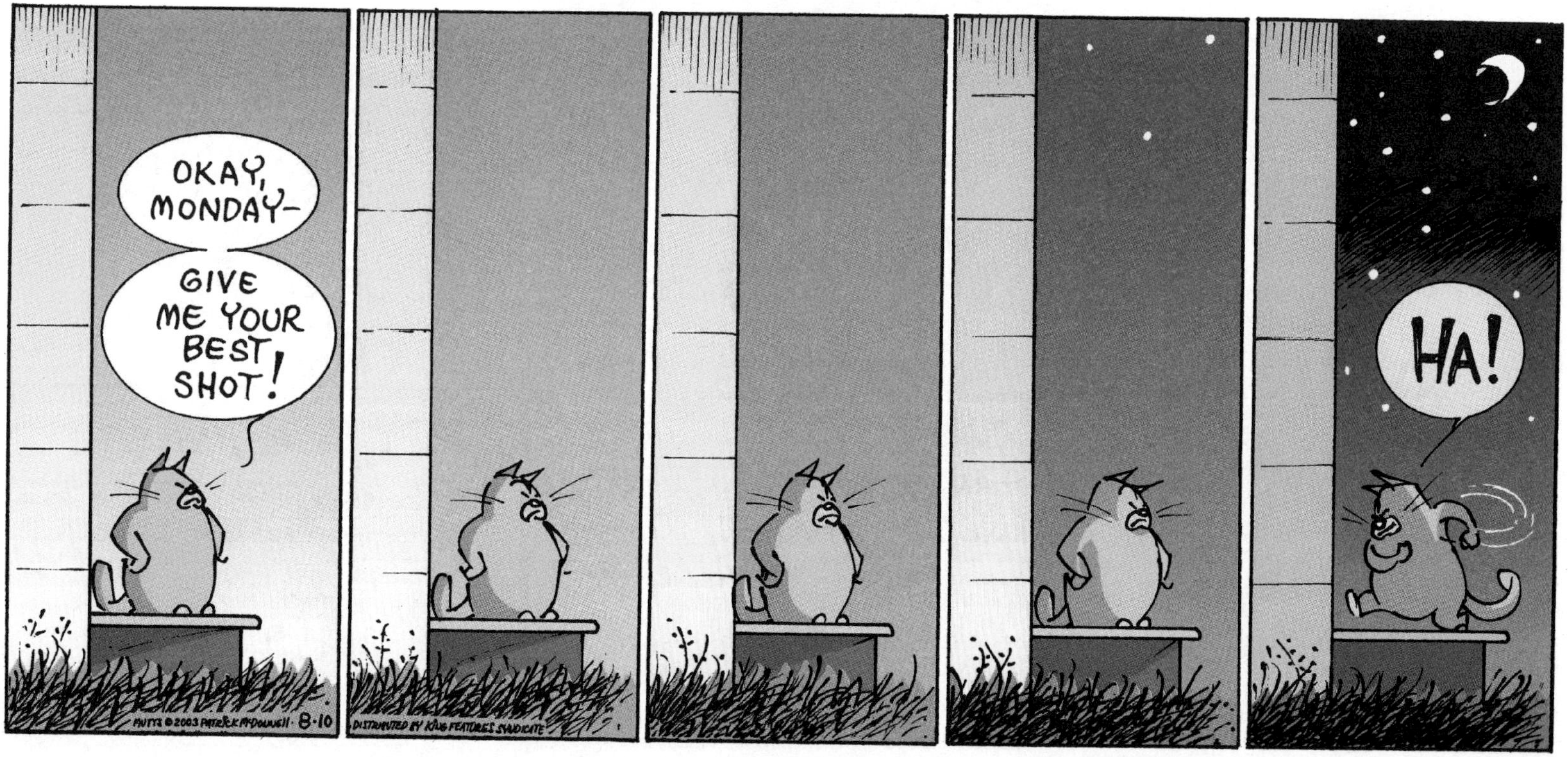

OKAY, MONDAY—
GIVE ME YOUR BEST SHOT!
MUTTS © 2003 PATRICK McDONNELL · 8-10
DISTRIBUTED BY KING FEATURES SYNDICATE
HA!

MUTTS
McDONNELL

THEY SAY IF YOU PUT A SEASHELL TO YOUR EAR YOU CAN HEAR THE OCEAN.
WOW.
8·17
MUTTS © 2003 PATRICK McDONNELL · DISTRIBUTED BY KING FEATURES SYNDICATE

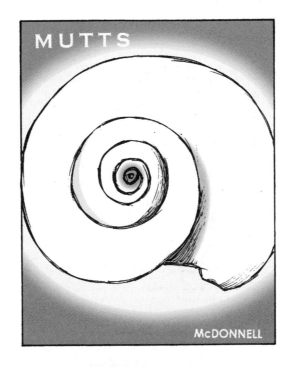

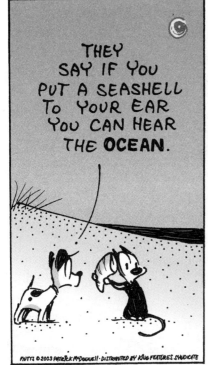

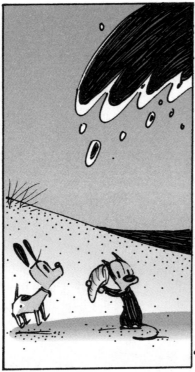

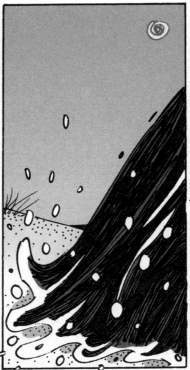

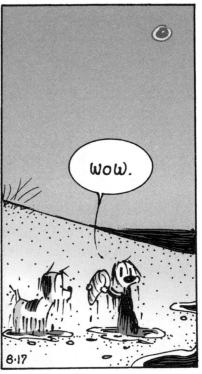

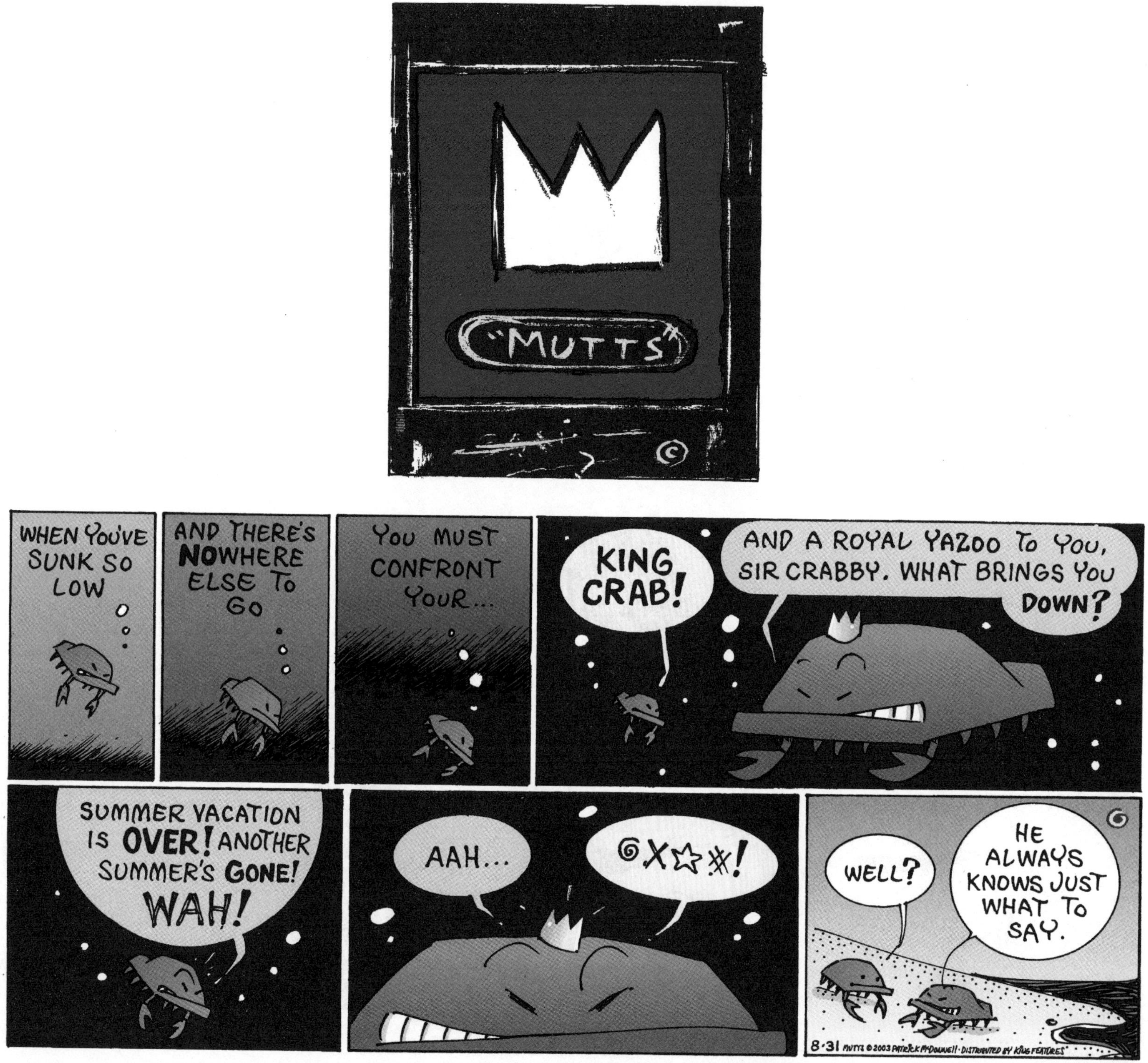
"MUTTS"
WHEN YOU'VE SUNK SO LOW
AND THERE'S NOWHERE ELSE TO GO
YOU MUST CONFRONT YOUR...
KING CRAB!
AND A ROYAL YAZOO TO YOU, SIR CRABBY. WHAT BRINGS YOU DOWN?
SUMMER VACATION IS OVER! ANOTHER SUMMER'S GONE! WAH!
AAH...
@X☆*#!
WELL?
HE ALWAYS KNOWS JUST WHAT TO SAY.
8·31 MUTTS © 2003 PATRICK McDONNELL · DISTRIBUTED BY KING FEATURES

NOTHING ELSE IS
MUTTS.
PATRICK McDONNELL

♫ LITTLE ♫ PINK SOCK
HO
HO!
THAT'S MY SOCK!!!
MINE!
NO-MINE!
NO-MINE!
MINE-YOU MUTT!
MINE-YOU PUSS!
AAH-IT'S YOURS, PAL.
NAH-IT'S YOURS, CHUM.
WHOSE "SOCK" IS THIS!?!
9.7
MUTTS © 2003 PATRICK McDONNELL · DISTRIBUTED BY KING FEATURES.

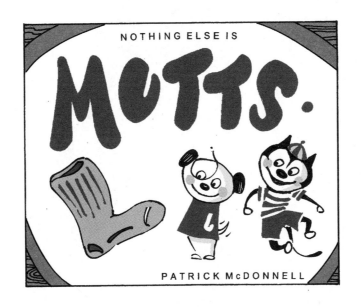

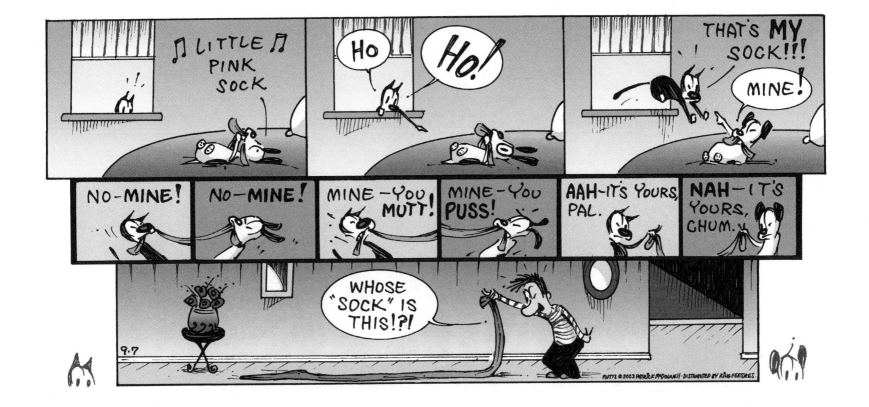

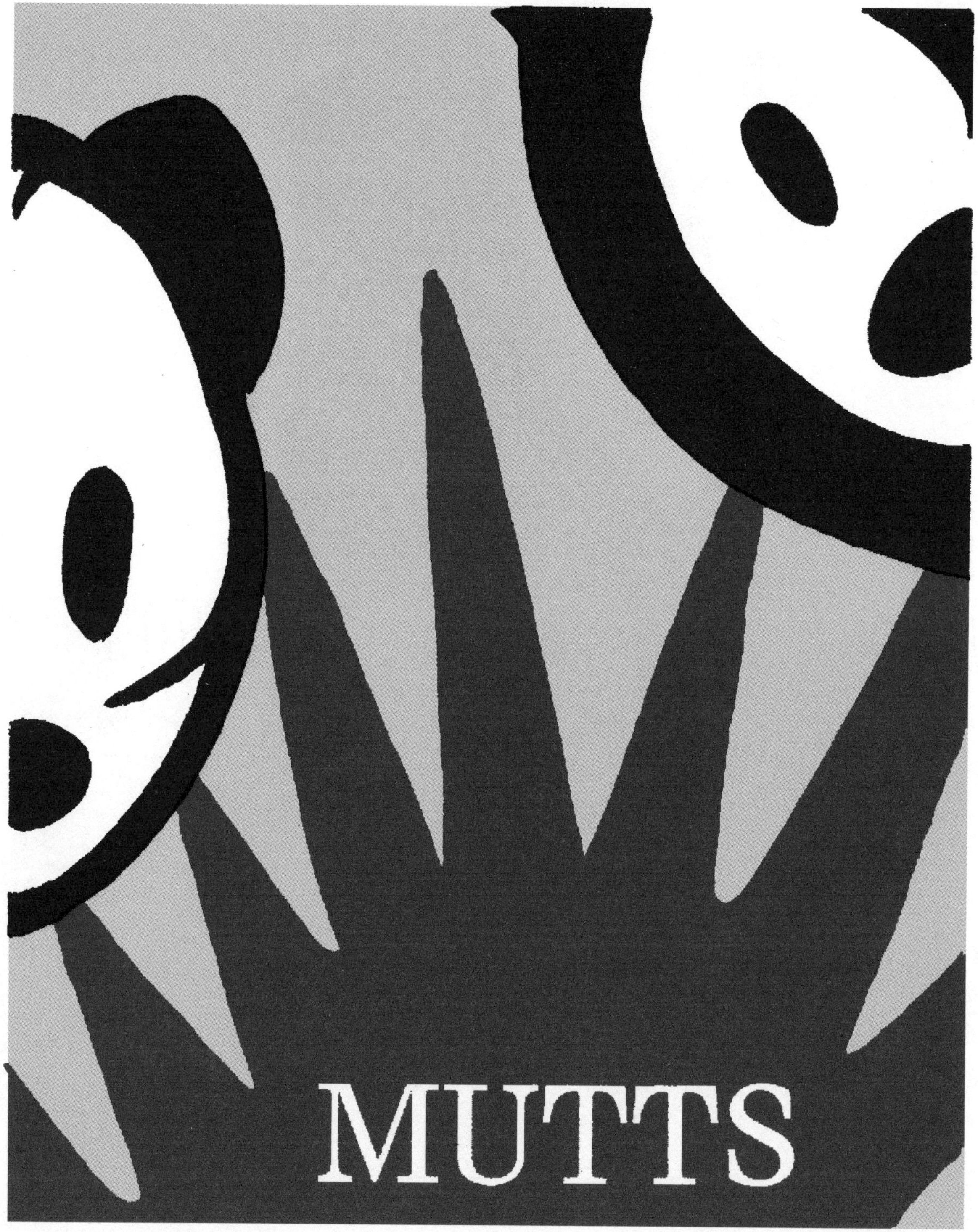
MUTTS

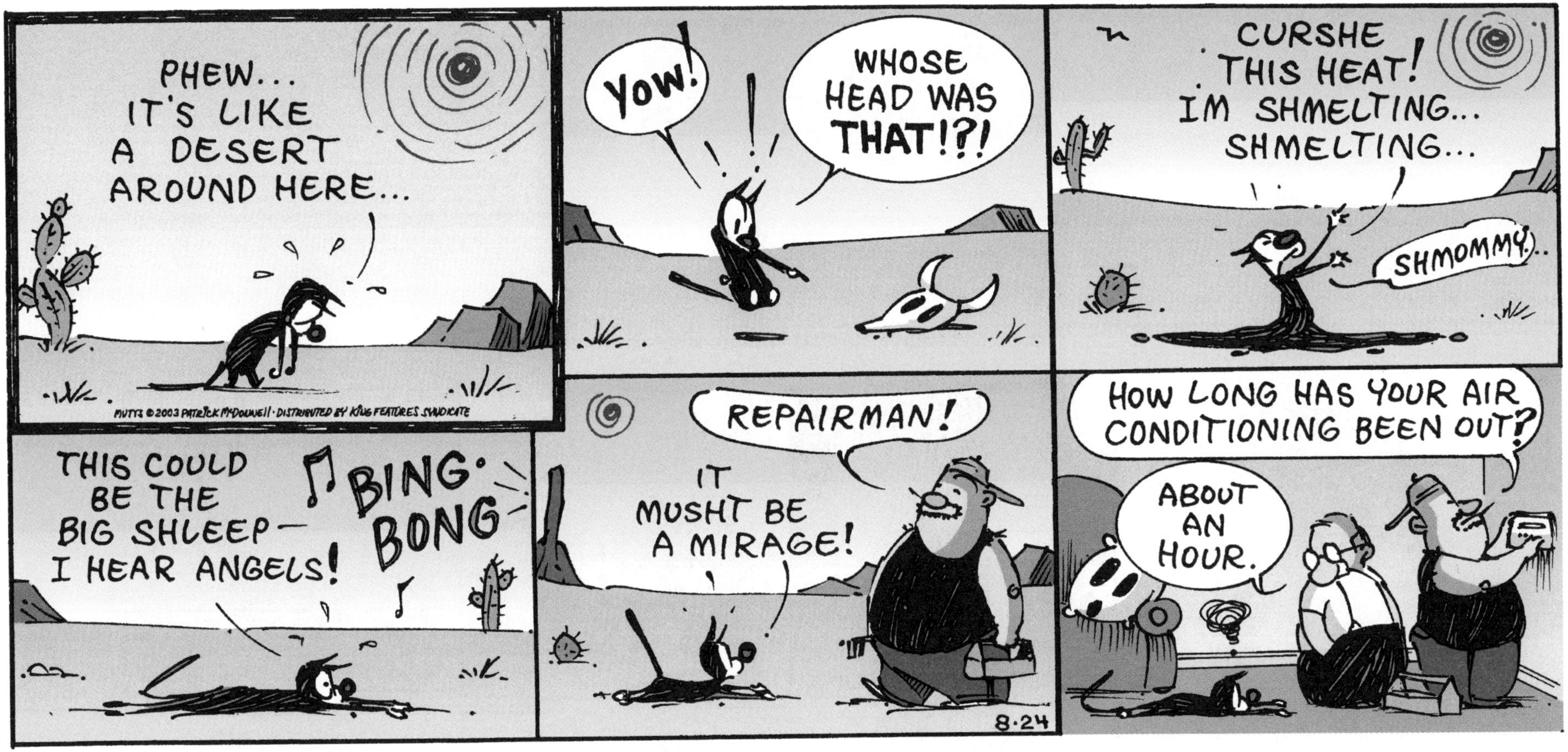
PHEW... IT'S LIKE A DESERT AROUND HERE...
MUTTS © 2003 PATRICK McDONNELL · DISTRIBUTED BY KING FEATURES SYNDICATE
YOW!
WHOSE HEAD WAS THAT!?!
CURSHE THIS HEAT! I'M SHMELTING... SHMELTING...
SHMOMMY...
THIS COULD BE THE BIG SHLEEP— I HEAR ANGELS!
BING· BONG
IT MUSHT BE A MIRAGE!
REPAIRMAN!
8·24
HOW LONG HAS YOUR AIR CONDITIONING BEEN OUT?
ABOUT AN HOUR.

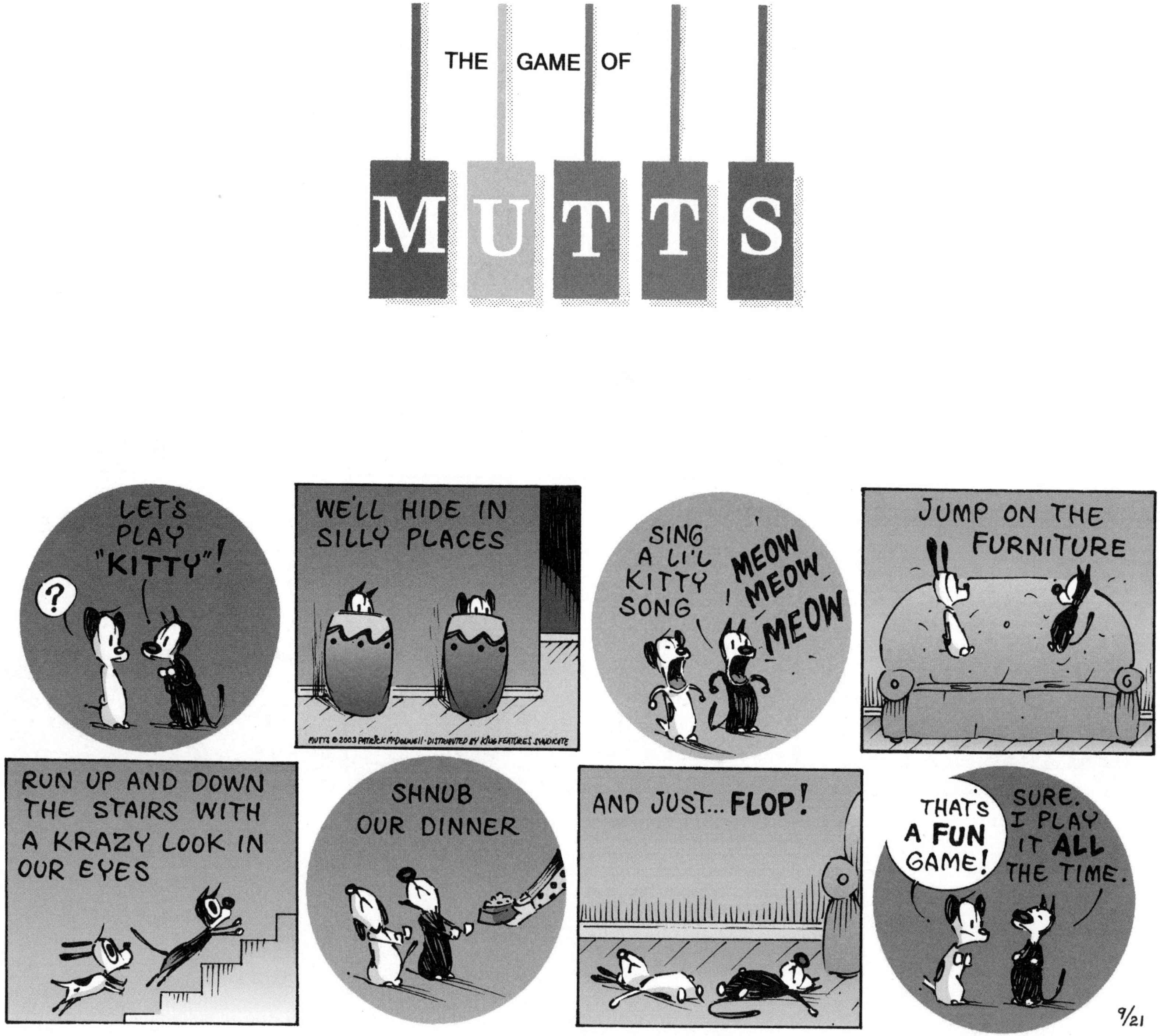
THE GAME OF
MUTTS
LET'S PLAY "KITTY"!
?
WE'LL HIDE IN SILLY PLACES
MUTTS © 2003 PATRICK McDONNELL · DISTRIBUTED BY KING FEATURES SYNDICATE
SING A LI'L KITTY SONG
MEOW MEOW MEOW
JUMP ON THE FURNITURE
RUN UP AND DOWN THE STAIRS WITH A KRAZY LOOK IN OUR EYES
SHNUB OUR DINNER
AND JUST... FLOP!
THAT'S A FUN GAME!
SURE. I PLAY IT ALL THE TIME.
9/21

THE GAME OF MUTTS

NOW— LET'S PLAY "DOGGY"!
?
WE'LL FETCH STICKS!
?
ROLL AROUND IN DIRT!
?
BARK AT THE MAILMAN!
SIT, STAY, HEEL, BEG, JUMP, SPEAK!
?
HOWL LIKE A LOON AT THE MOON!
?
HOOWL
AND CHASE OUR OWN TAILS!
?
LET'S QUIT.
I CAN'T.
MUTTS © 2003 PATRICK McDONNELL · DISTRIBUTED BY KING FEATURES SYNDICATE
10/5

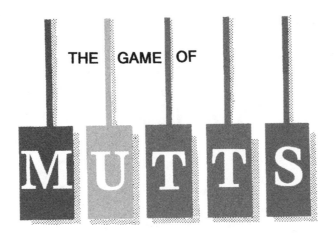

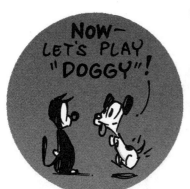

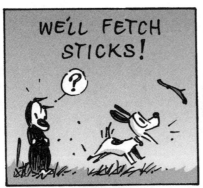

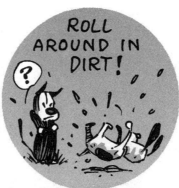

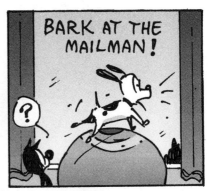

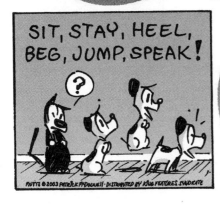

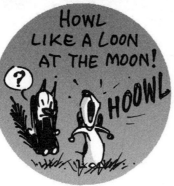

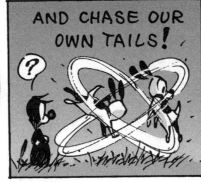

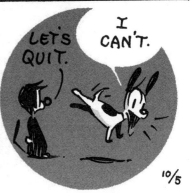

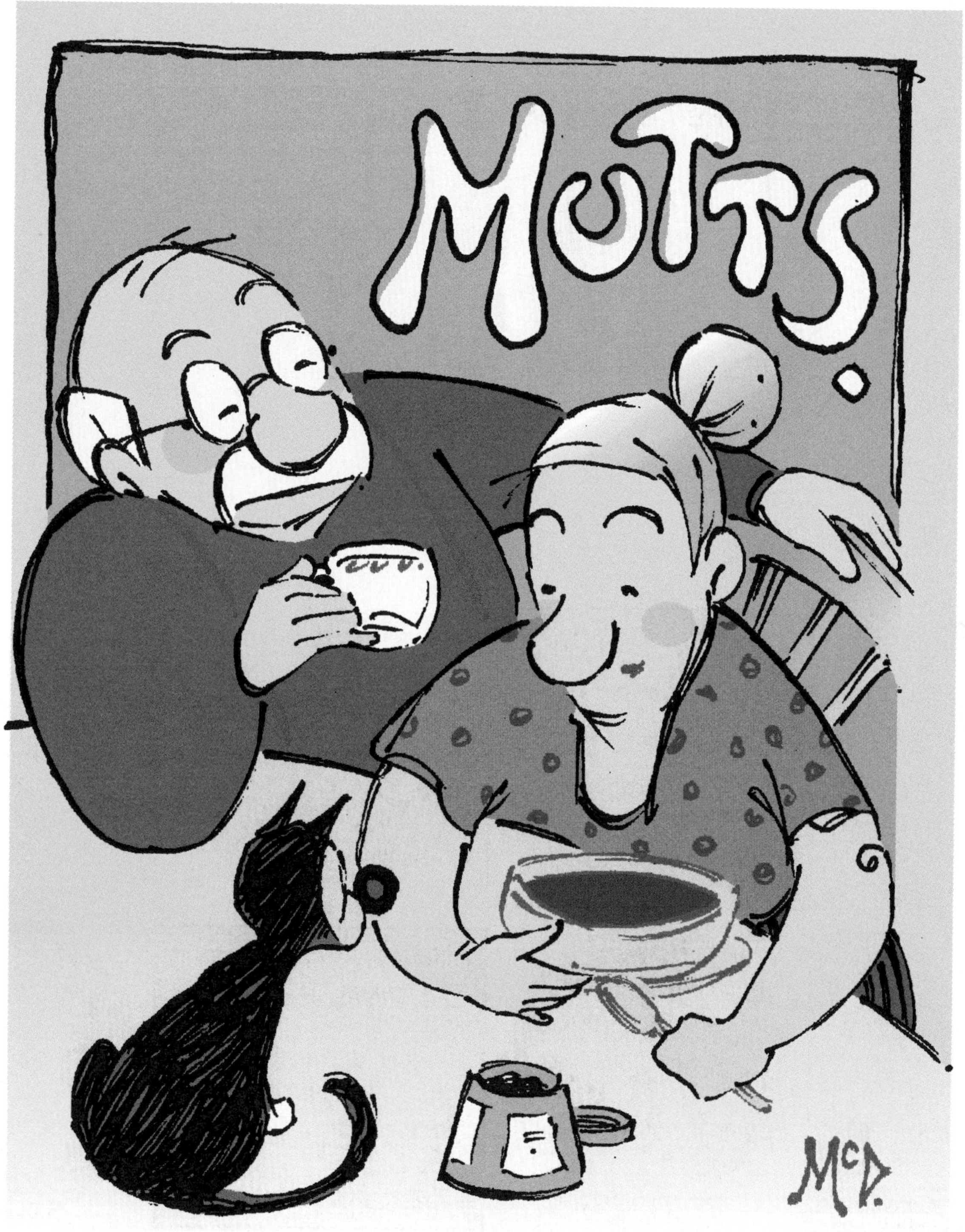
MUTTS
McD.

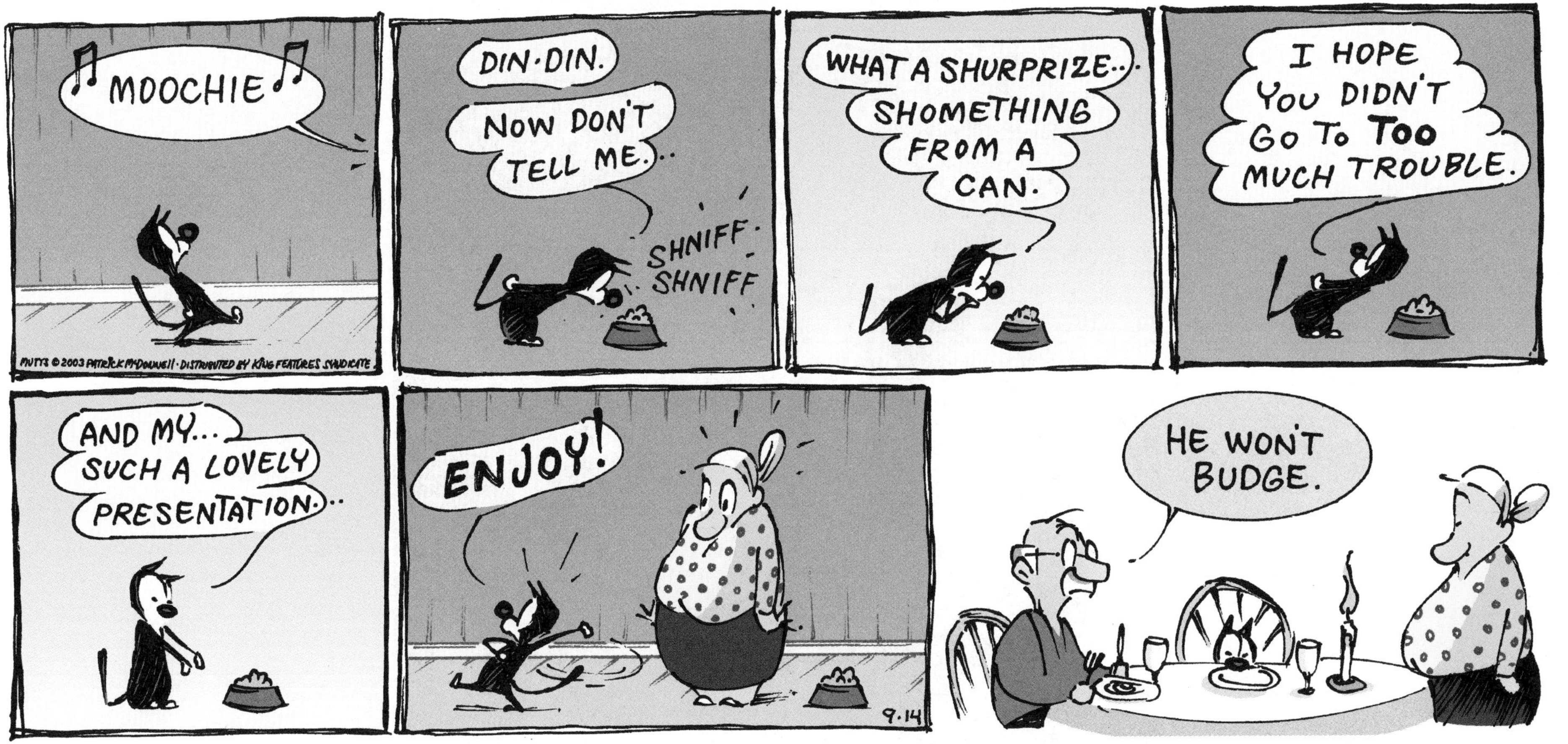
MOOCHIE
MUTTS © 2003 PATRICK McDONNELL · DISTRIBUTED BY KING FEATURES SYNDICATE
DIN·DIN.
NOW DON'T TELL ME...
SHNIFF· SHNIFF
WHAT A SHURPRIZE...
SHOMETHING FROM A CAN.
I HOPE YOU DIDN'T GO TO **TOO** MUCH TROUBLE.
AND MY...
SUCH A LOVELY PRESENTATION...
ENJOY!
9·14
HE WON'T BUDGE.

MUTTS
CARTOON

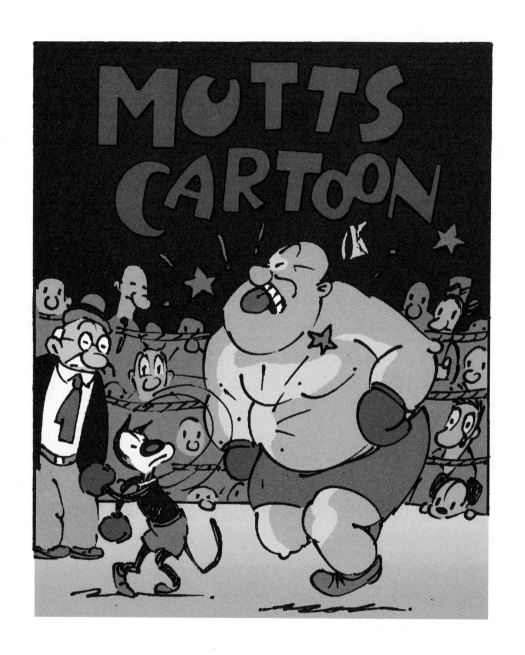

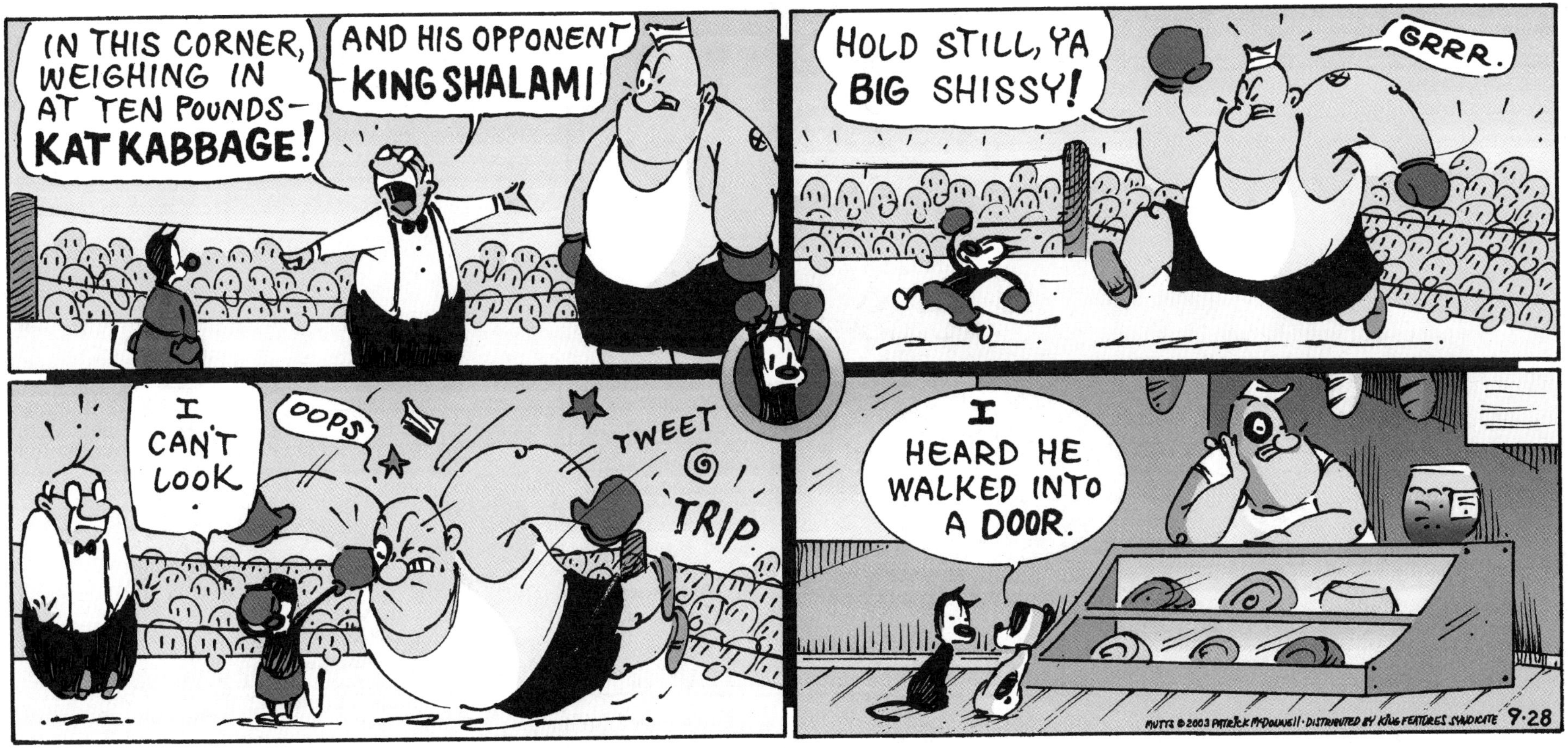
IN THIS CORNER, WEIGHING IN AT TEN POUNDS- KAT KABBAGE!
AND HIS OPPONENT -KING SHALAMI
HOLD STILL, YA BIG SHISSY!
GRRR.
I CAN'T LOOK.
OOPS
TWEET
TRIP
I HEARD HE WALKED INTO A DOOR.
MUTTS © 2003 PATRICK McDONNELL · DISTRIBUTED BY KING FEATURES SYNDICATE 9·28

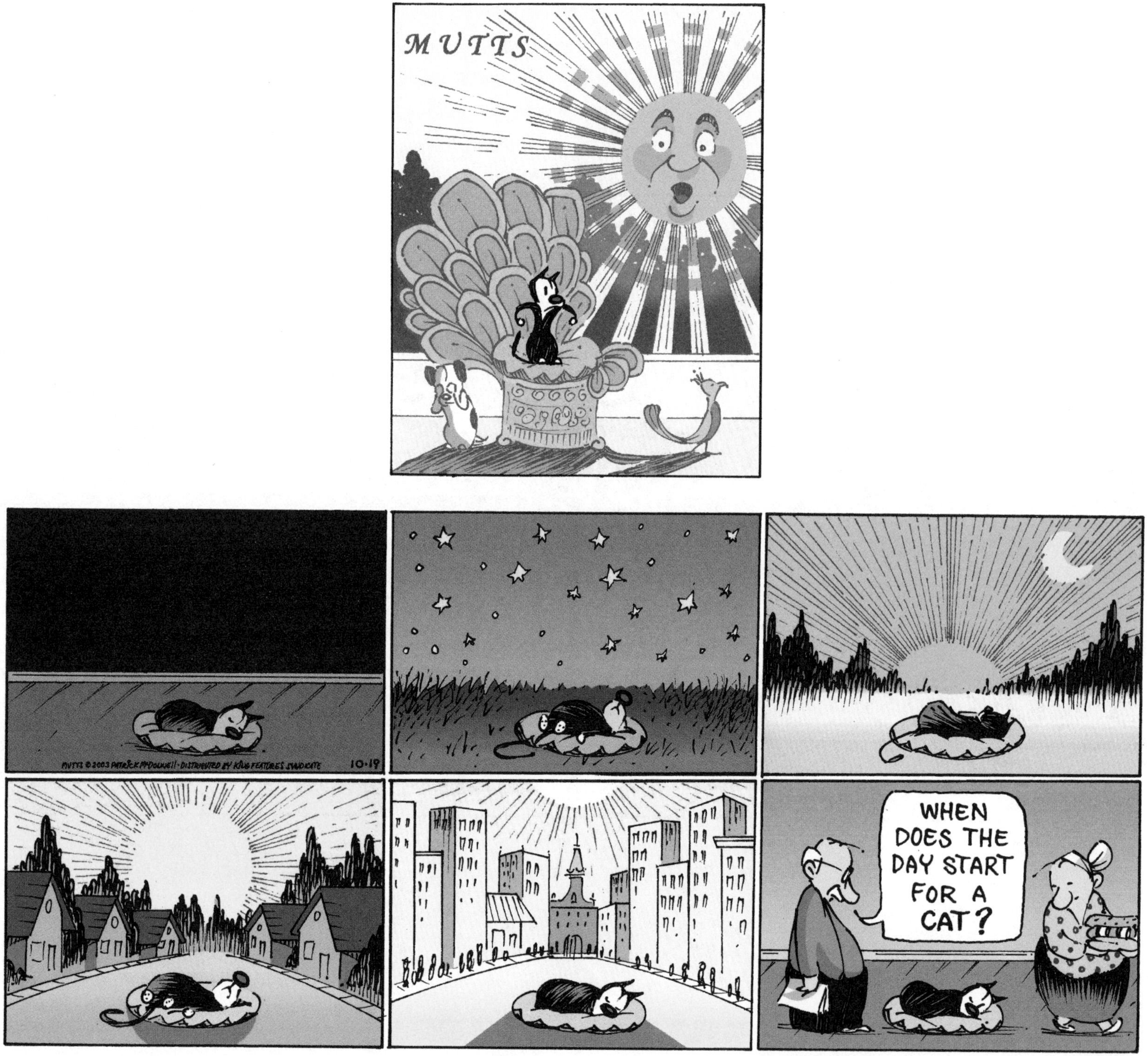
MUTTS
MUTTS © 2003 PATRICK McDONNELL · DISTRIBUTED BY KING FEATURES SYNDICATE
10-19
WHEN DOES THE DAY START FOR A CAT?

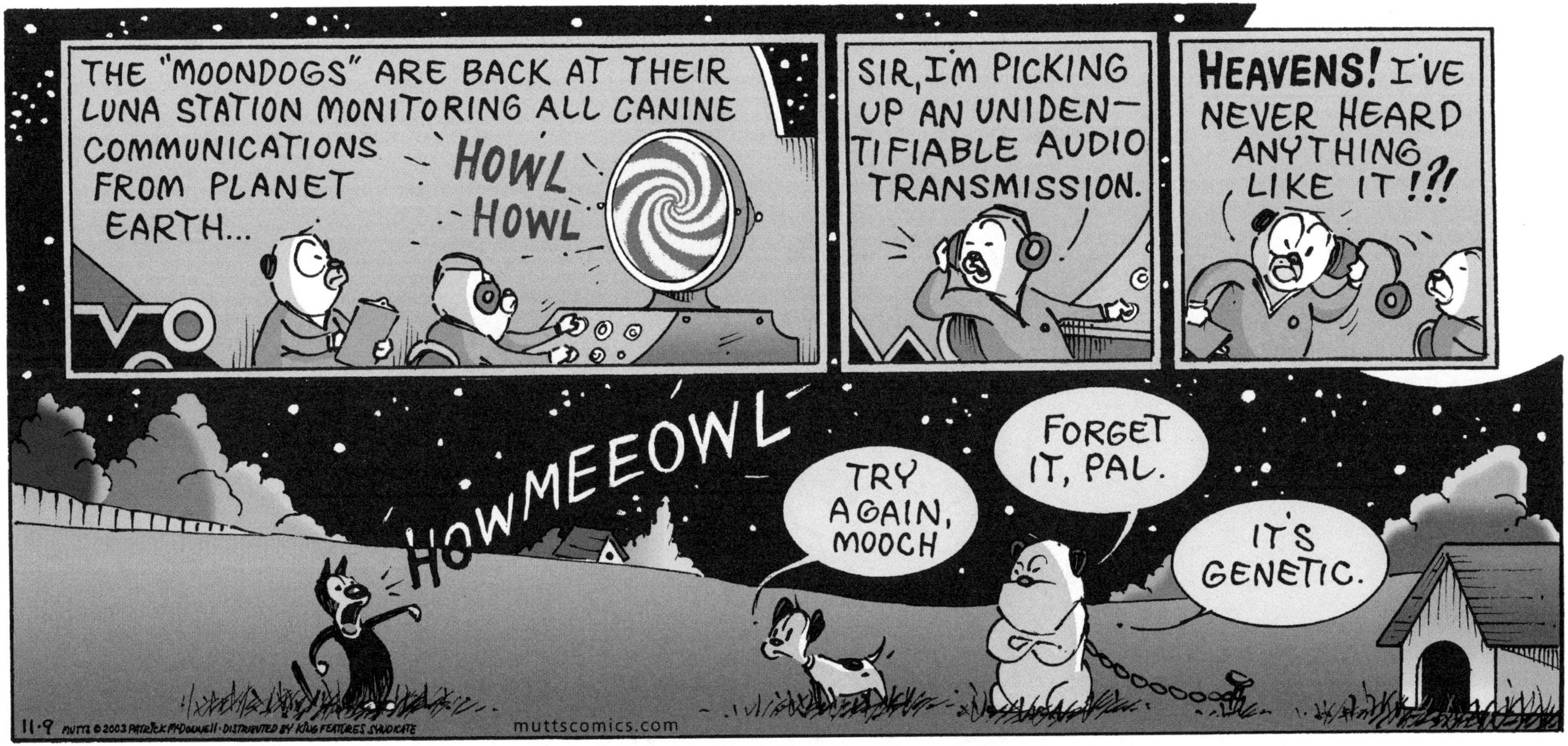
THE "MOONDOGS" ARE BACK AT THEIR LUNA STATION MONITORING ALL CANINE COMMUNICATIONS FROM PLANET EARTH...
HOWL
HOWL
SIR, I'M PICKING UP AN UNIDEN-TIFIABLE AUDIO TRANSMISSION.
HEAVENS! I'VE NEVER HEARD ANYTHING LIKE IT!?!
HOWMEEOWL
TRY AGAIN, MOOCH
FORGET IT, PAL.
IT'S GENETIC.
11·9 MUTTS © 2003 PATRICK McDONNELL · DISTRIBUTED BY KING FEATURES SYNDICATE
muttscomics.com

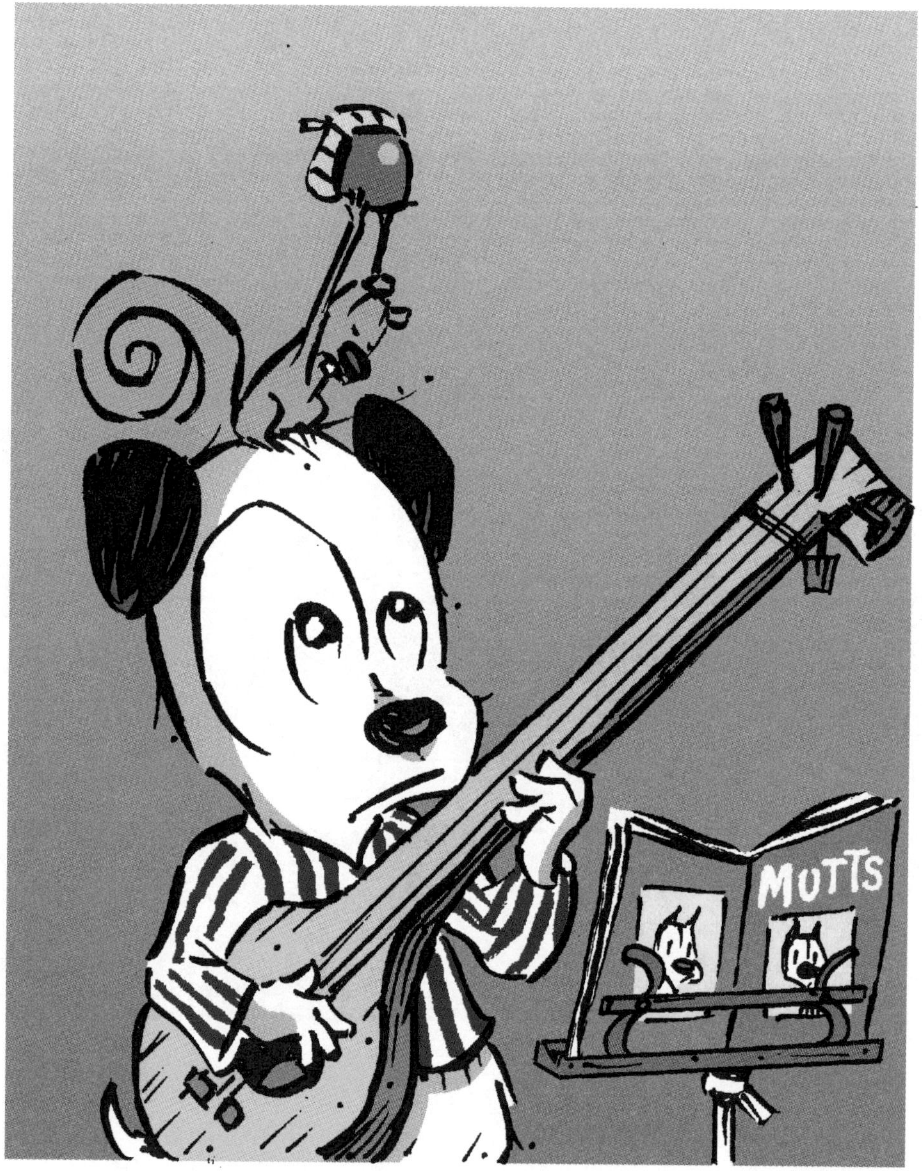
MUTTS

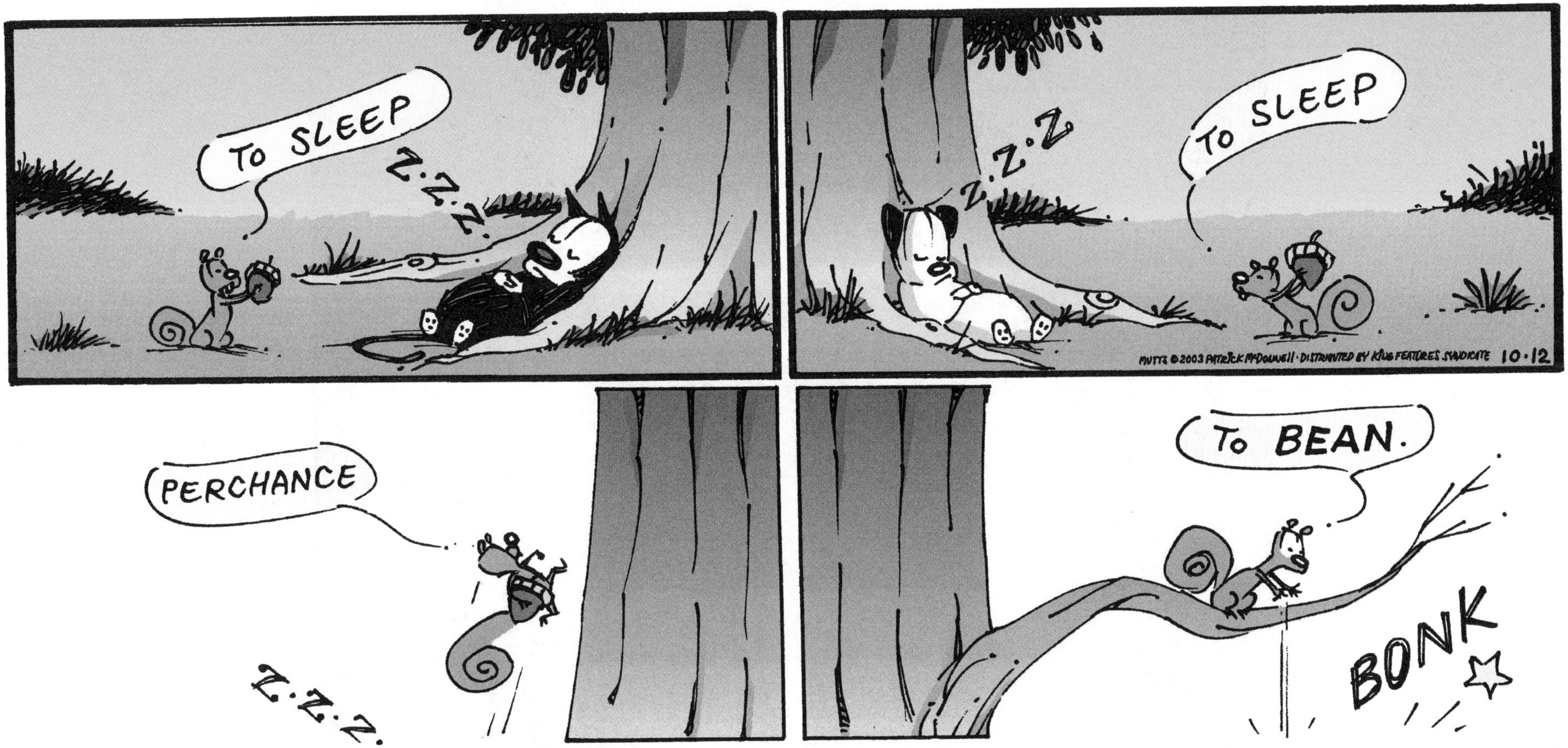
TO SLEEP
Z·Z·Z
Z·Z·Z
TO SLEEP
MUTTS © 2003 PATRICK McDONNELL · DISTRIBUTED BY KING FEATURES SYNDICATE 10·12
PERCHANCE
Z·Z·Z·
TO BEAN.
BONK

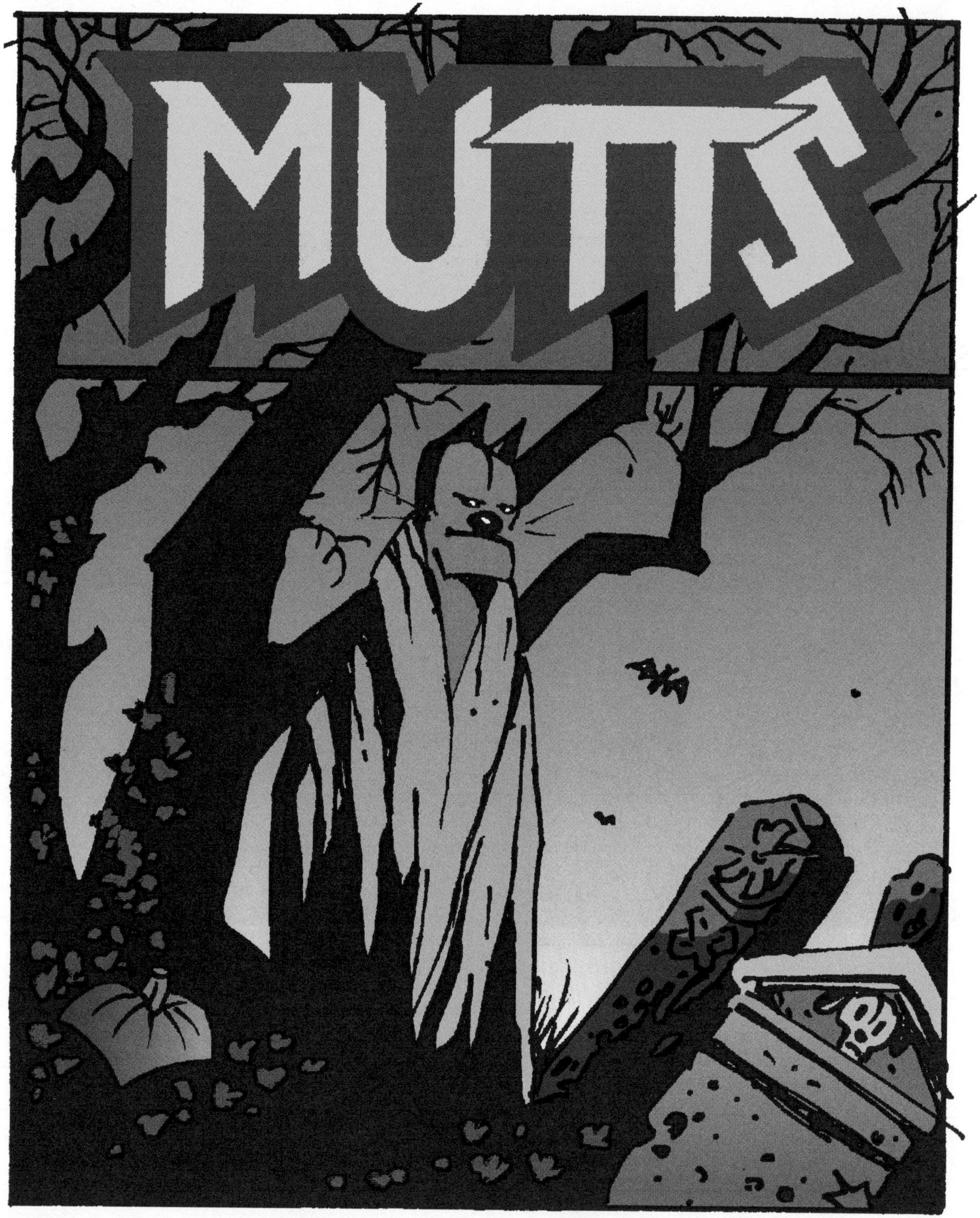
MUTTS

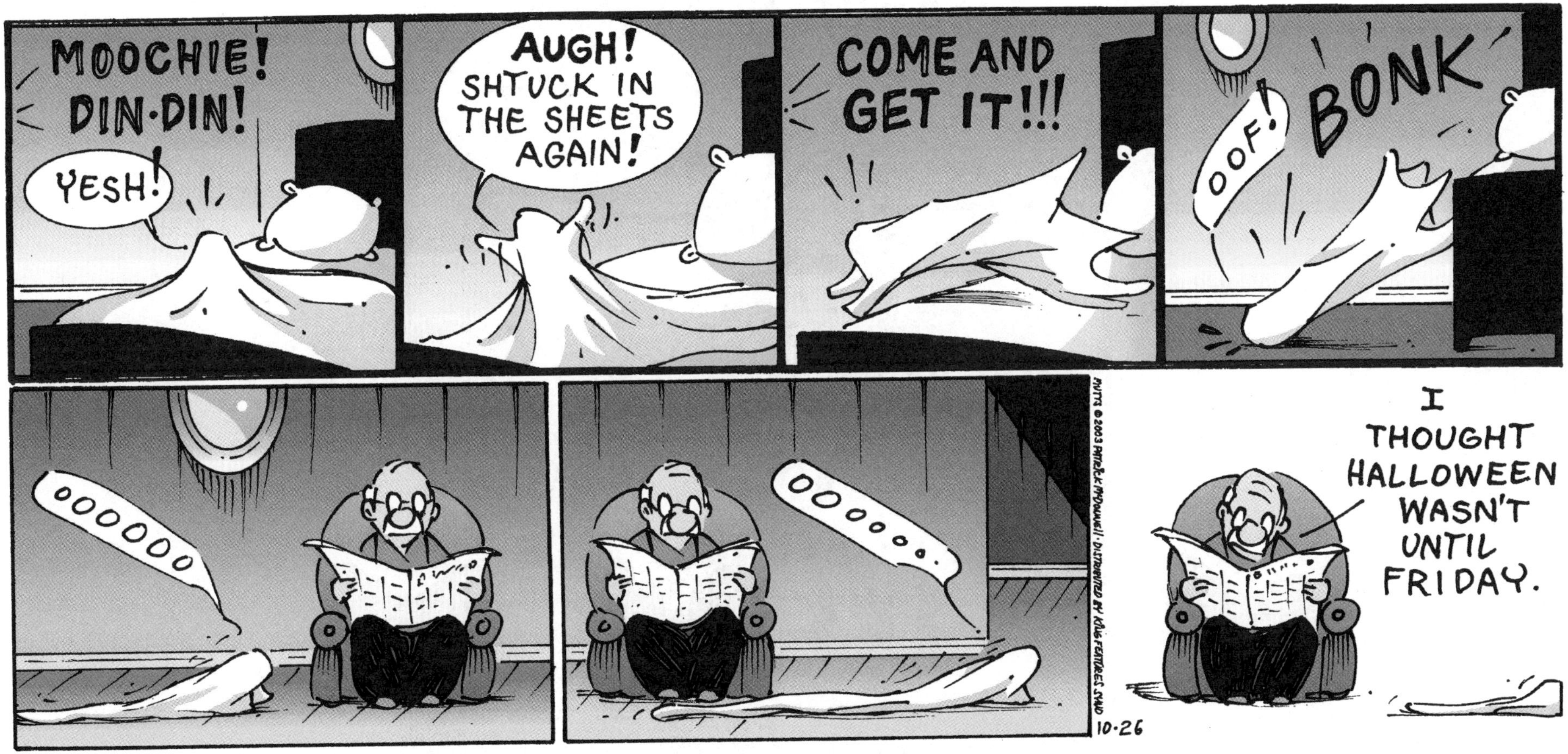
MOOCHIE! DIN-DIN!
YESH!
AUGH! SHTUCK IN THE SHEETS AGAIN!
COME AND GET IT!!!
OOF!
BONK
OOOOOO
OOOOOO..
I THOUGHT HALLOWEEN WASN'T UNTIL FRIDAY.
10-26

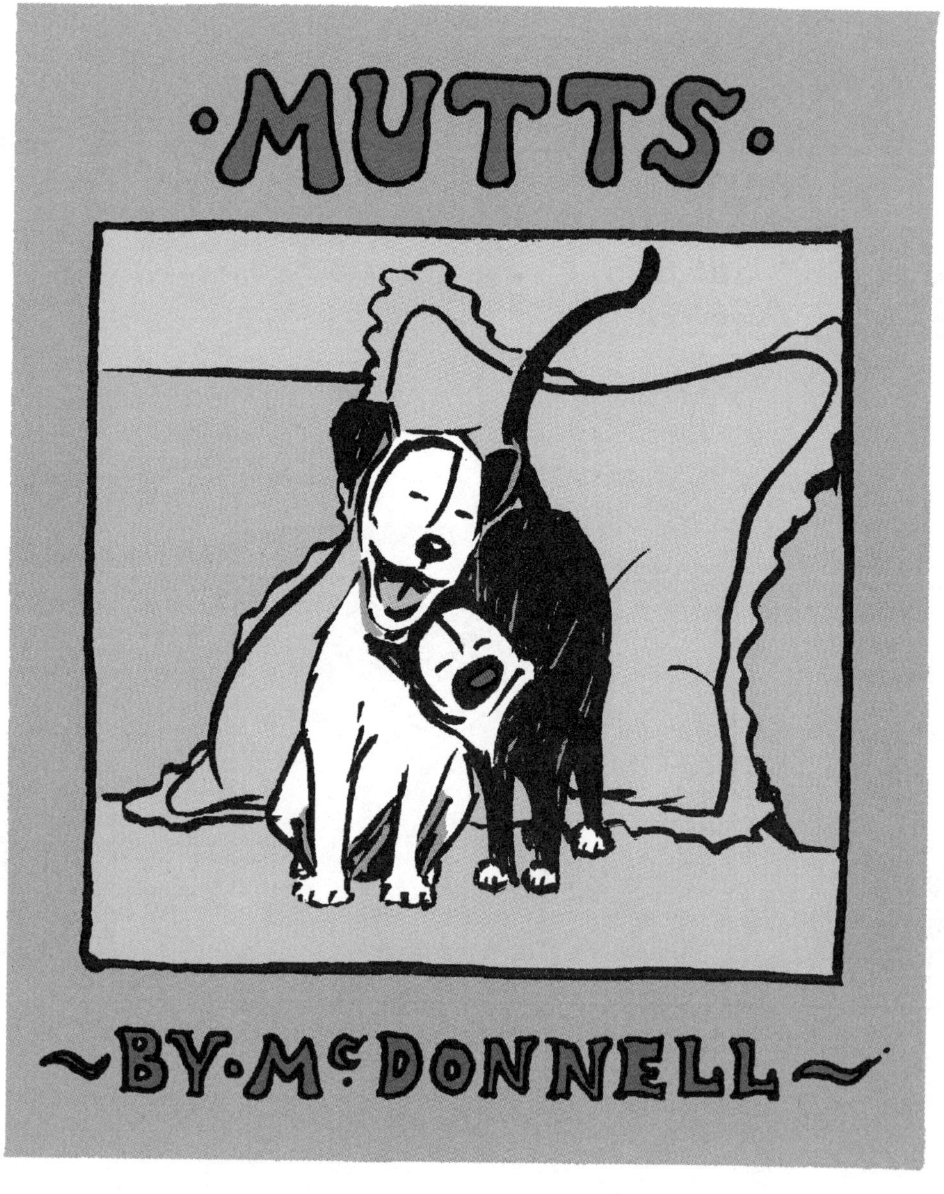
·MUTTS·
~BY·M^C DONNELL~

SHELTER STORY NEWS

MUTTS © 2003 PATRICK M^cDONNELL. DISTRIBUTED BY KING FEATURES SYNDICATE

Beau: Found wandering the streets. Help him find a home.

Peanut: Lost and forgotten, a tiny kitten with a big heart.

Chickpea and her brother: Surrendered littermates.

Uma: Dropped off. Give her a second chance.

Rosie: Abandoned, rescued and waiting.

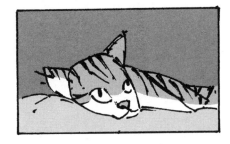

Stanley: Lived under a truck. Loves everybody.

11·2

67

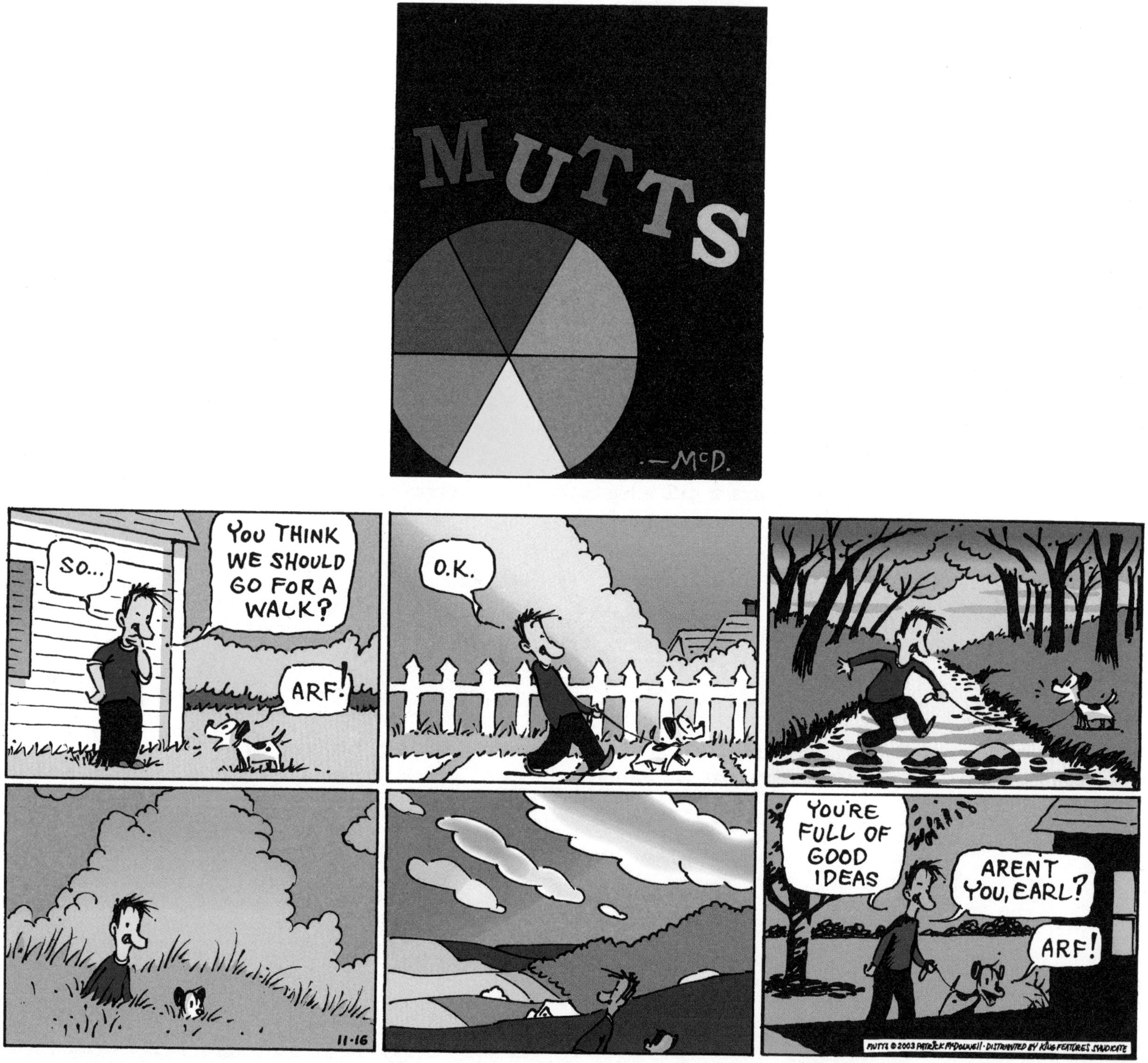
MUTTS
—McD.
SO...
YOU THINK WE SHOULD GO FOR A WALK?
ARF!
O.K.
11-16
YOU'RE FULL OF GOOD IDEAS
ARENT YOU, EARL?
ARF!
MUTTS © 2003 PATRICK McDONNELL · DISTRIBUTED BY KING FEATURES SYNDICATE

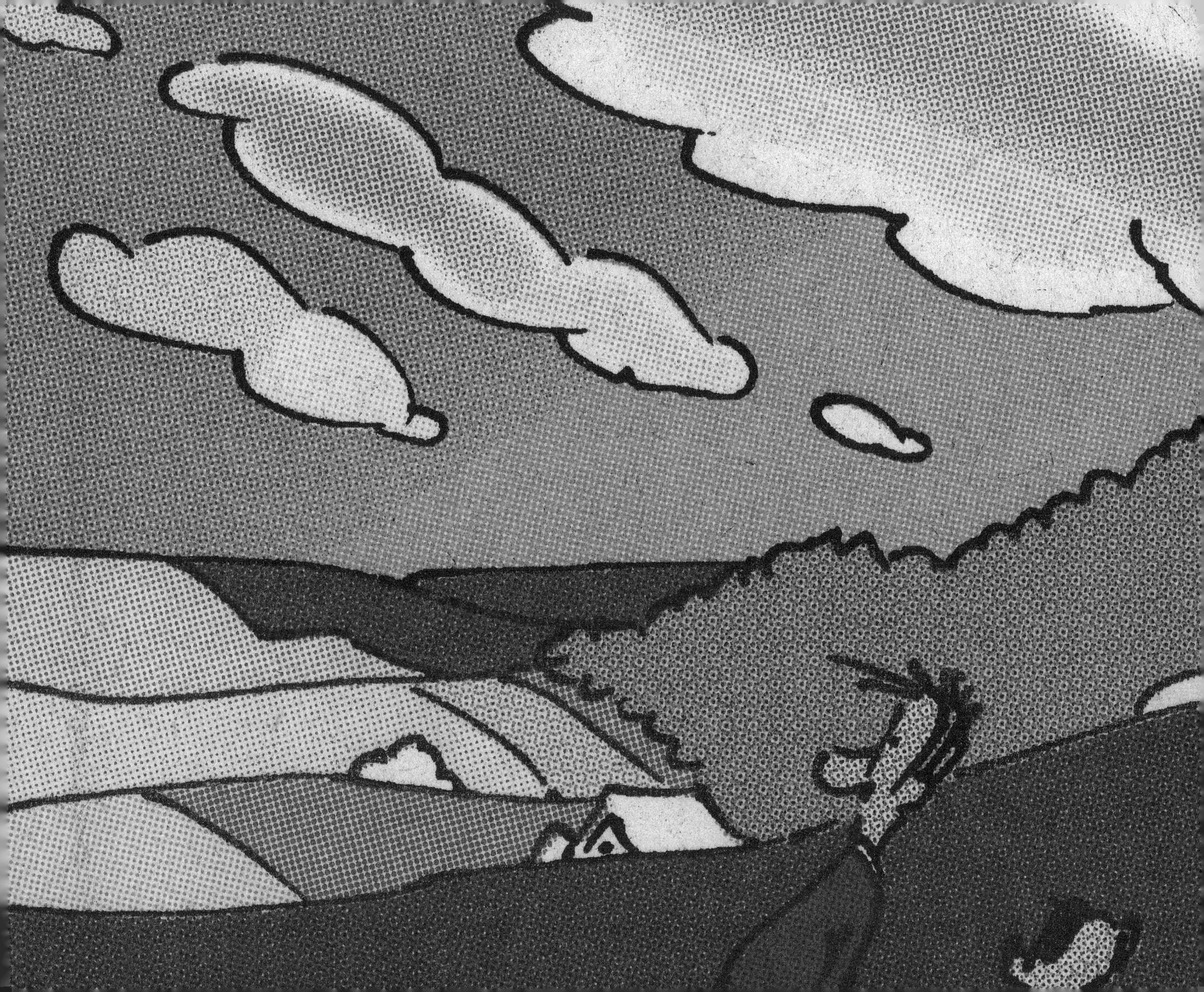

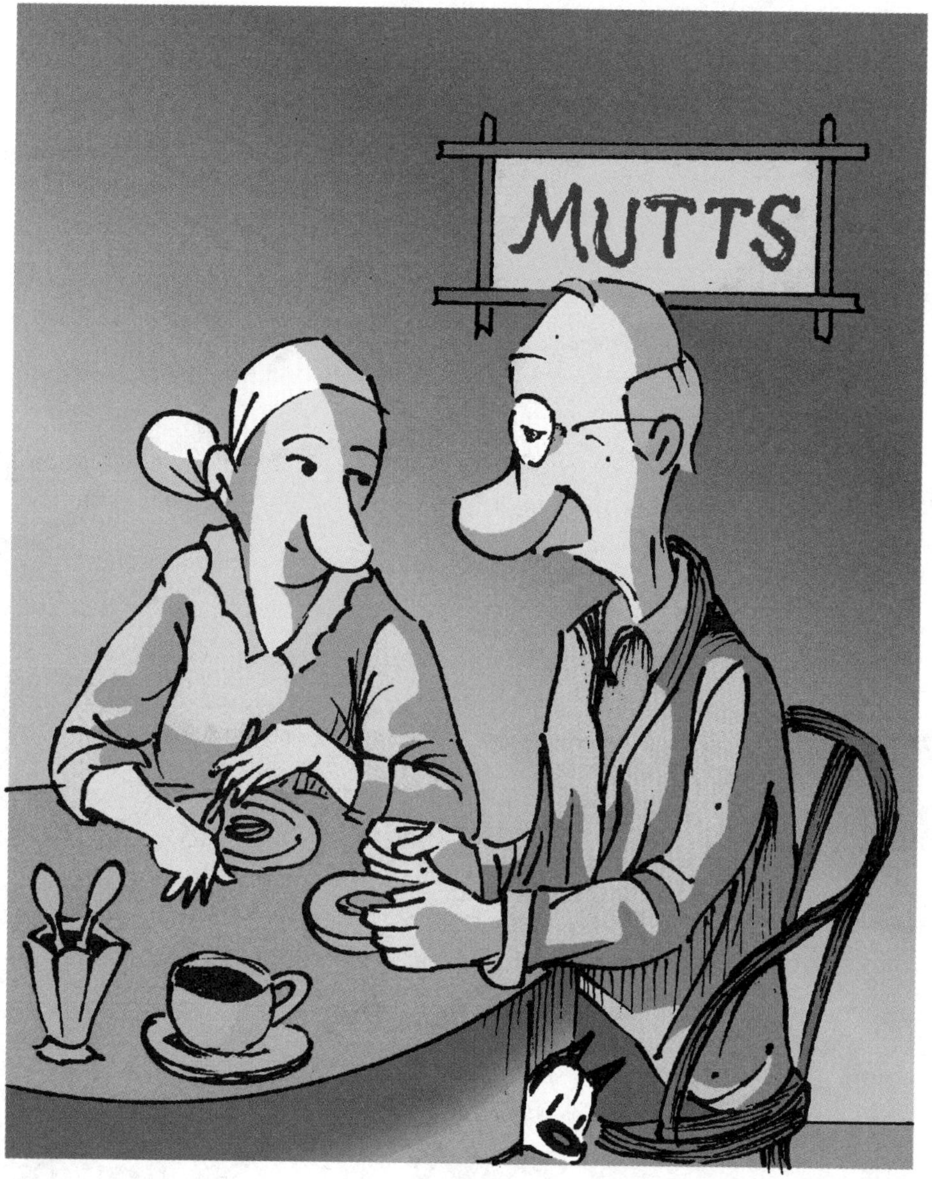
MUTTS

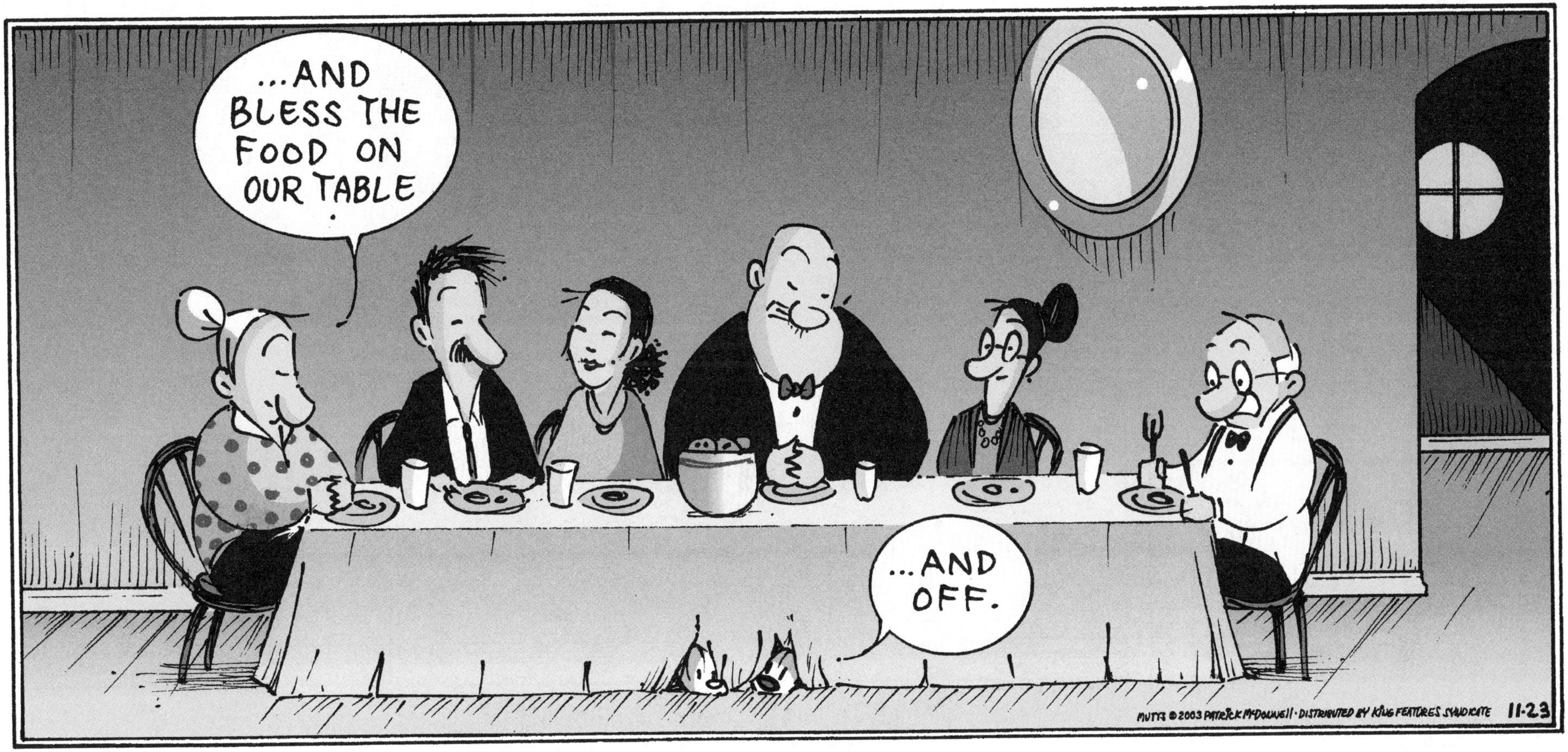
...AND BLESS THE FOOD ON OUR TABLE.
...AND OFF.
MUTTS © 2003 PATRICK McDONNELL · DISTRIBUTED BY KING FEATURES SYNDICATE 11-23

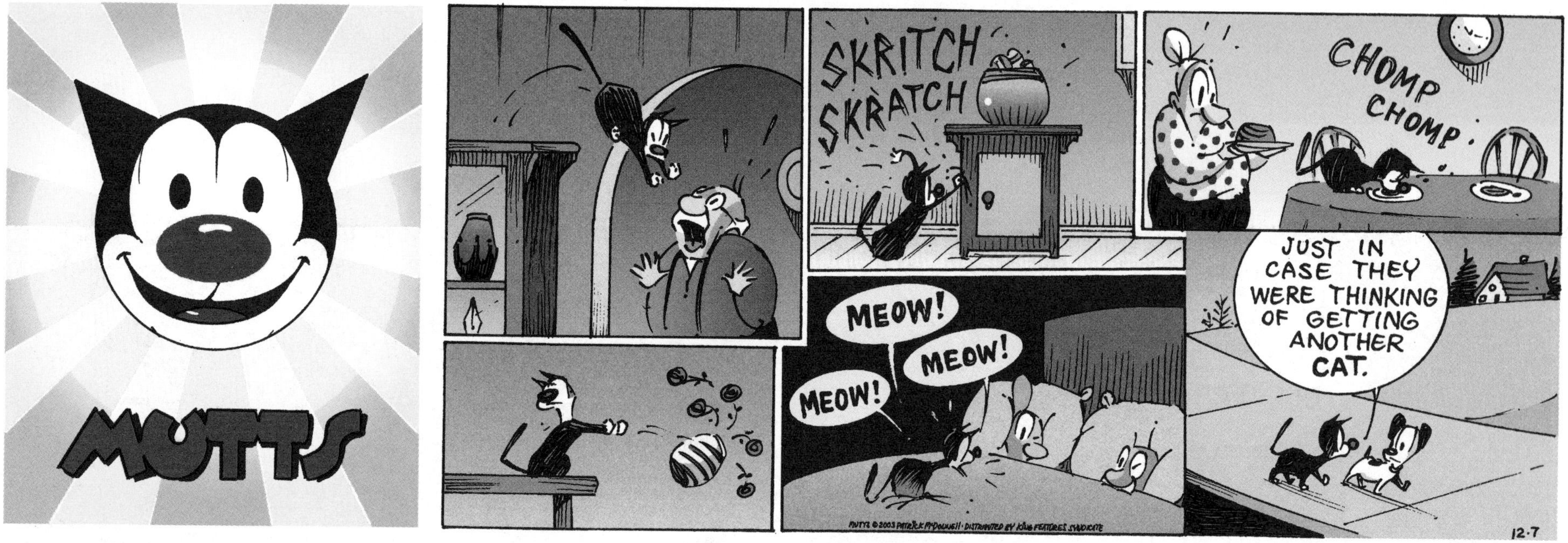
MUTTS
SKRITCH SKRATCH
CHOMP CHOMP
MEOW!
MEOW!
MEOW!
MUTTS © 2003 PATRICK McDONNELL · DISTRIBUTED BY KING FEATURES SYNDICATE
JUST IN CASE THEY WERE THINKING OF GETTING ANOTHER CAT.
12·7

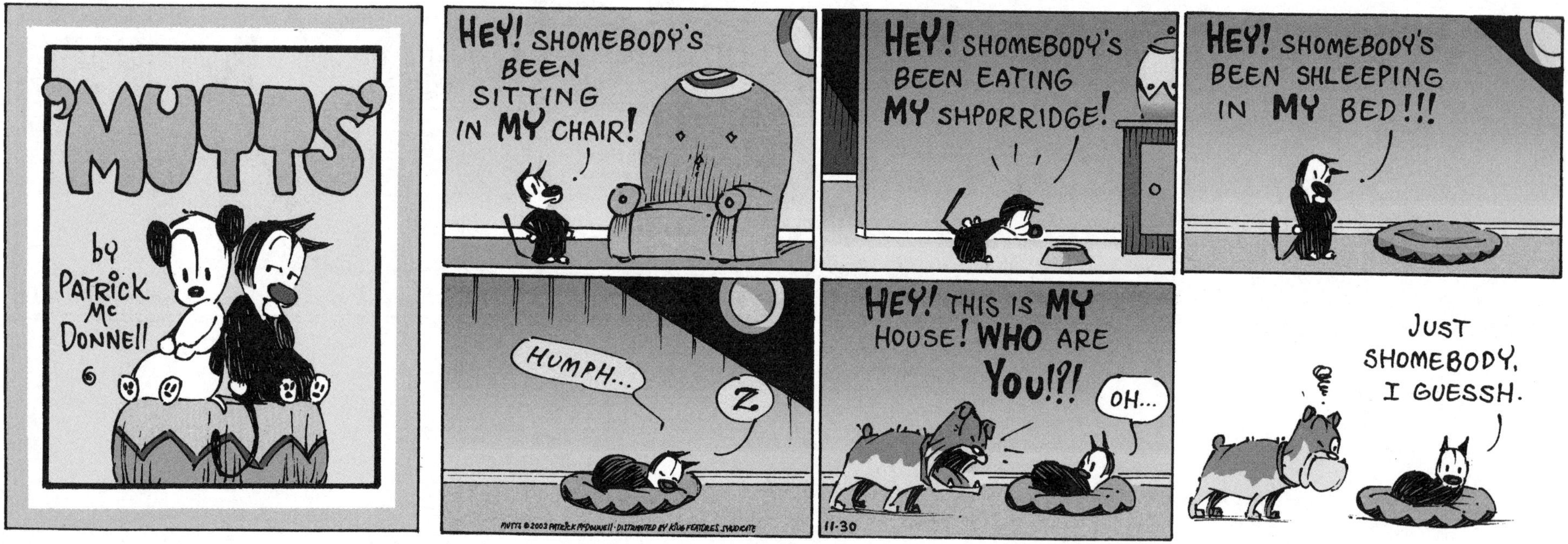
"MUTTS"
by PATRICK Mc DONNELL
HEY! SHOMEBODY'S BEEN SITTING IN MY CHAIR!
HEY! SHOMEBODY'S BEEN EATING MY SHPORRIDGE!
HEY! SHOMEBODY'S BEEN SHLEEPING IN MY BED!!!
HUMPH...
Z
MUTTS © 2003 PATRICK McDONNELL · DISTRIBUTED BY KING FEATURES SYNDICATE
HEY! THIS IS MY HOUSE! WHO ARE YOU!?!
OH...
11·30
JUST SHOMEBODY, I GUESSH.

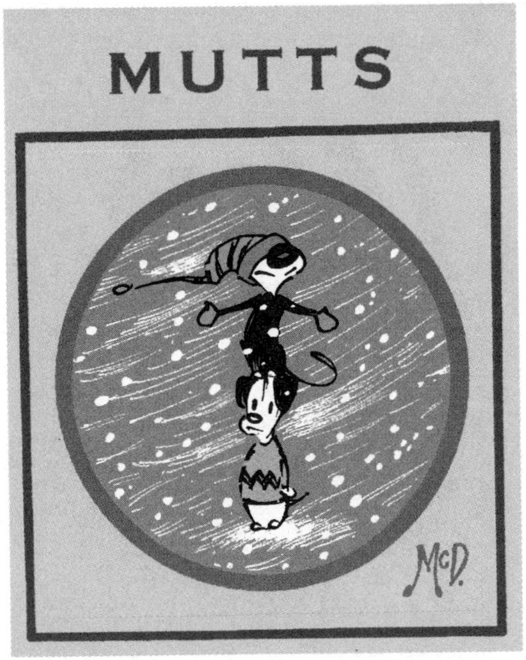
MUTTS
McD.

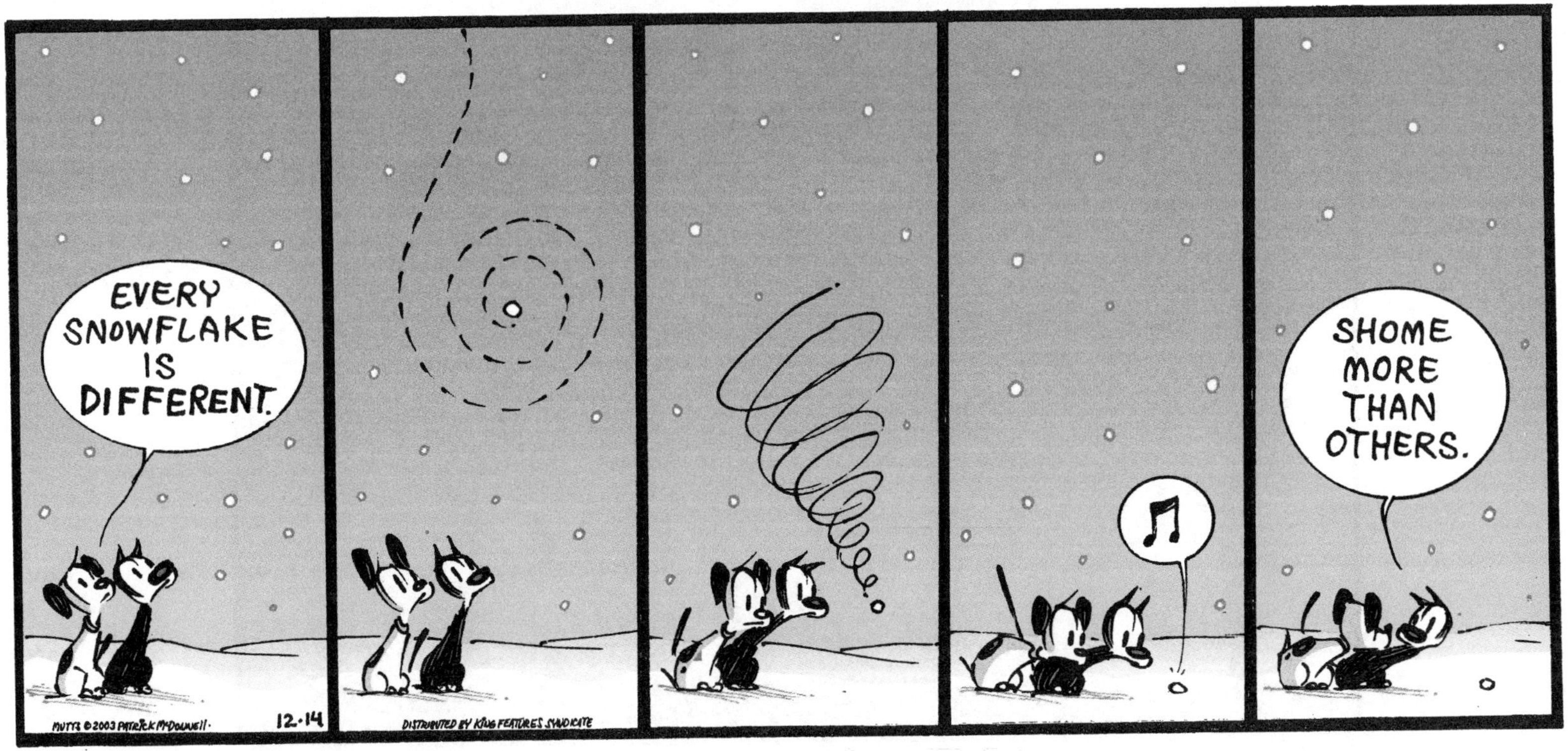
EVERY SNOWFLAKE IS DIFFERENT.
MUTTS © 2003 PATRICK McDONNELL·
12·14
DISTRIBUTED BY KING FEATURES SYNDICATE
♫
SHOME MORE THAN OTHERS.

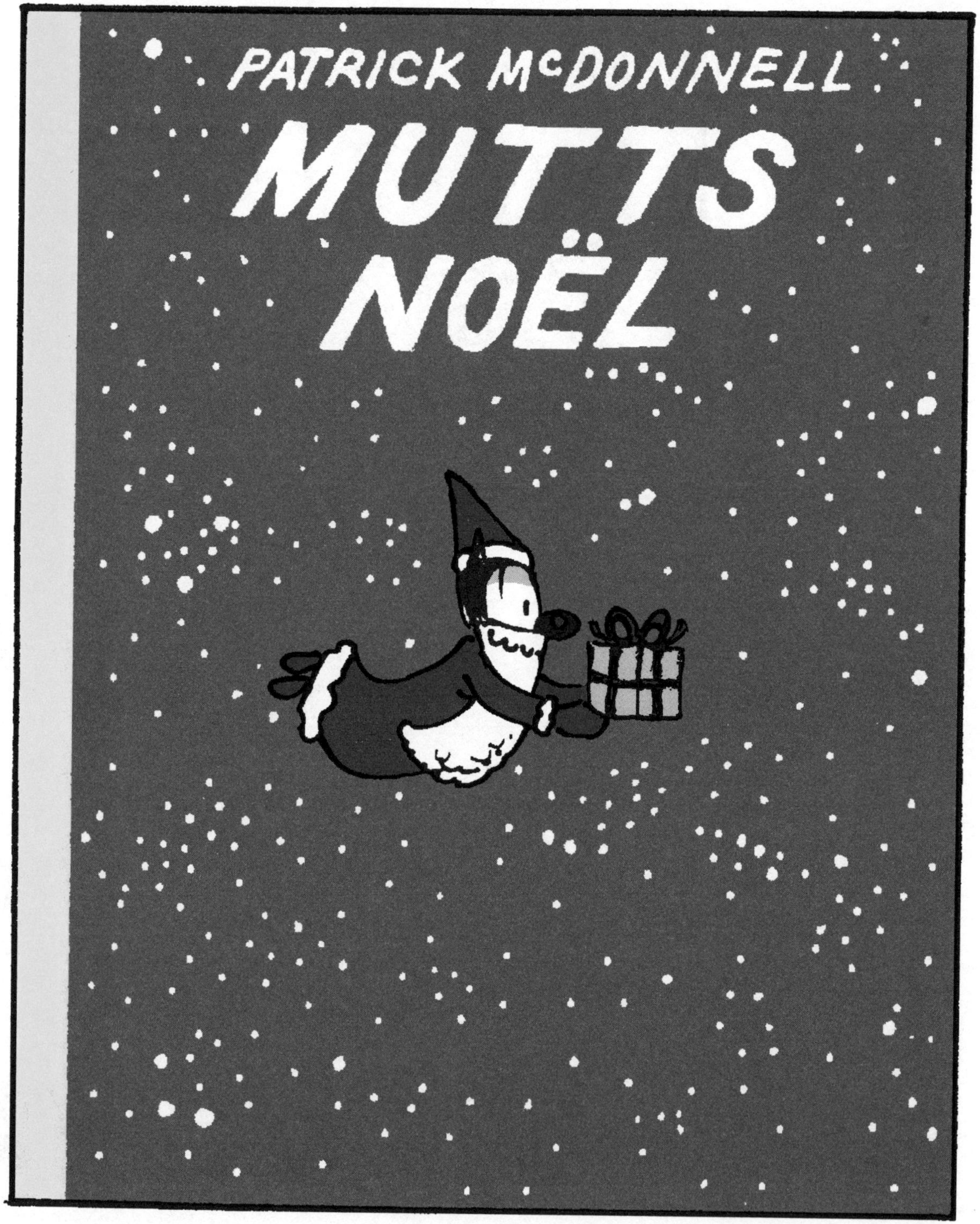
PATRICK McDONNELL
MUTTS
NOËL

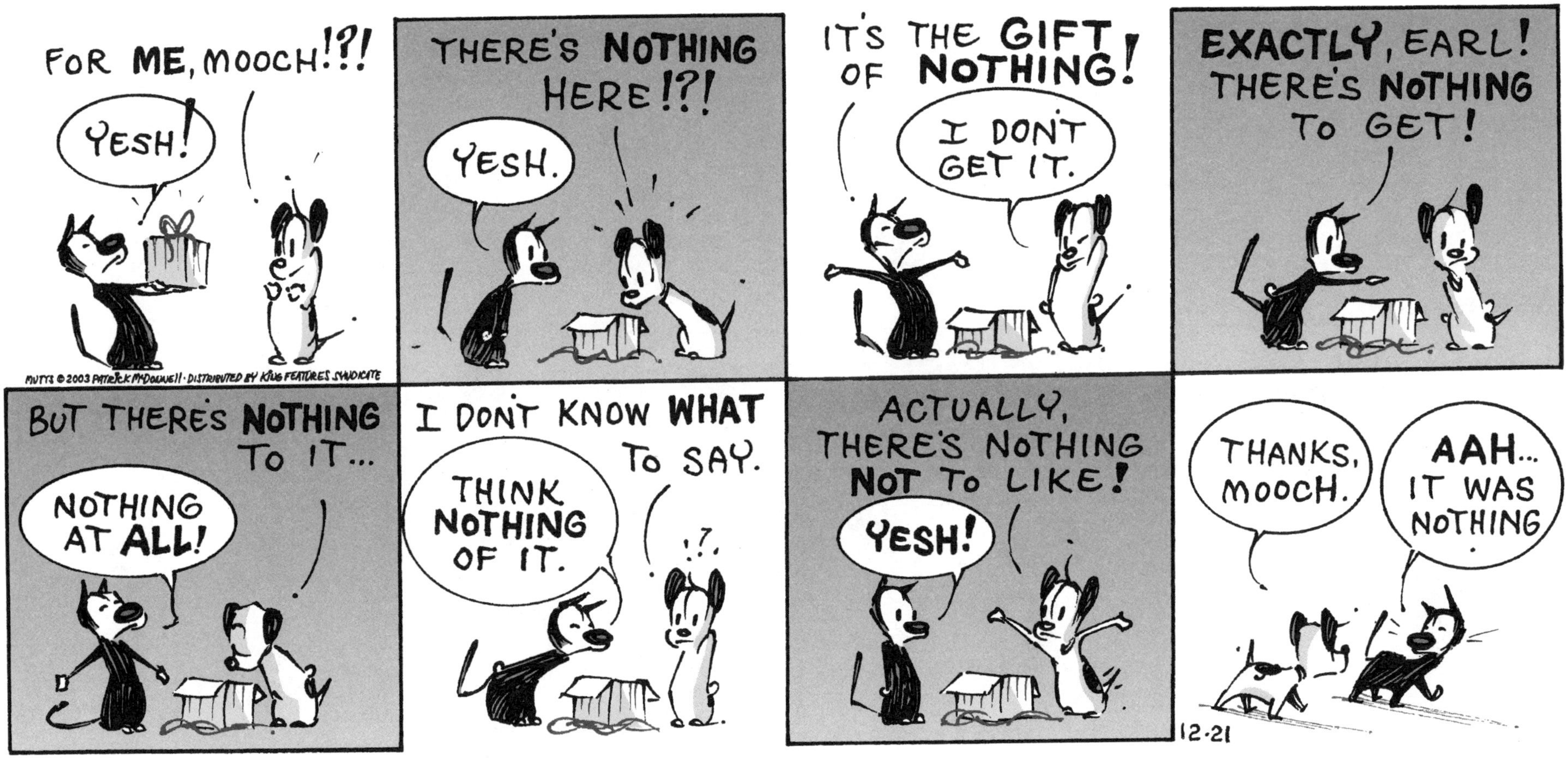
FOR ME, MOOCH!?!
YESH!
MUTTS © 2003 PATRICK McDONNELL · DISTRIBUTED BY KING FEATURES SYNDICATE
THERE'S NOTHING HERE!?!
YESH.
IT'S THE GIFT OF NOTHING!
I DON'T GET IT.
EXACTLY, EARL! THERE'S NOTHING TO GET!
BUT THERE'S NOTHING TO IT...
NOTHING AT ALL!
I DON'T KNOW WHAT TO SAY.
THINK NOTHING OF IT.
ACTUALLY, THERE'S NOTHING NOT TO LIKE!
YESH!
THANKS, MOOCH.
AAH... IT WAS NOTHING.
12-21

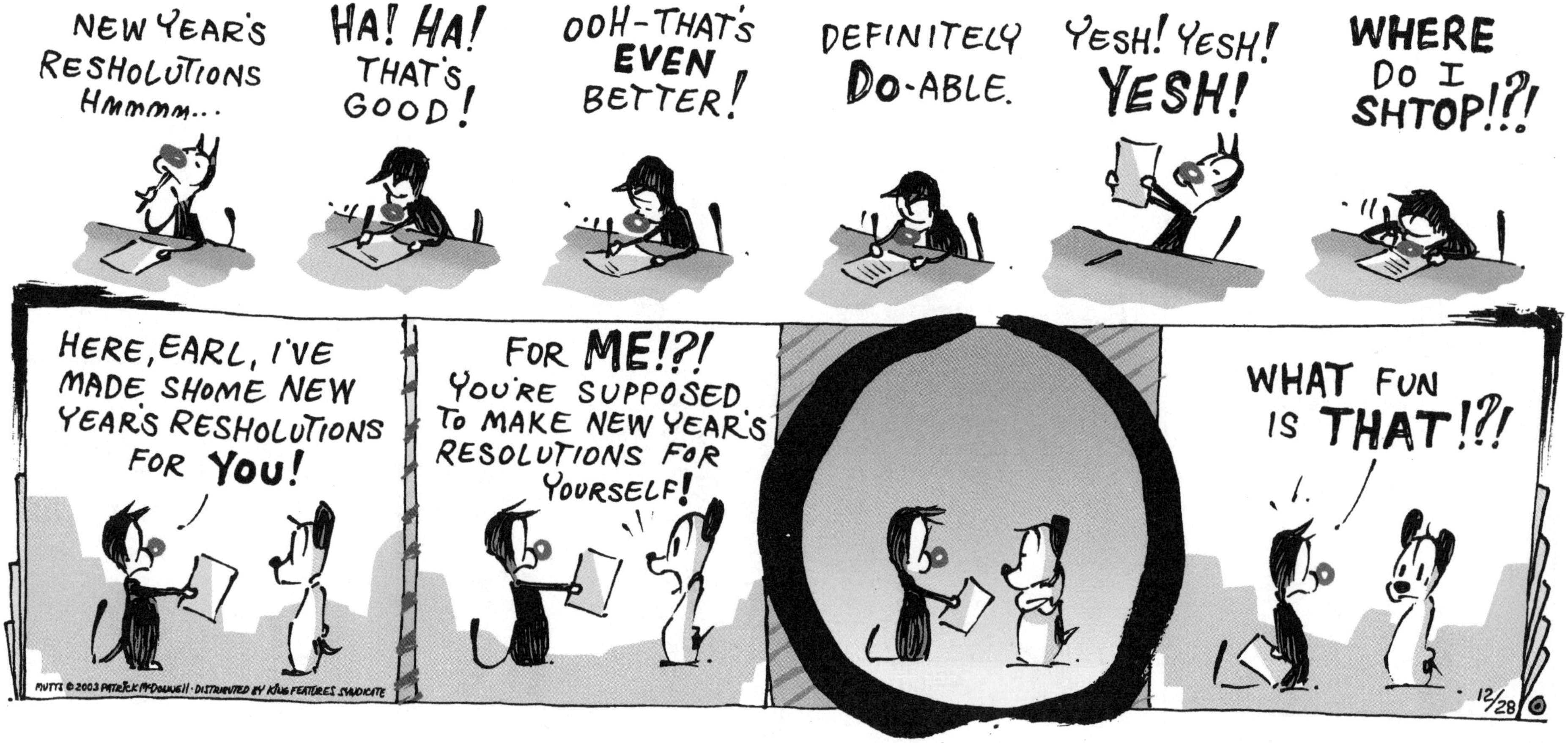
NEW YEAR'S RESHOLUTIONS Hmmmm...
HA! HA! THAT'S GOOD!
OOH–THAT'S EVEN BETTER!
DEFINITELY DO-ABLE.
YESH! YESH! YESH!
WHERE DO I SHTOP!?!
HERE, EARL, I'VE MADE SHOME NEW YEAR'S RESHOLUTIONS FOR YOU!
FOR ME!?! YOU'RE SUPPOSED TO MAKE NEW YEAR'S RESOLUTIONS FOR YOURSELF!
WHAT FUN IS THAT!?!
MUTTS © 2003 PATRICK McDONNELL · DISTRIBUTED BY KING FEATURES SYNDICATE
12/28

MUTTS
McDONNELL

I WAS THINKING OF ALL MY PROBLEMS.
I WAS THINKING OF ALL THE PAIN OF THE PAST AND...
I WAS THINKING OF ALL THE UNCERTAINTY OF THE FUTURE.
AND I WAS THINKING POOR, POOR ME —
MY SAD LIFE.
AND THEN I WAS THINKING HOW LITTLE TIME THERE IS...
AND I'M REALLY THINKING IT'S ALL JUST... HOPELESS.
...WHAT CAN I DO?
MUTTS © 2004 PATRICK McDONNELL · DISTRIBUTED BY KING FEATURES SYNDICATE
SHTOP THINKING.
1·11

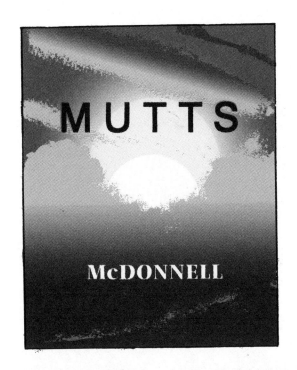

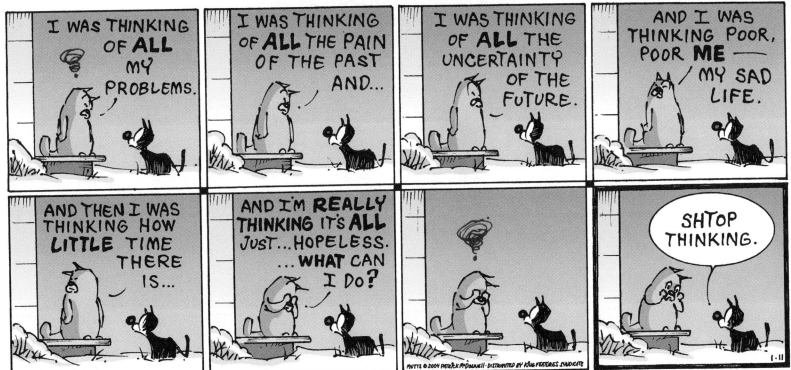

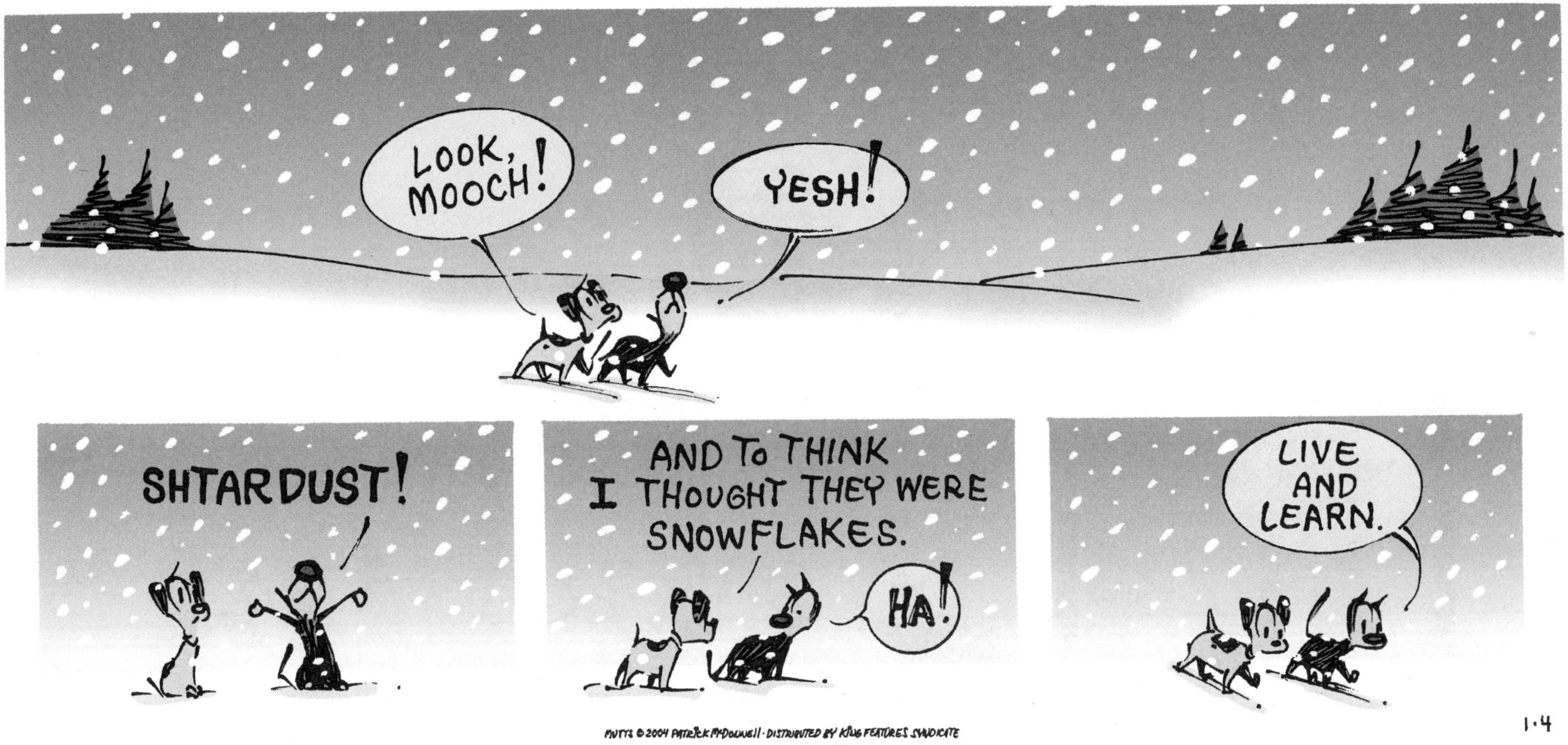
LOOK, MOOCH!
YESH!
SHTARDUST!
AND TO THINK I THOUGHT THEY WERE SNOWFLAKES.
HA!
LIVE AND LEARN.
MUTTS © 2004 PATRICK McDONNELL · DISTRIBUTED BY KING FEATURES SYNDICATE
1·4

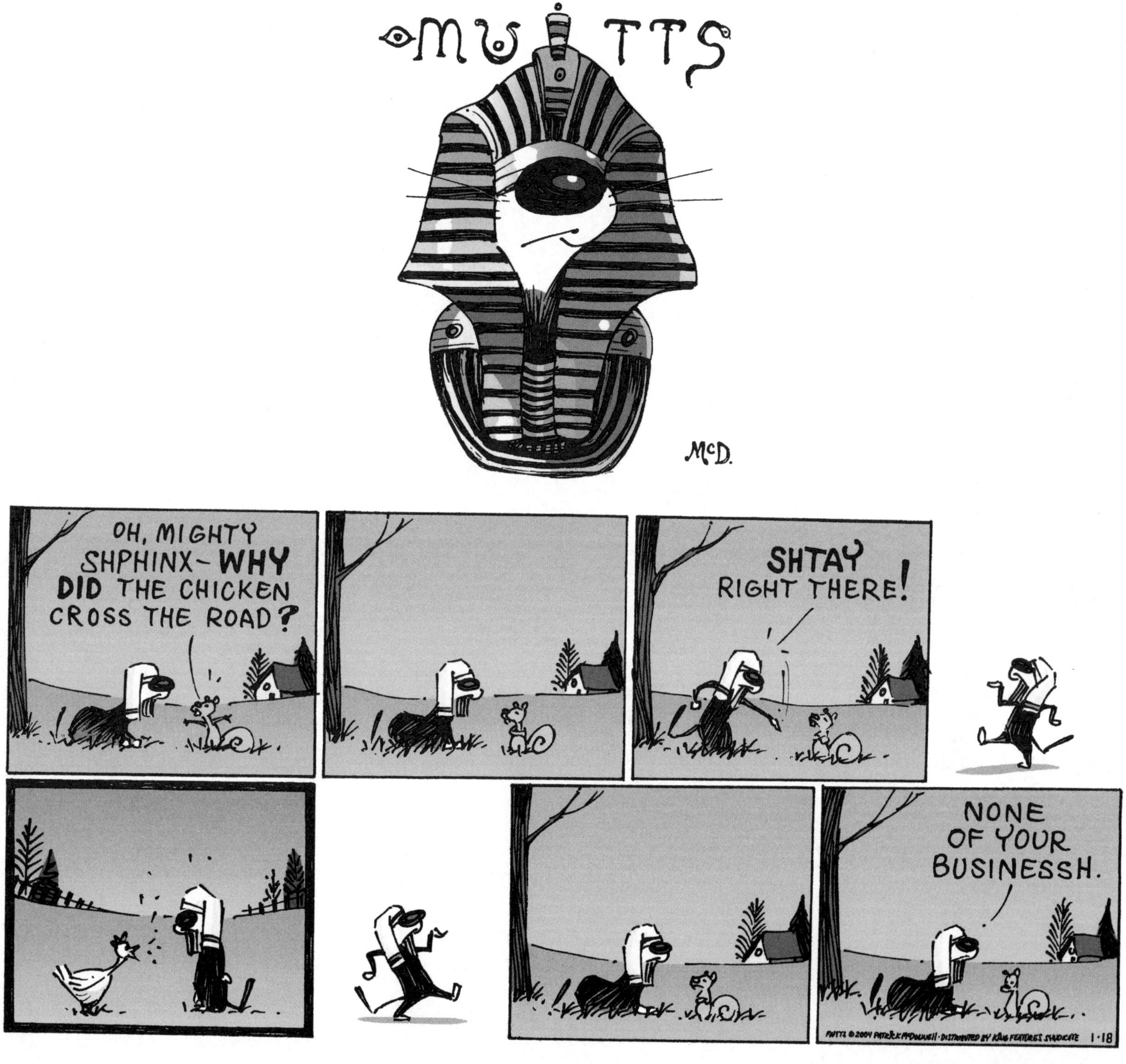
MUTTS
McD.
OH, MIGHTY SHPHINX- WHY DID THE CHICKEN CROSS THE ROAD?
SHTAY RIGHT THERE!
NONE OF YOUR BUSINESSH.
MUTTS © 2004 PATRICK McDONNELL · DISTRIBUTED BY KING FEATURES SYNDICATE 1·18

LAMONT
The Groundhog in
MUTTS
by
PATRICK McDONNELL

COME TOMORROW MORNING THE WORLD WILL BE RIVETED ON THE DRAMA OF **ME** AND **MY SHADOW**!
IT'S **CURIOSITY**, MY FELINE FRIEND! **WHAT** WILL THE FUTURE HOLD?
IT MIGHT BE A TENDER MOMENT OF SURPRISE AND JOY...
WHAT - **NO** SHADOW?
'TIS! IT 'TIS! **NO** MORE WINTER!
FA LA FA LA FA **LA**
OR PERHAPS A... DRAMATIC, TRAGIC **TOUR·DE·FORCE**... "... **MY** ... SHADOW..."
SOB
SIX MORE WEEKS OF **COLD**!!! WHY!?! WHY? **WHY?** AGONY!
AGONY!
WAH
WHICH WILL IT BE? IT'S IMPROVISATIONAL THEATRE AT ITS BEST! MY EAGER PUBLIC AWAITS!
CIAO!
WHAT DO **YOU** HOPE FOR, MOOCH?
HE OVER-SHLEEPS
MUTTS © 2004 PATRICK McDONNELL · DISTRIBUTED BY KING FEATURES. 2·1

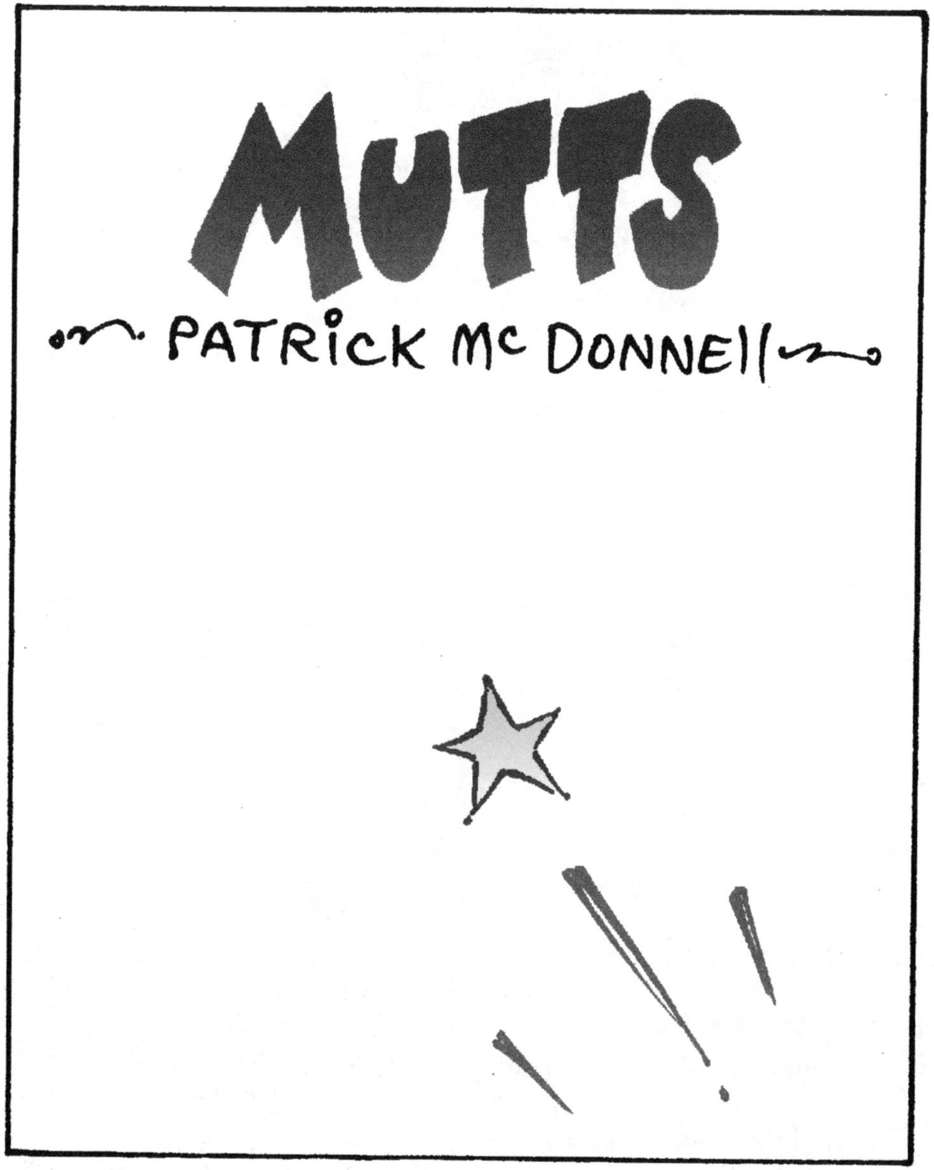
MUTTS
PATRICK McDONNELL

1·25 MUTTS © 2004 PATRICK McDONNELL · DISTRIBUTED BY KING FEATURES SYNDICATE

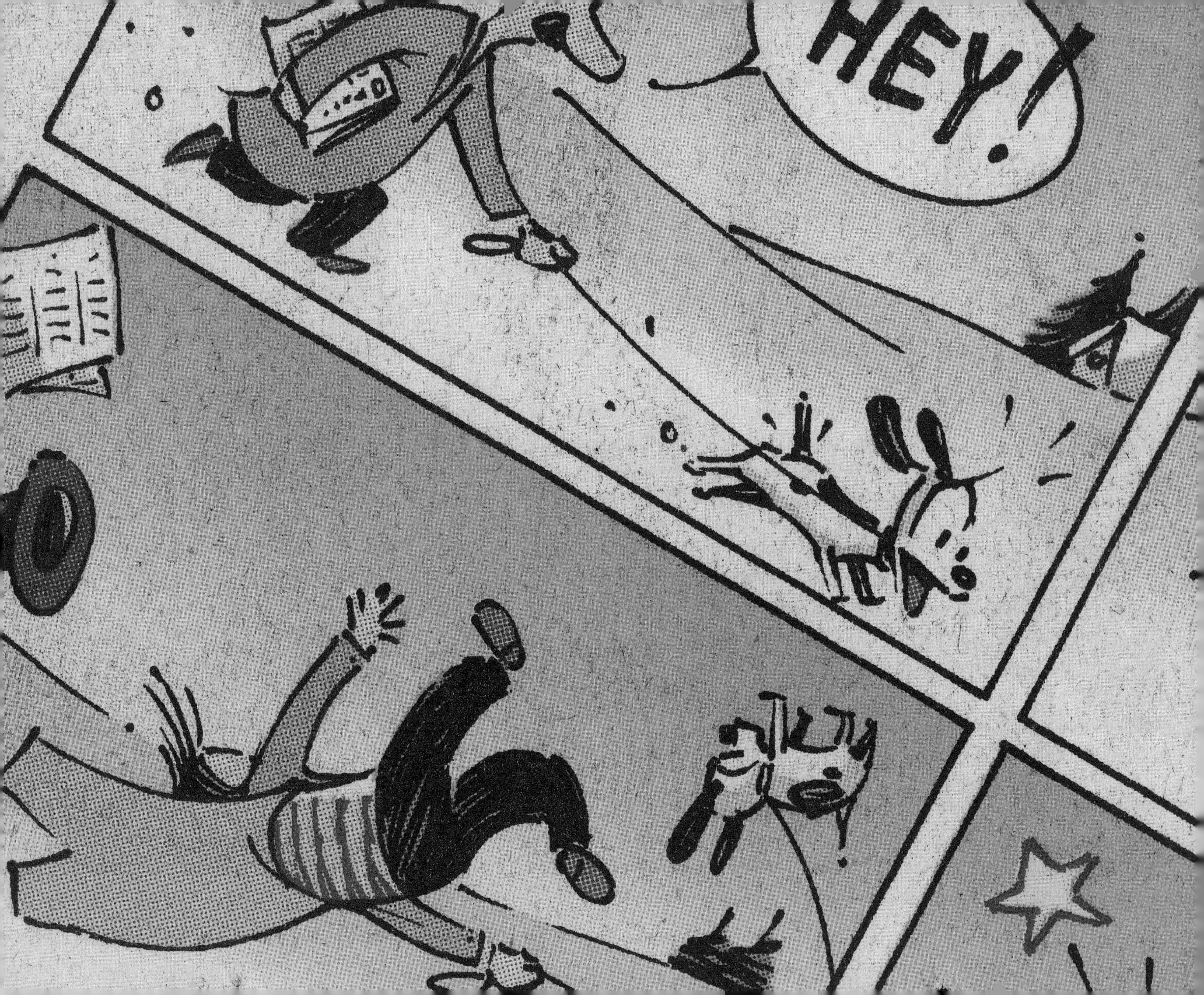
HEY!

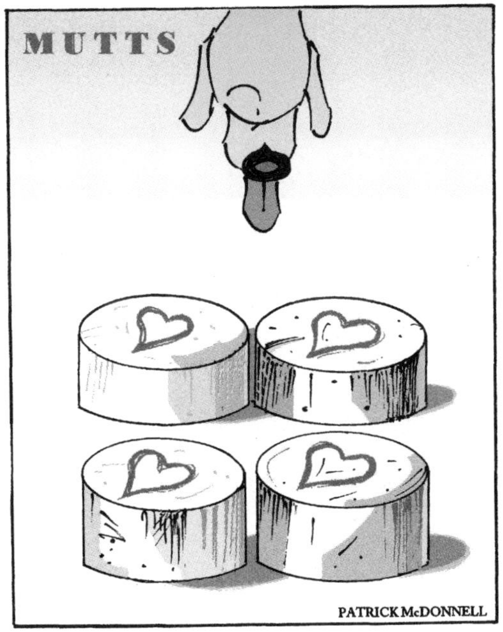
MUTTS
PATRICK McDONNELL

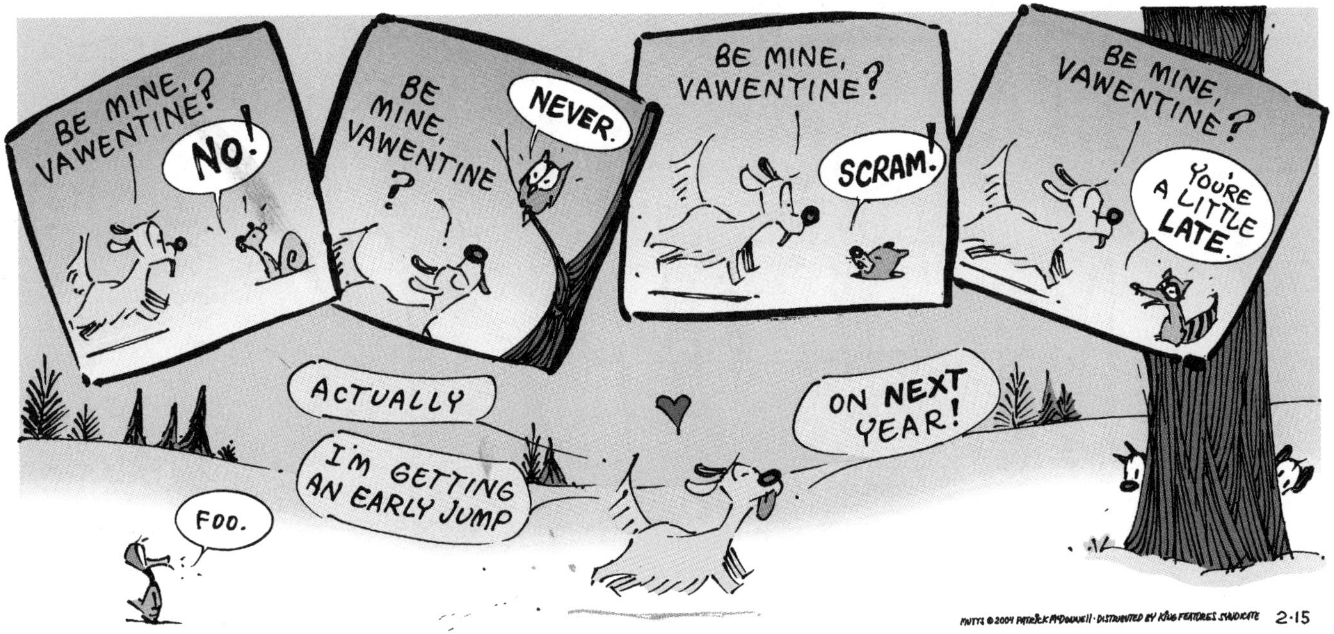
BE MINE, VAWENTINE?
NO!
BE MINE, VAWENTINE?
NEVER.
BE MINE, VAWENTINE?
SCRAM!
BE MINE, VAWENTINE?
YOU'RE A LITTLE LATE.
ACTUALLY
I'M GETTING AN EARLY JUMP
ON NEXT YEAR!
FOO.
MUTTS © 2004 PATRICK McDONNELL · DISTRIBUTED BY KING FEATURES SYNDICATE 2·15

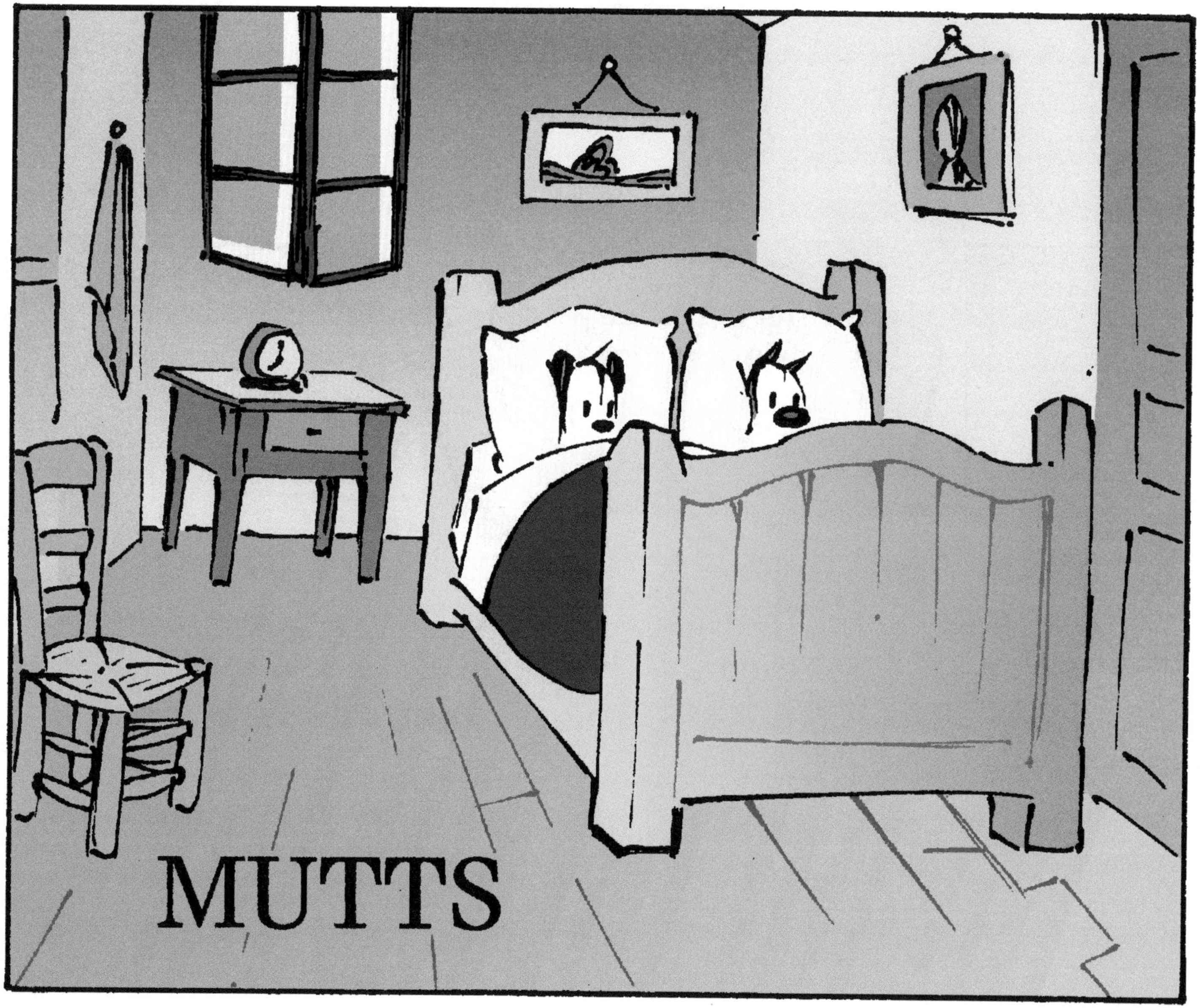
MUTTS

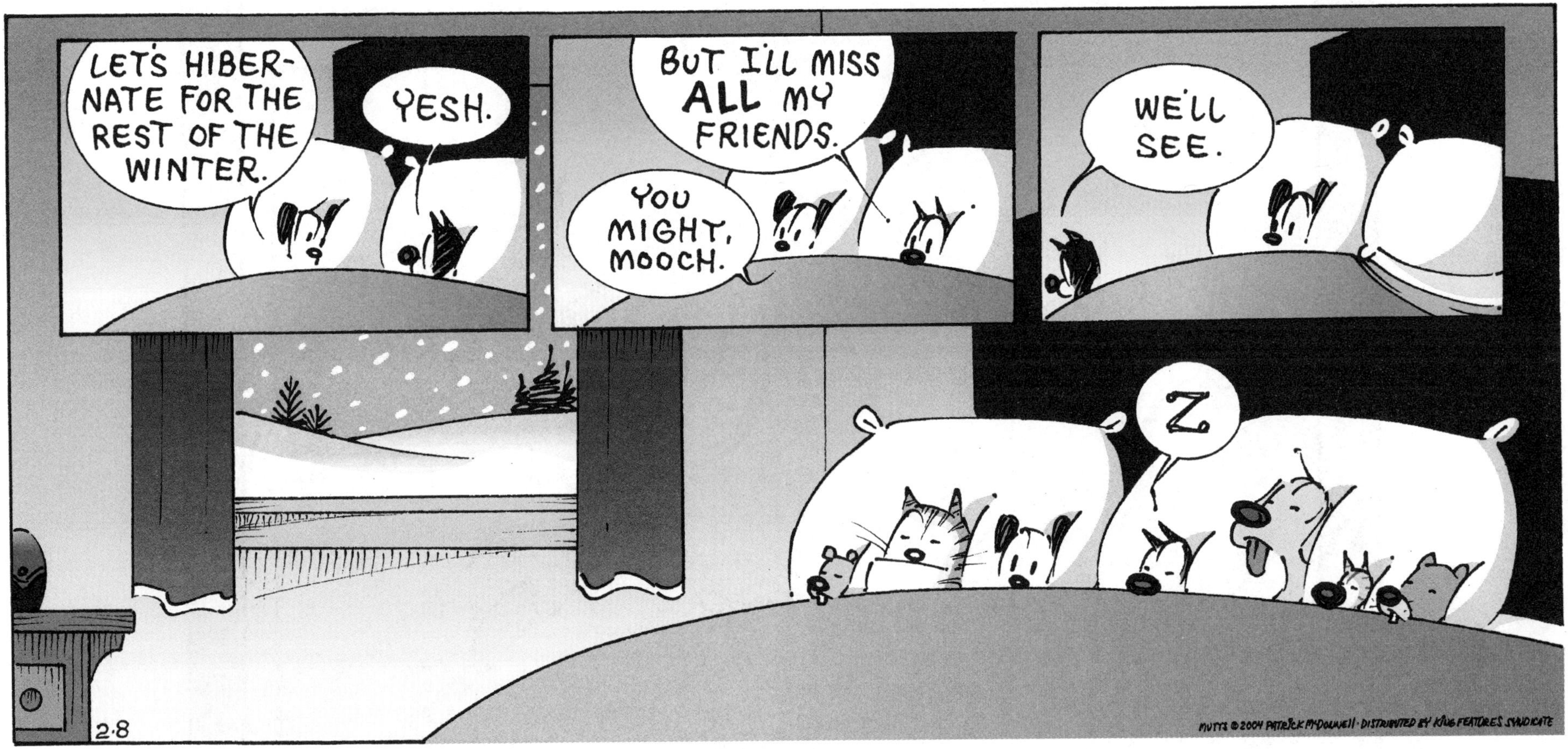
LET'S HIBERNATE FOR THE REST OF THE WINTER.
YESH.
BUT I'LL MISS ALL MY FRIENDS.
YOU MIGHT, MOOCH.
WE'LL SEE.
Z
2·8
MUTTS © 2004 PATRICK McDONNELL · DISTRIBUTED BY KING FEATURES SYNDICATE

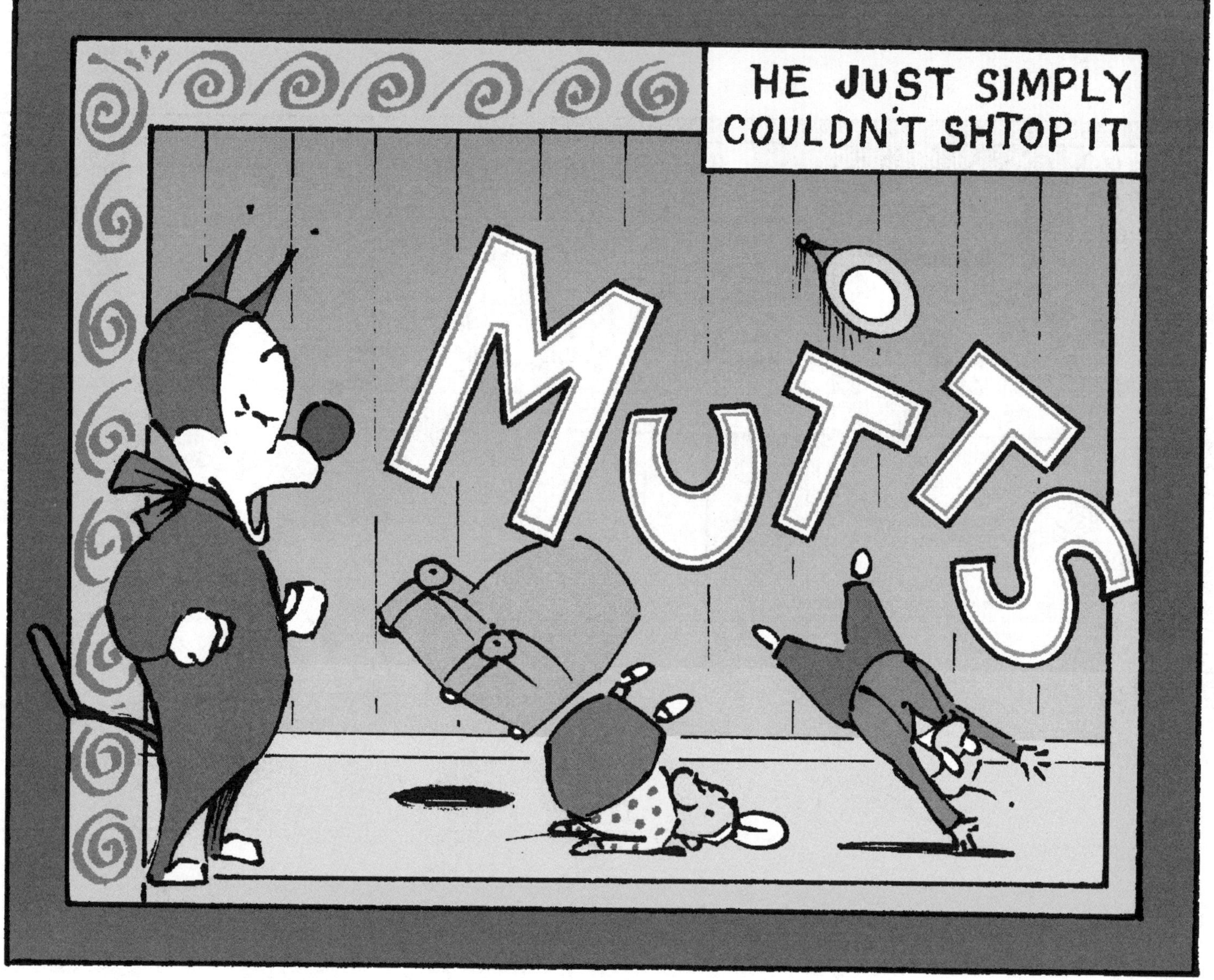
HE JUST SIMPLY COULDN'T SHTOP IT
MUTTS

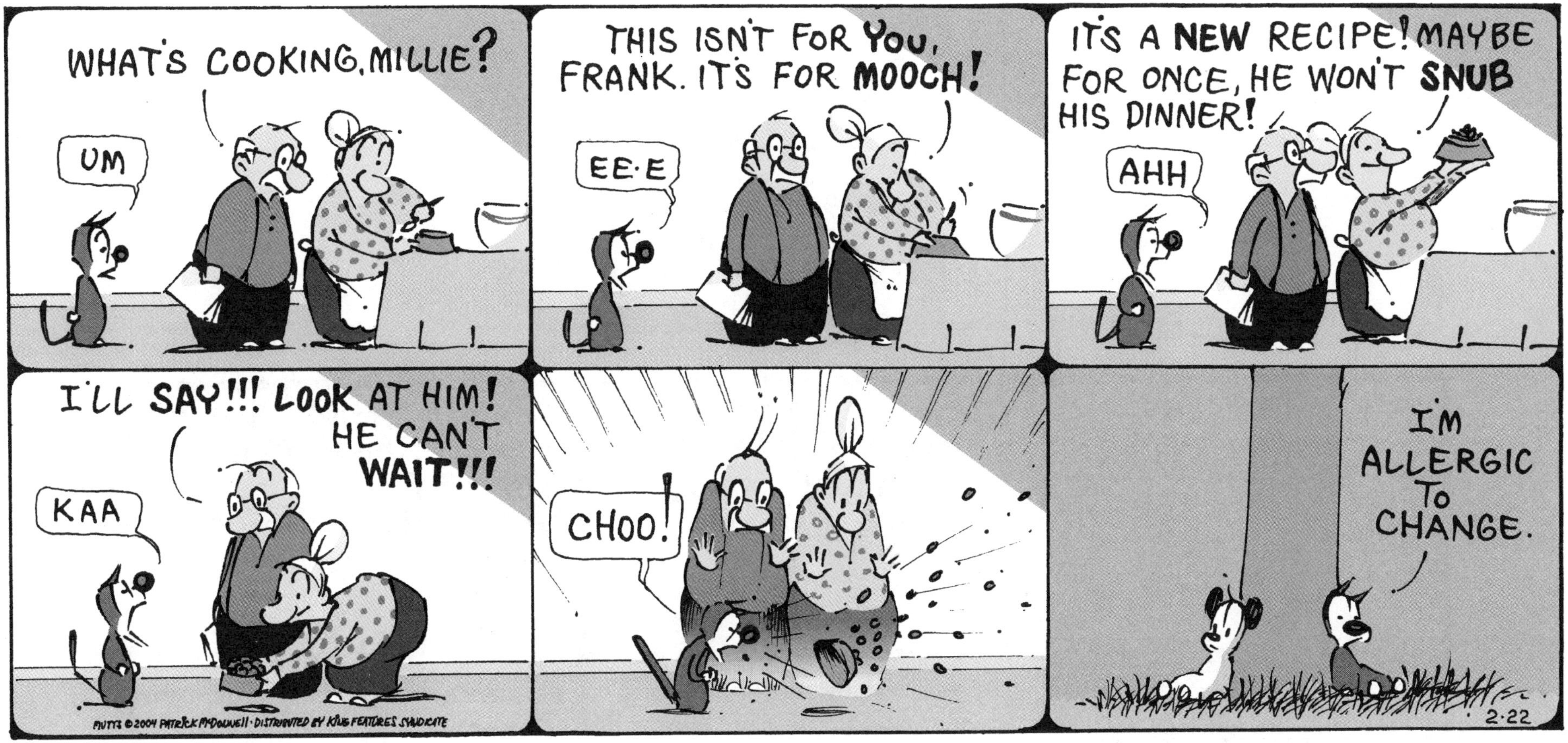
WHAT'S COOKING, MILLIE?
UM
THIS ISN'T FOR YOU, FRANK. IT'S FOR MOOCH!
EE·E
IT'S A NEW RECIPE! MAYBE FOR ONCE, HE WON'T SNUB HIS DINNER!
AHH
I'LL SAY!!! LOOK AT HIM! HE CAN'T WAIT!!!
KAA
MUTTS © 2004 PATRICK McDONNELL · DISTRIBUTED BY KING FEATURES SYNDICATE
CHOO!
I'M ALLERGIC TO CHANGE.
2·22

MUTTS JOKE·A·DAY

CALENDAR

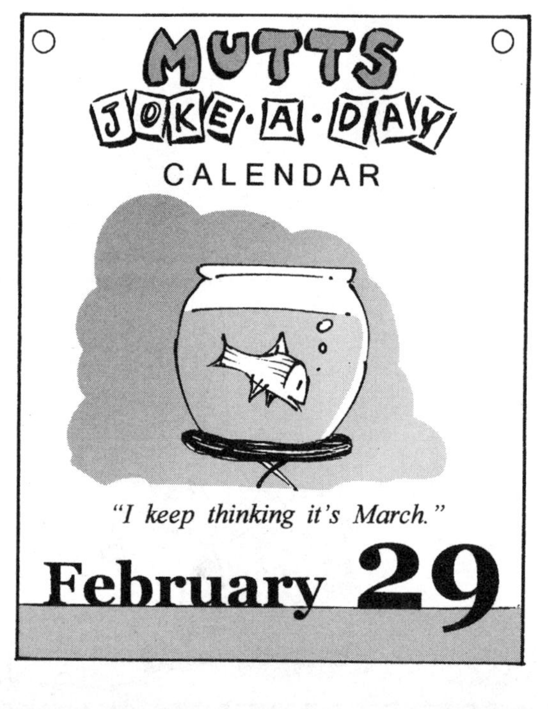

"I keep thinking it's March."

February 29

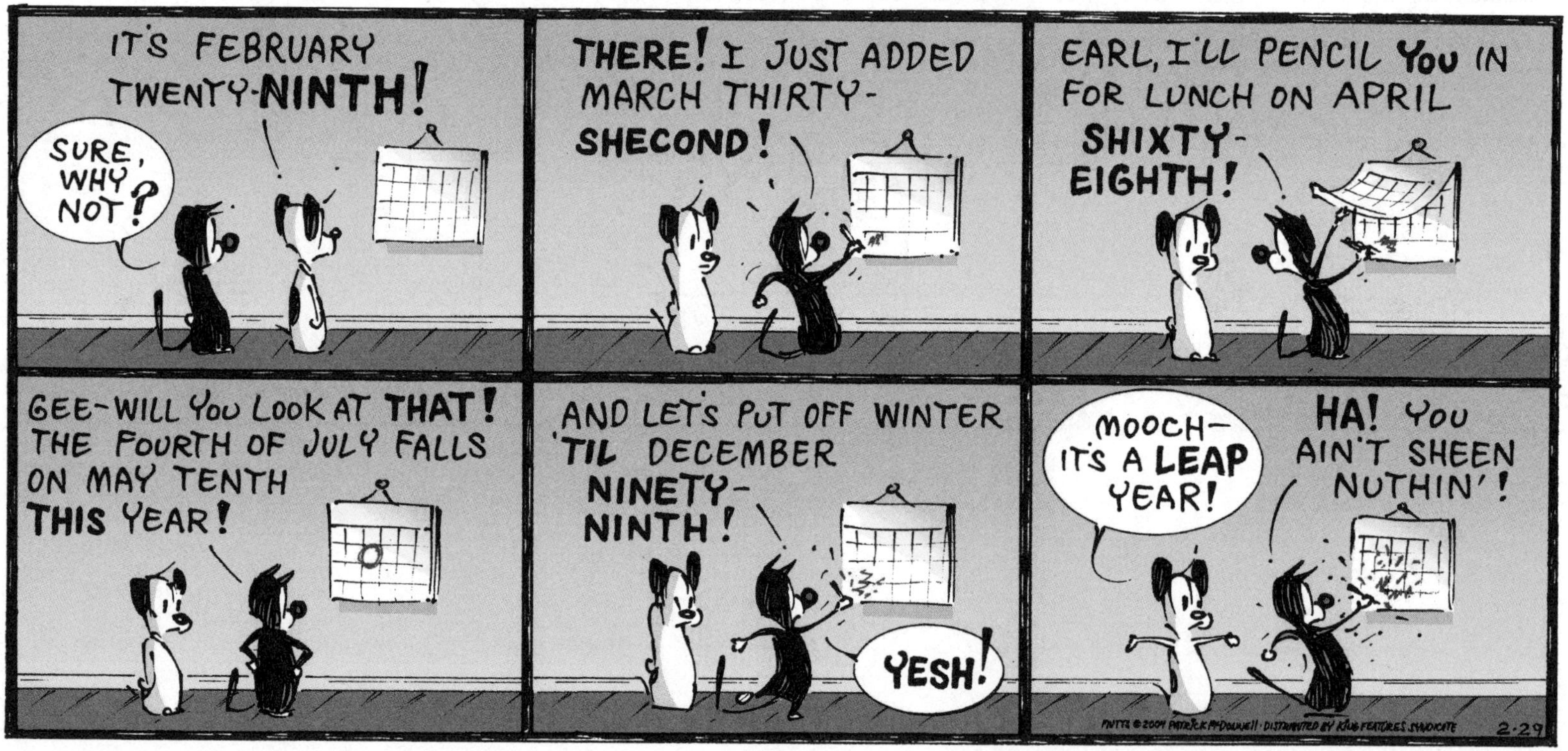
IT'S FEBRUARY TWENTY-NINTH!
SURE, WHY NOT?
THERE! I JUST ADDED MARCH THIRTY-SHECOND!
EARL, I'LL PENCIL YOU IN FOR LUNCH ON APRIL SHIXTY-EIGHTH!
GEE-WILL YOU LOOK AT THAT! THE FOURTH OF JULY FALLS ON MAY TENTH THIS YEAR!
AND LET'S PUT OFF WINTER 'TIL DECEMBER NINETY-NINTH!
YESH!
MOOCH— IT'S A LEAP YEAR!
HA! YOU AIN'T SHEEN NUTHIN'!
MUTTS © 2004 PATRICK McDONNELL · DISTRIBUTED BY KING FEATURES SYNDICATE
2-29

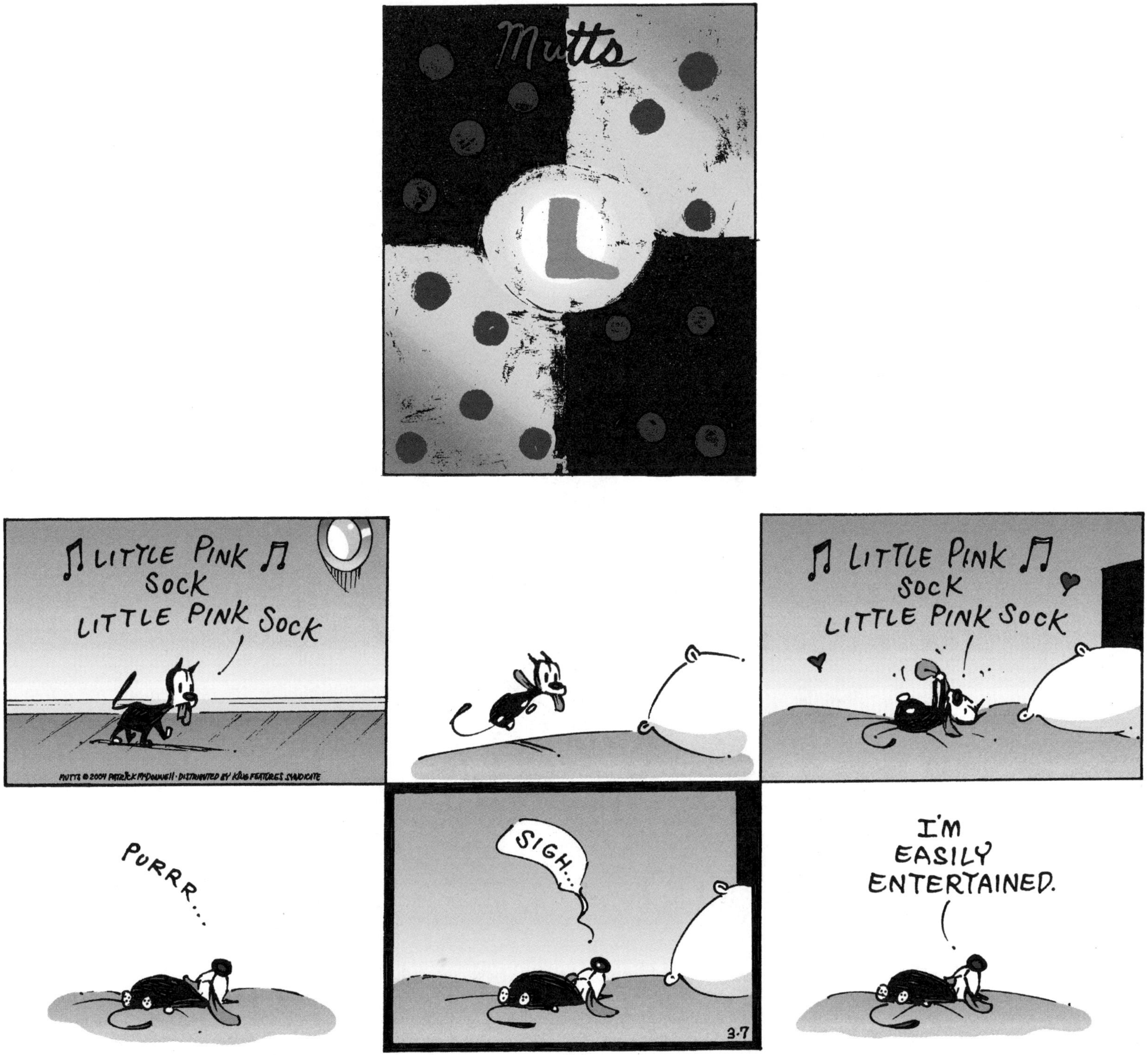
Mutts
♫ LITTLE PINK ♫ SOCK LITTLE PINK SOCK
MUTTS © 2004 PATRICK McDONNELL · DISTRIBUTED BY KING FEATURES SYNDICATE
♫ LITTLE PINK ♫ SOCK LITTLE PINK SOCK
PURRR...
SIGH...
I'M EASILY ENTERTAINED.
3·7

MUTTS
PATRICK McDONNELL

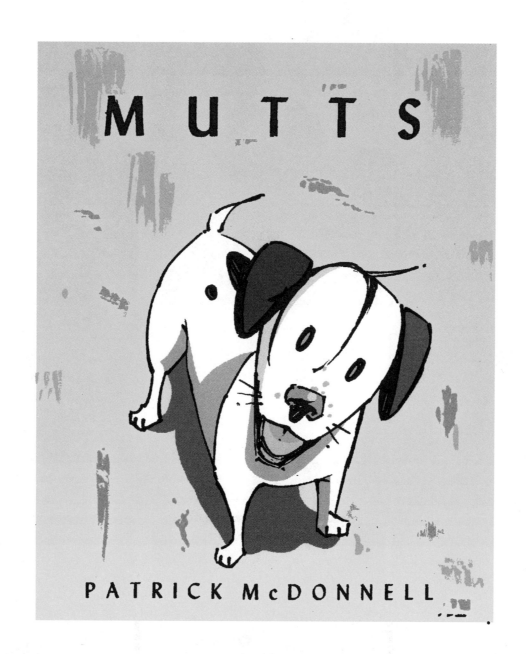

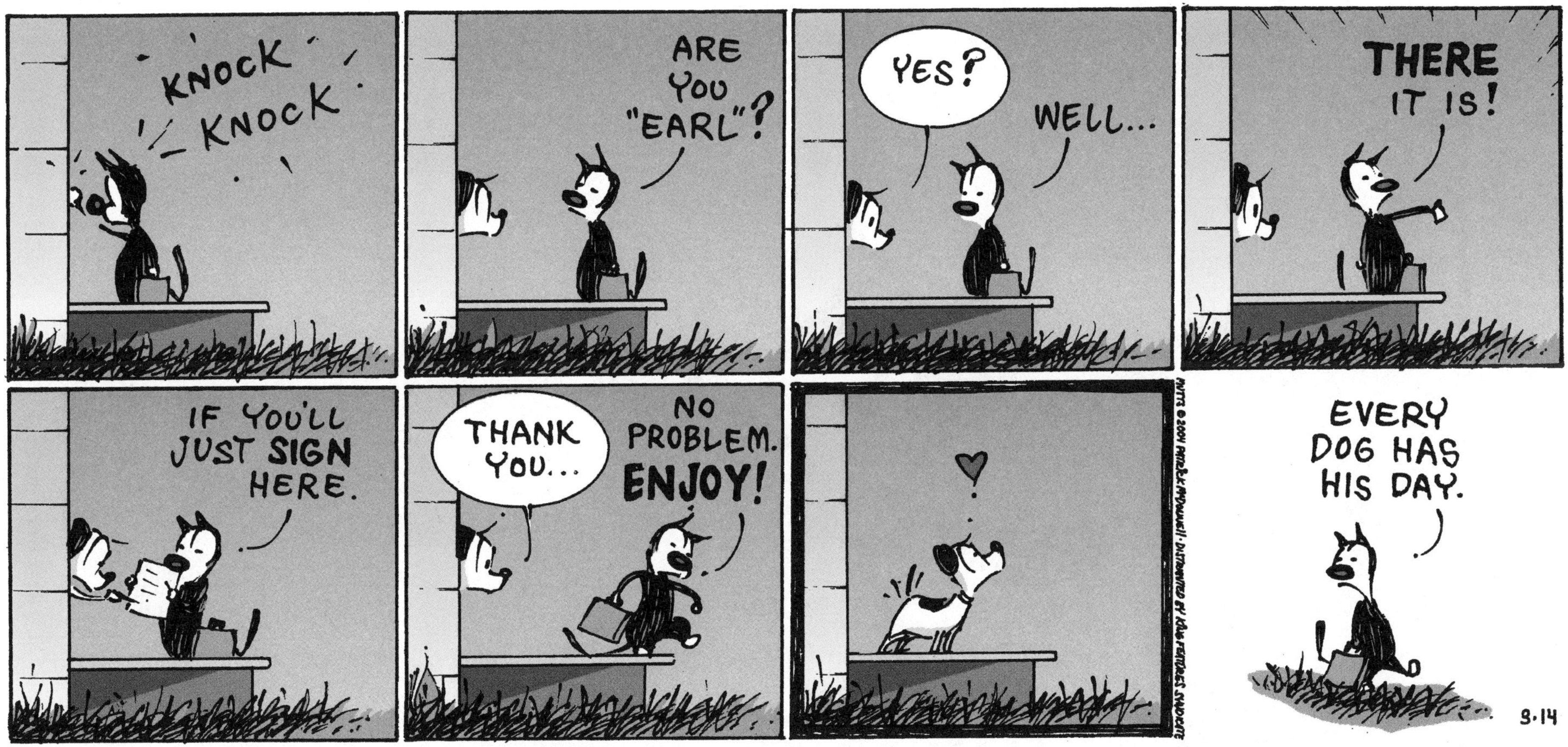
KNOCK KNOCK
ARE YOU "EARL"?
YES?
WELL...
THERE IT IS!
IF YOU'LL JUST SIGN HERE.
THANK YOU...
NO PROBLEM. ENJOY!
MUTTS ©2004 PATRICK McDONNELL · DISTRIBUTED BY KING FEATURES SYNDICATE
EVERY DOG HAS HIS DAY.
8·14

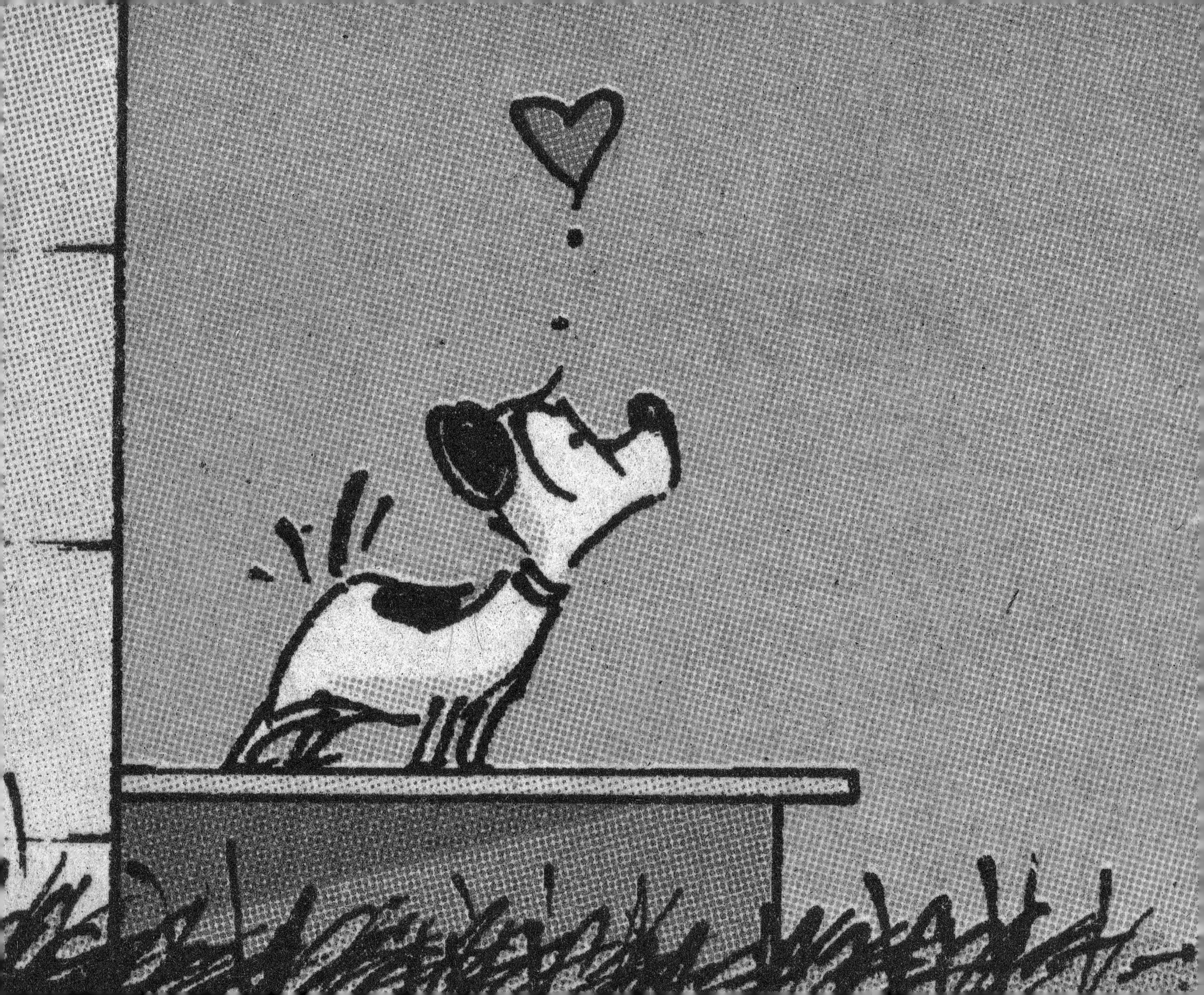

Here Today!
·MUTTS·
OZZIE
and
EARL

EARL,
WATCH
ME.
SIT.
BEG.
ROLL OVER
PLAY DEAD.
WOW!
WHAT
ELSHE CAN
HE DO?
MUTTS © 2004 PATRICK McDONNELL · DISTRIBUTED BY KING FEATURES SYNDICATE
3-28

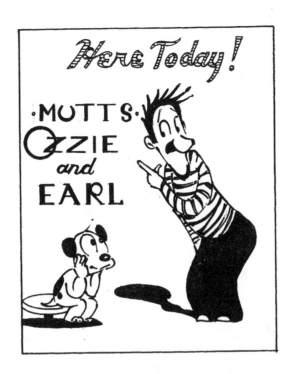

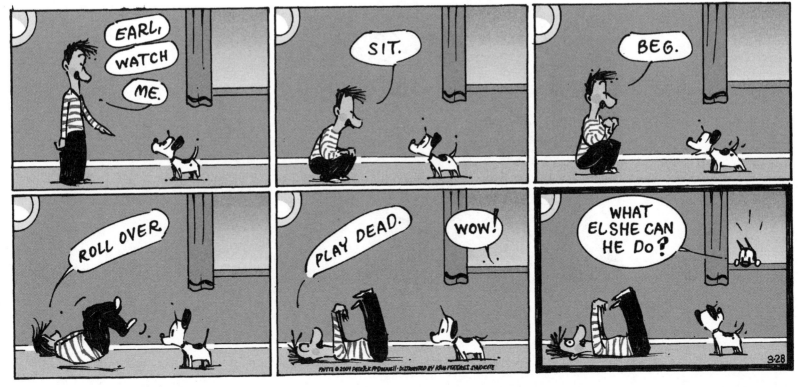

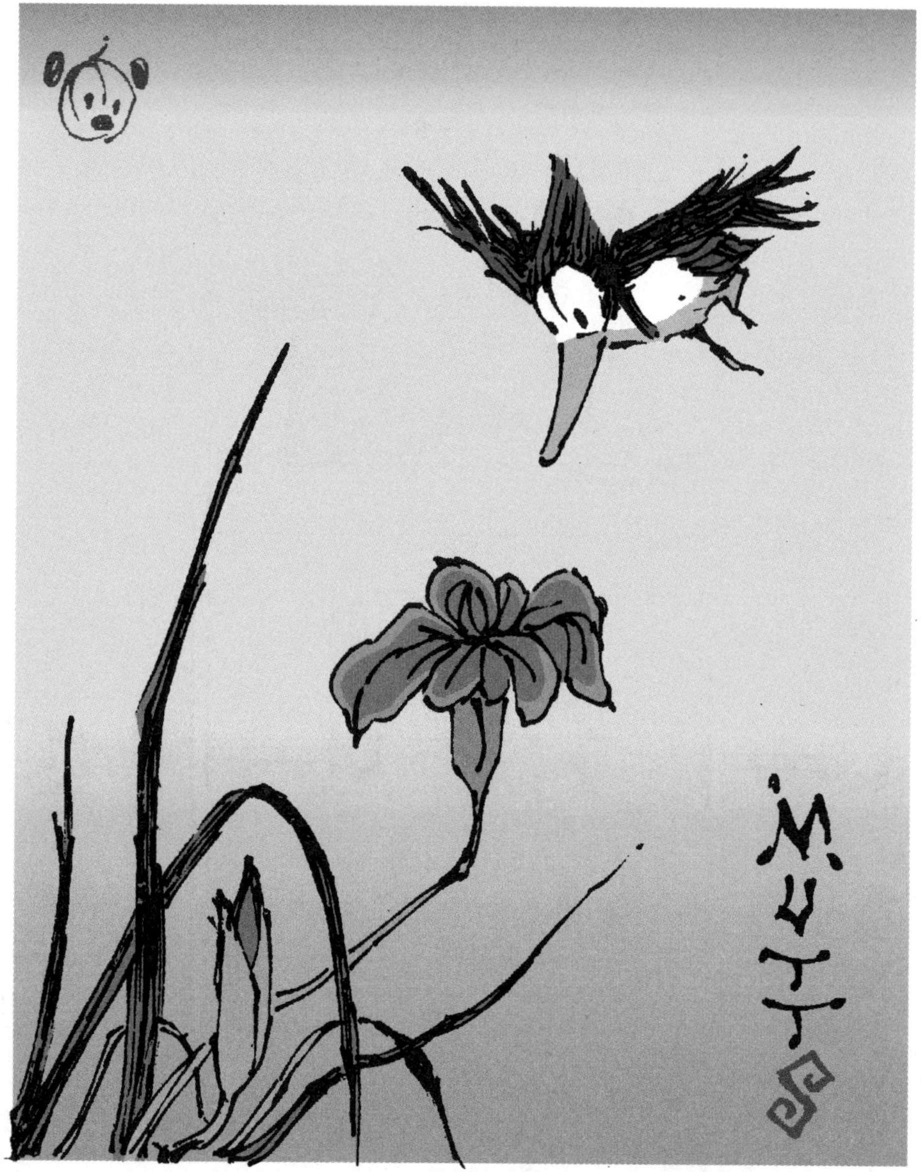
MUTT

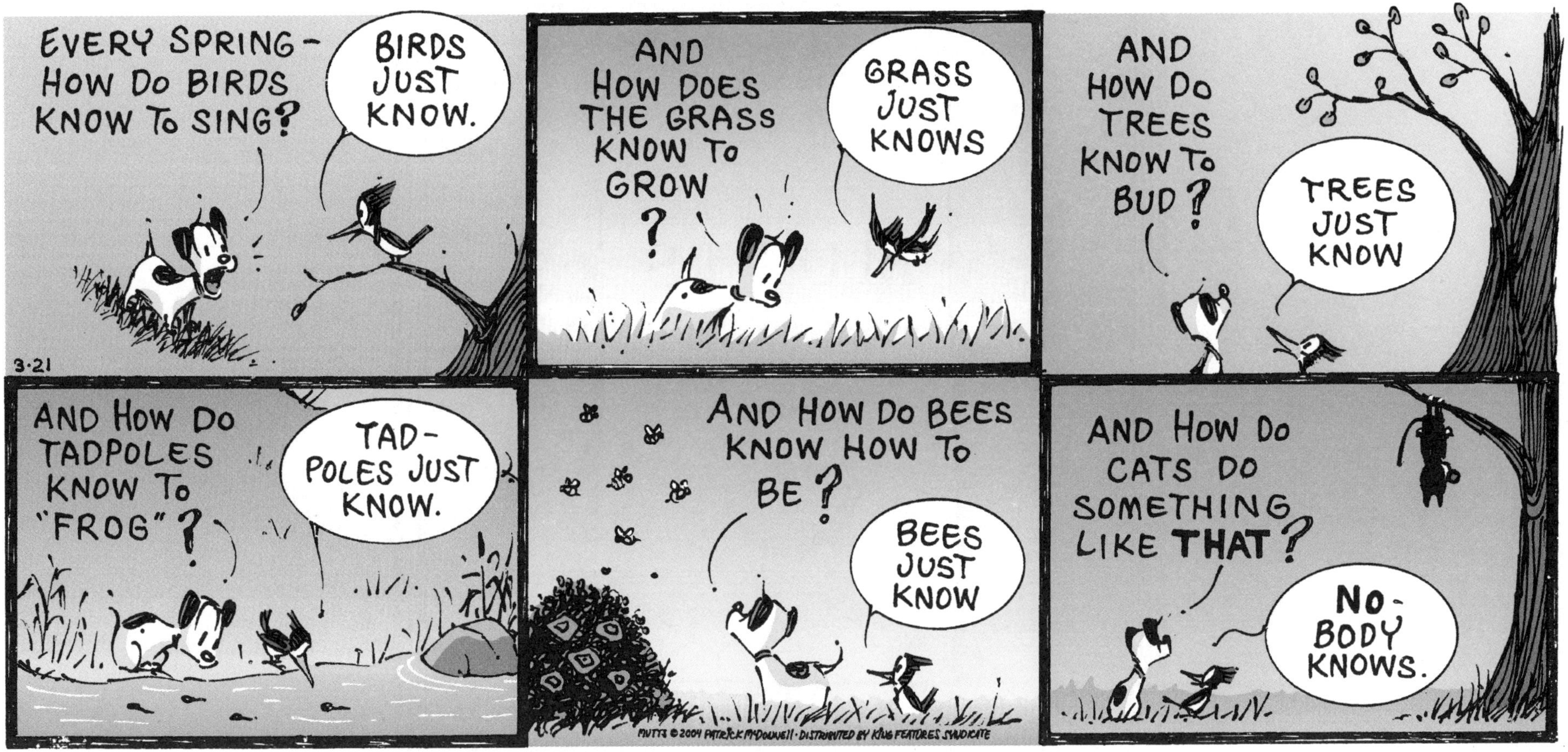
3·21
EVERY SPRING - HOW DO BIRDS KNOW TO SING?
BIRDS JUST KNOW.
AND HOW DOES THE GRASS KNOW TO GROW ?
GRASS JUST KNOWS
AND HOW DO TREES KNOW TO BUD?
TREES JUST KNOW
AND HOW DO TADPOLES KNOW TO "FROG"?
TAD-POLES JUST KNOW.
AND HOW DO BEES KNOW HOW TO BE?
BEES JUST KNOW
AND HOW DO CATS DO SOMETHING LIKE THAT?
NO-BODY KNOWS.
MUTTS © 2004 PATRICK McDONNELL · DISTRIBUTED BY KING FEATURES SYNDICATE

MUTTS
PATRICK McDONNELL

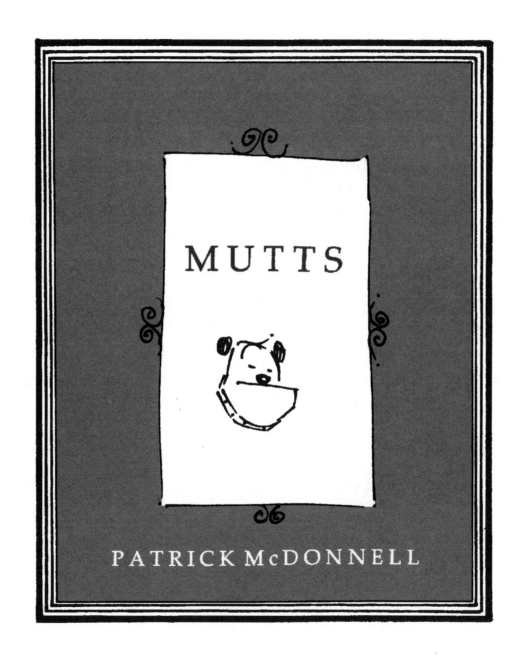

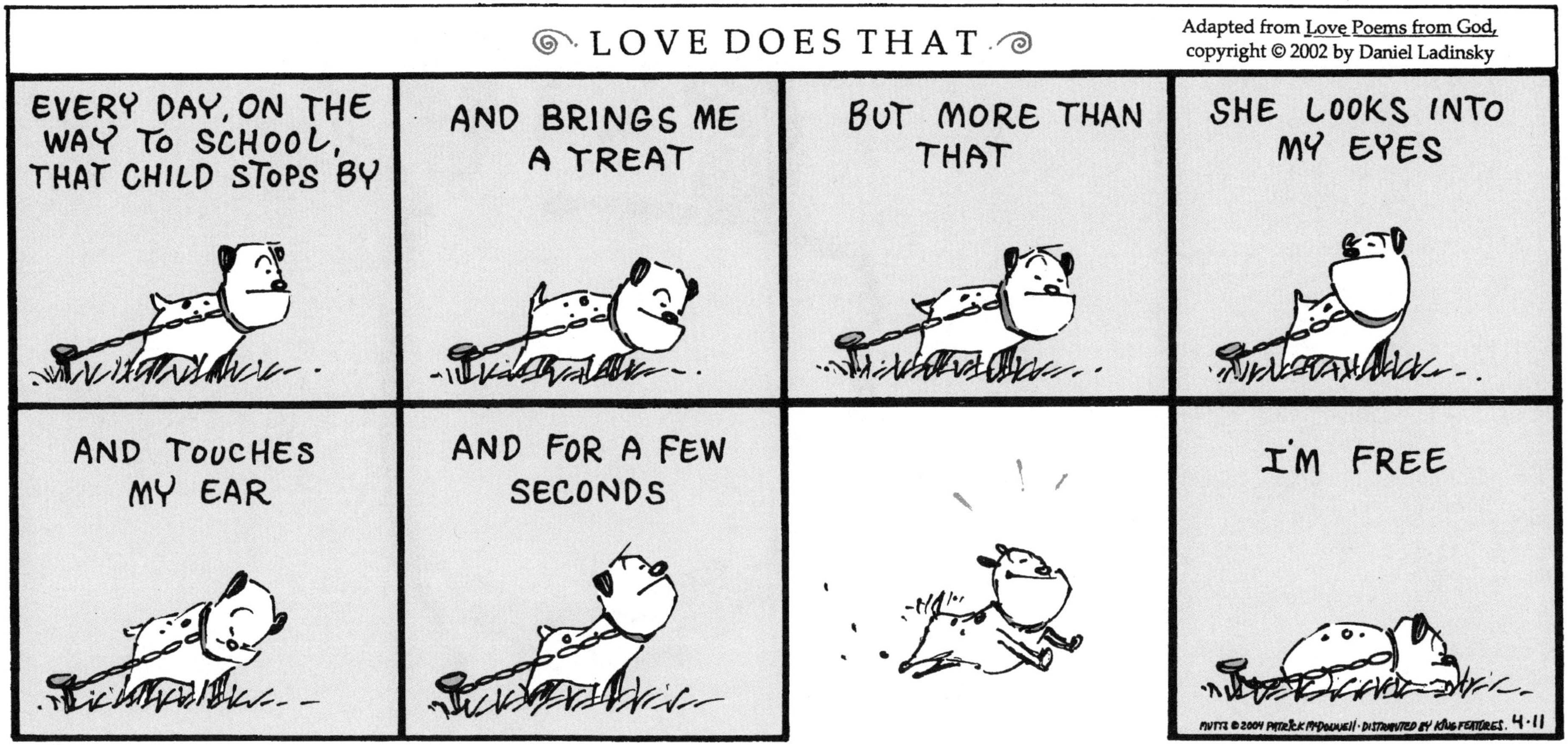
LOVE DOES THAT
Adapted from Love Poems from God, copyright © 2002 by Daniel Ladinsky
EVERY DAY, ON THE WAY TO SCHOOL, THAT CHILD STOPS BY
AND BRINGS ME A TREAT
BUT MORE THAN THAT
SHE LOOKS INTO MY EYES
AND TOUCHES MY EAR
AND FOR A FEW SECONDS
I'M FREE
MUTTS © 2004 PATRICK McDONNELL · DISTRIBUTED BY KING FEATURES. 4·11

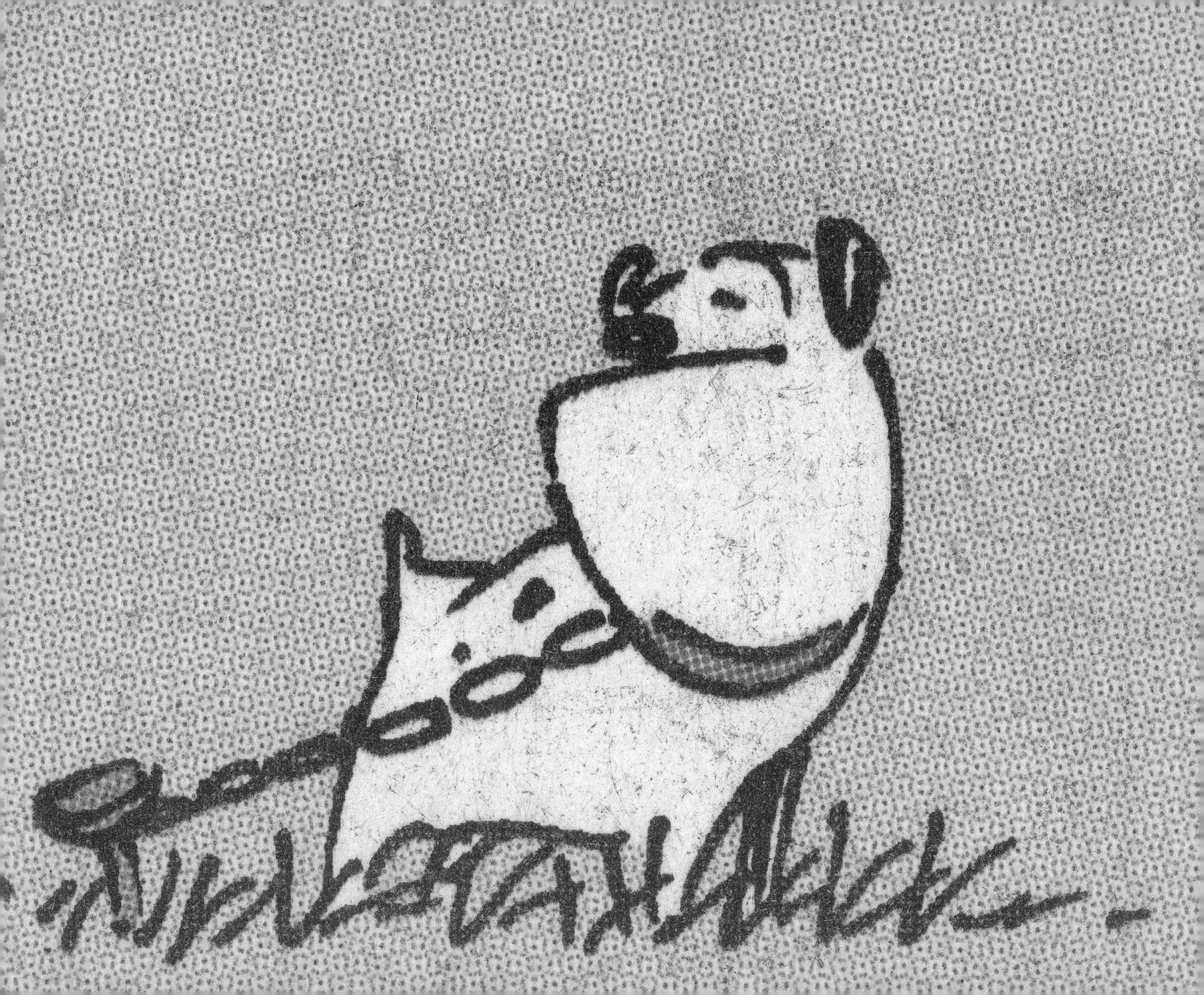

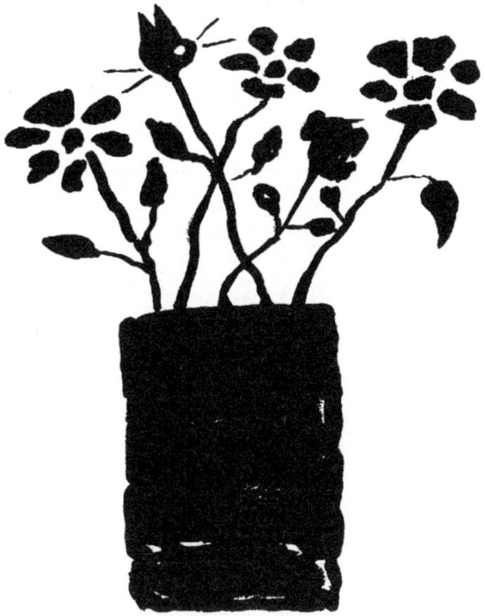

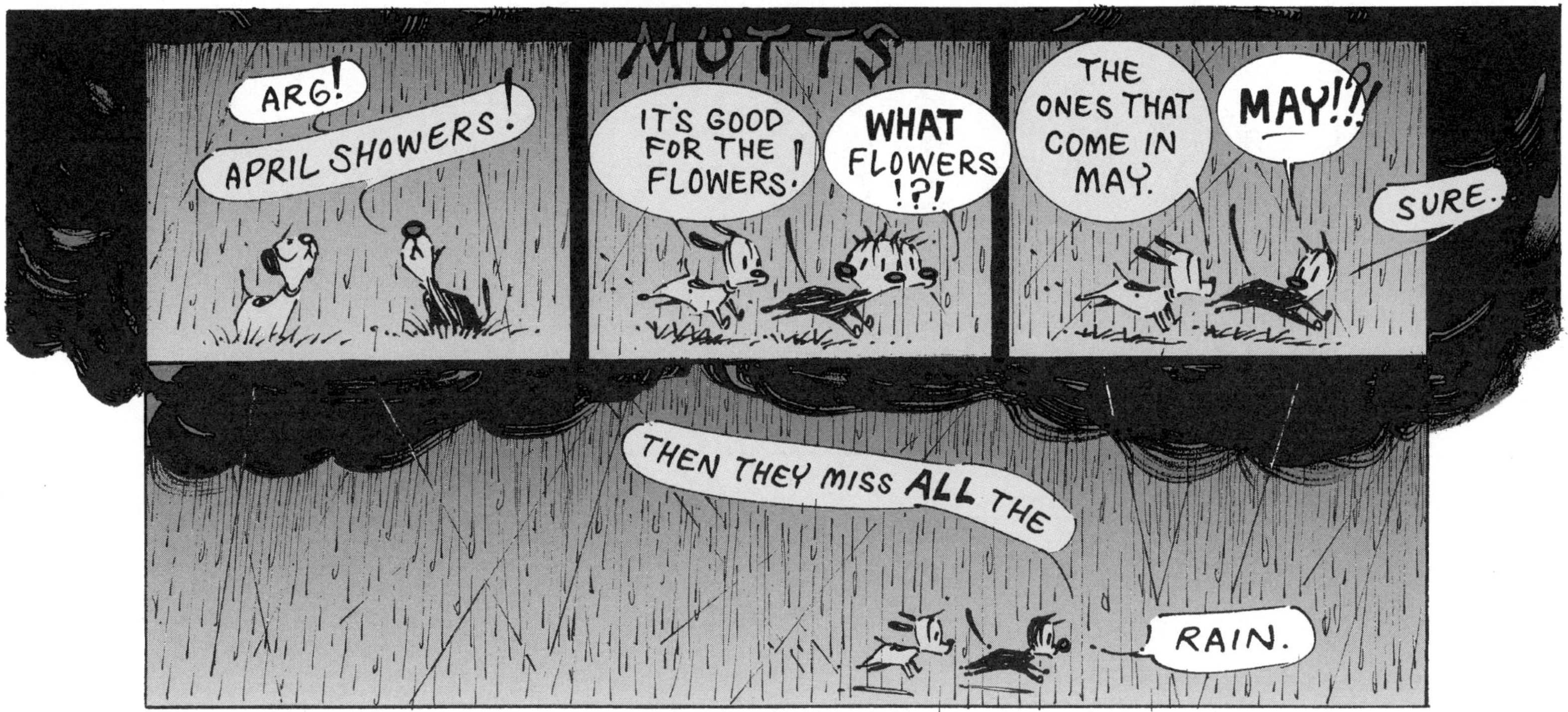
MUTTS
ARG!
APRIL SHOWERS!
IT'S GOOD FOR THE FLOWERS!
WHAT FLOWERS !?!
THE ONES THAT COME IN MAY.
MAY!?!
SURE.
THEN THEY MISS ALL THE
RAIN.

4.4

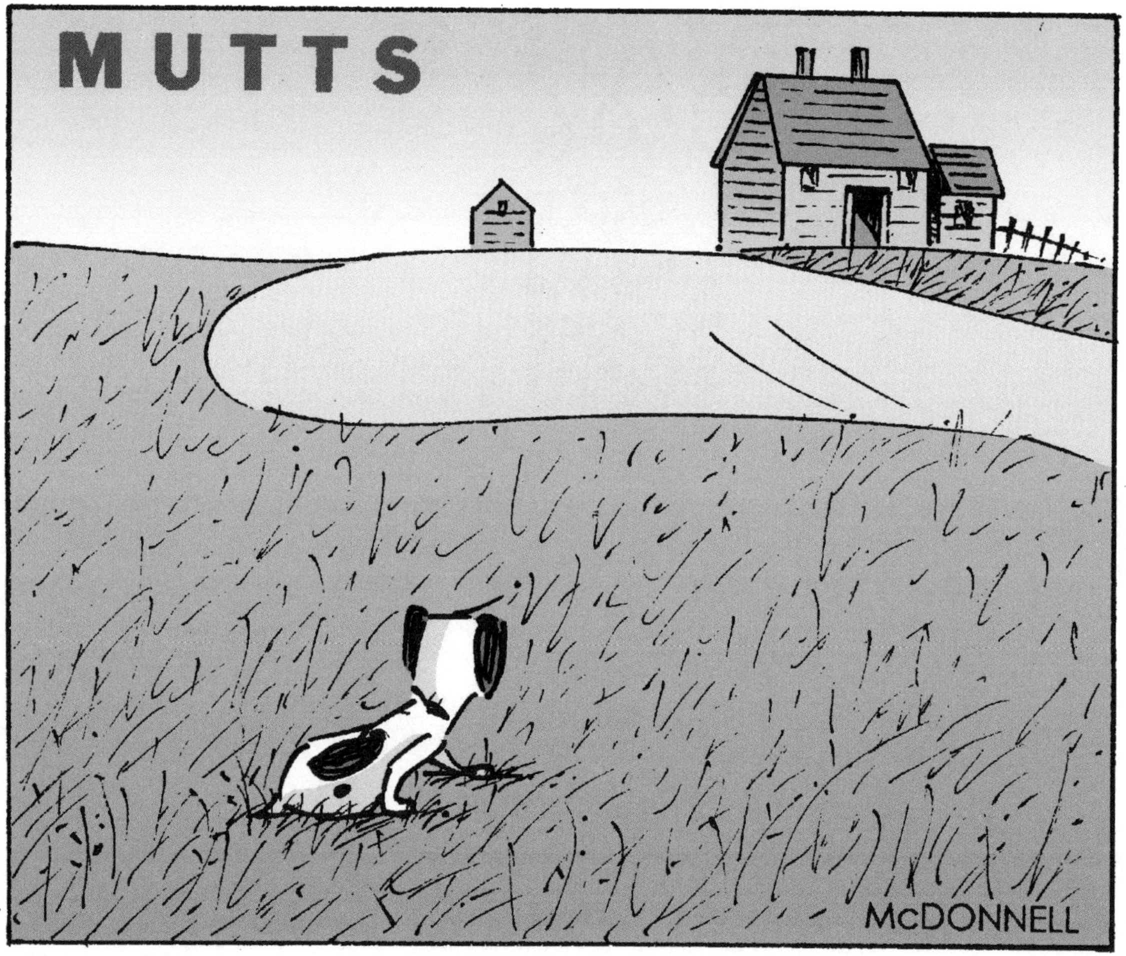
MUTTS
McDONNELL

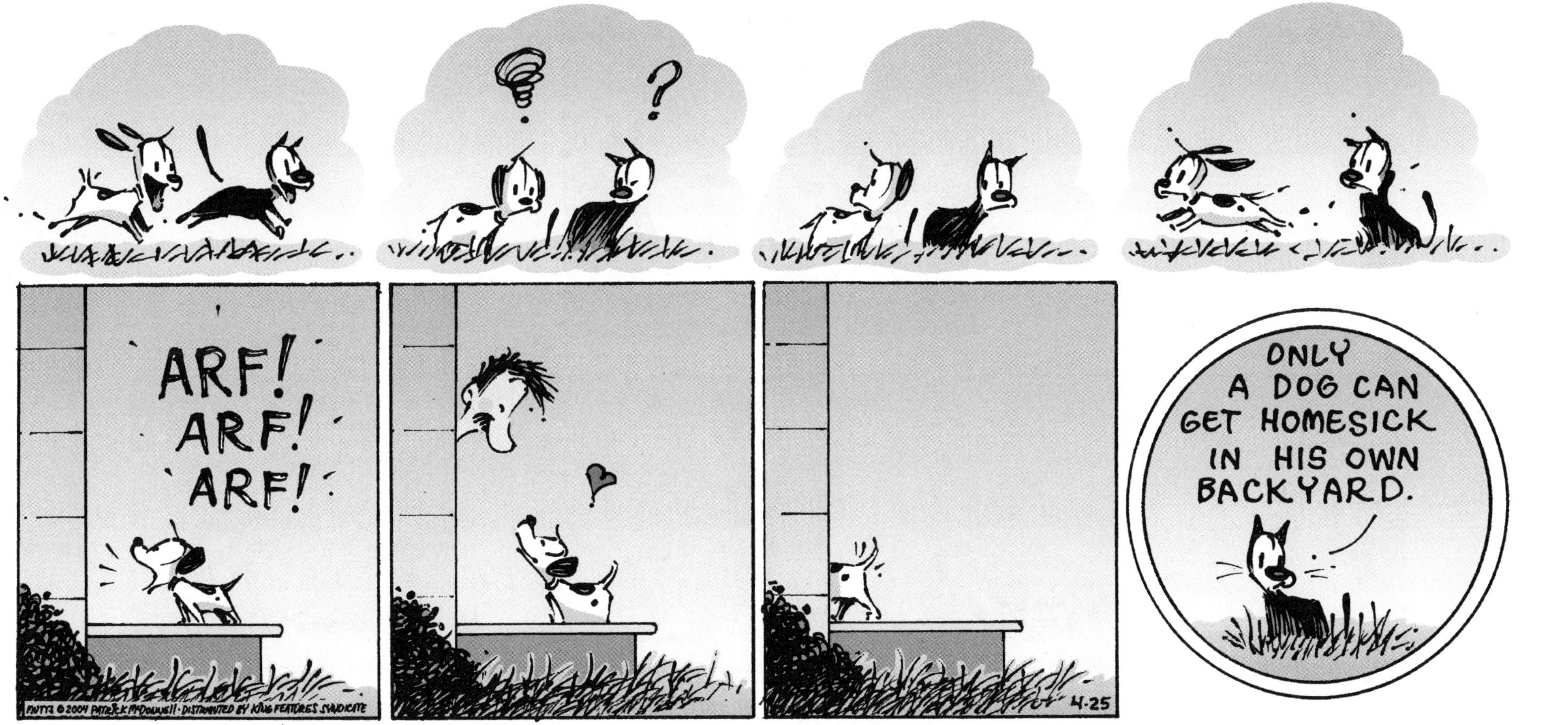
ARF! ARF! ARF!
ONLY A DOG CAN GET HOMESICK IN HIS OWN BACKYARD.
MUTTS © 2004 PATRICK McDONNELL · DISTRIBUTED BY KING FEATURES SYNDICATE
4-25

FOR THE LOVE OF MUTTS!
by PATRICK McDONNELL

ANIMAL SHELTER
MUTTS © 2004 PATRICK McDONNELL · DISTRIBUTED BY KING FEATURES SYNDICATE
ANIMAL SHELTER
HOWOOO
ARF
ARF ARF ARF
MEEYOW!
ANIMAL SHELTER
PURRR
LICK LICK LICK LICK LICK
ANIMAL SHELTER
GOOD DEEDS SHOULD BE REWARDED
YESH!
5·2

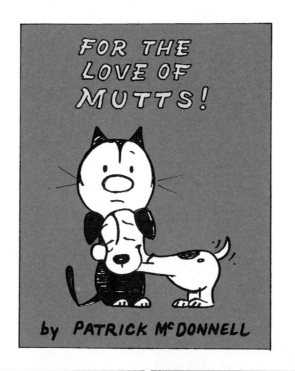

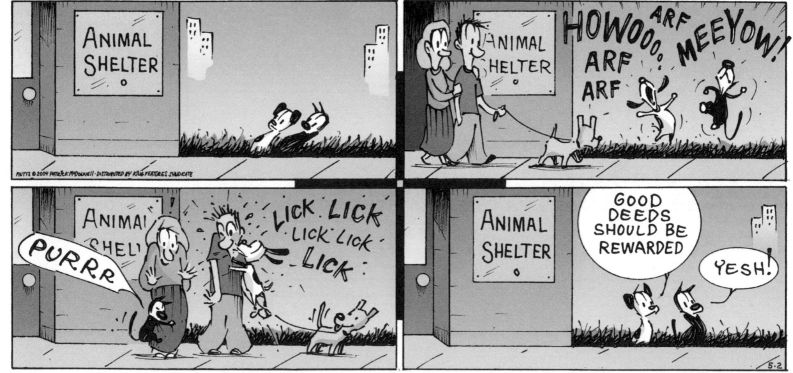

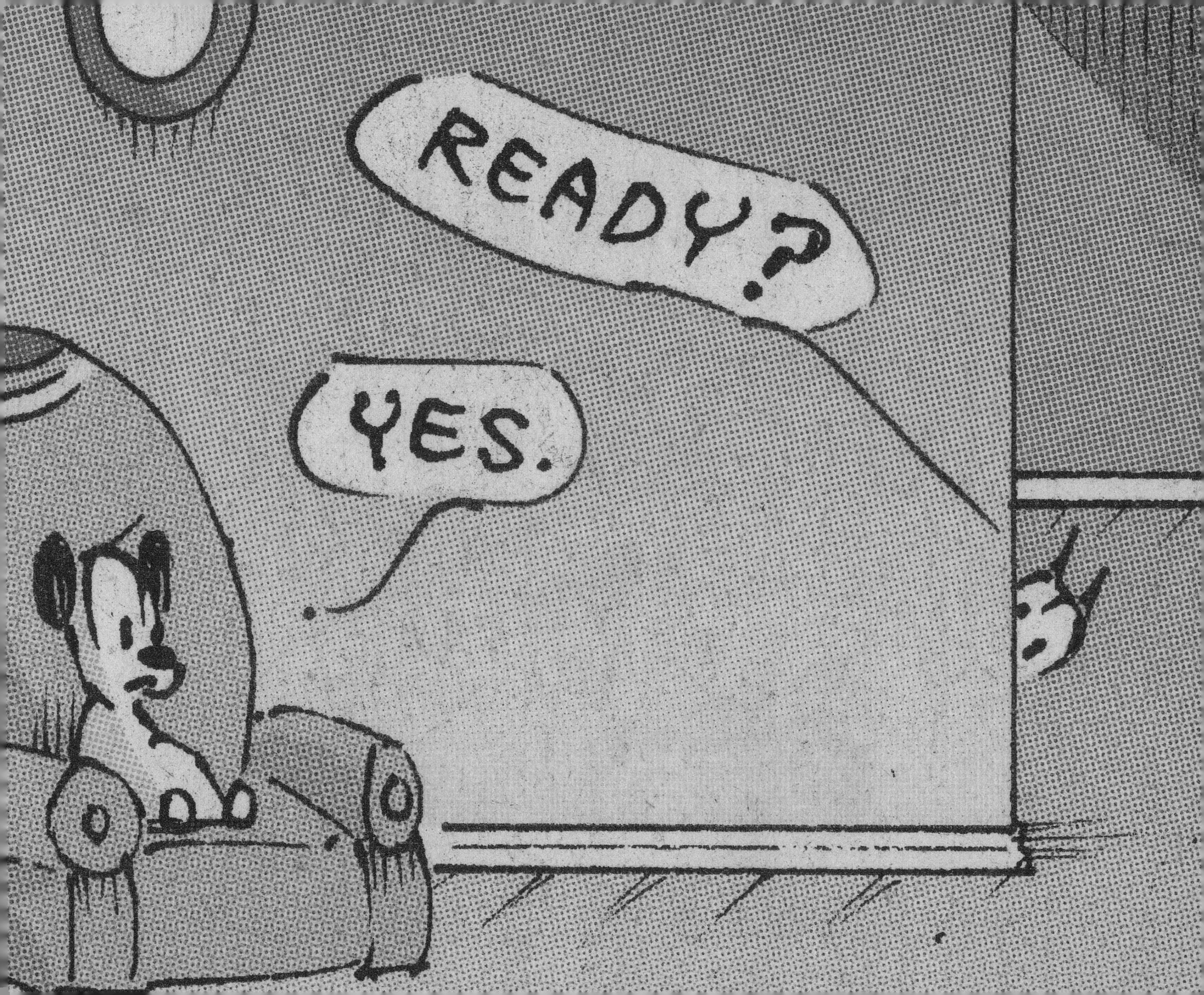
READY?
YES.

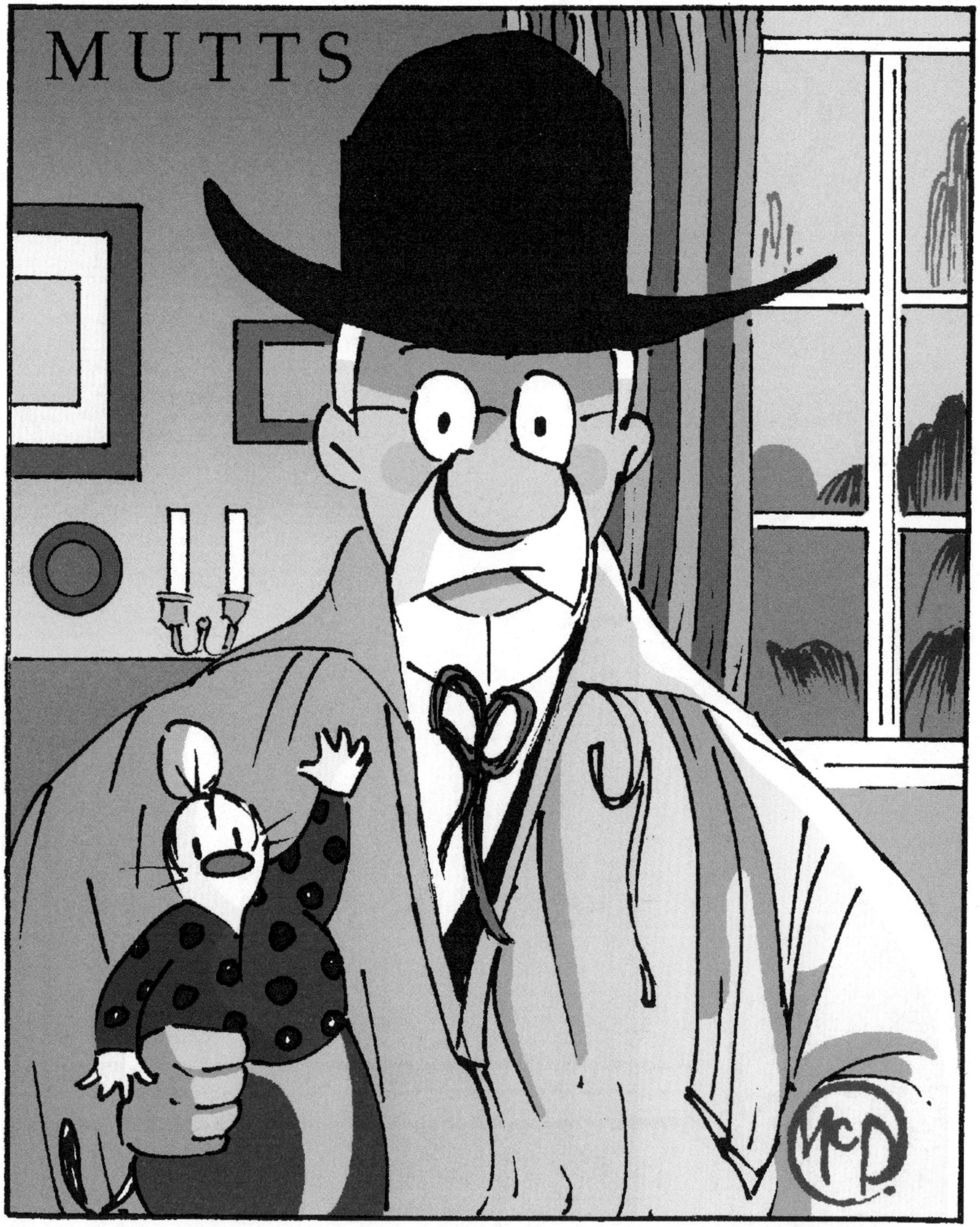
MUTTS
McD.

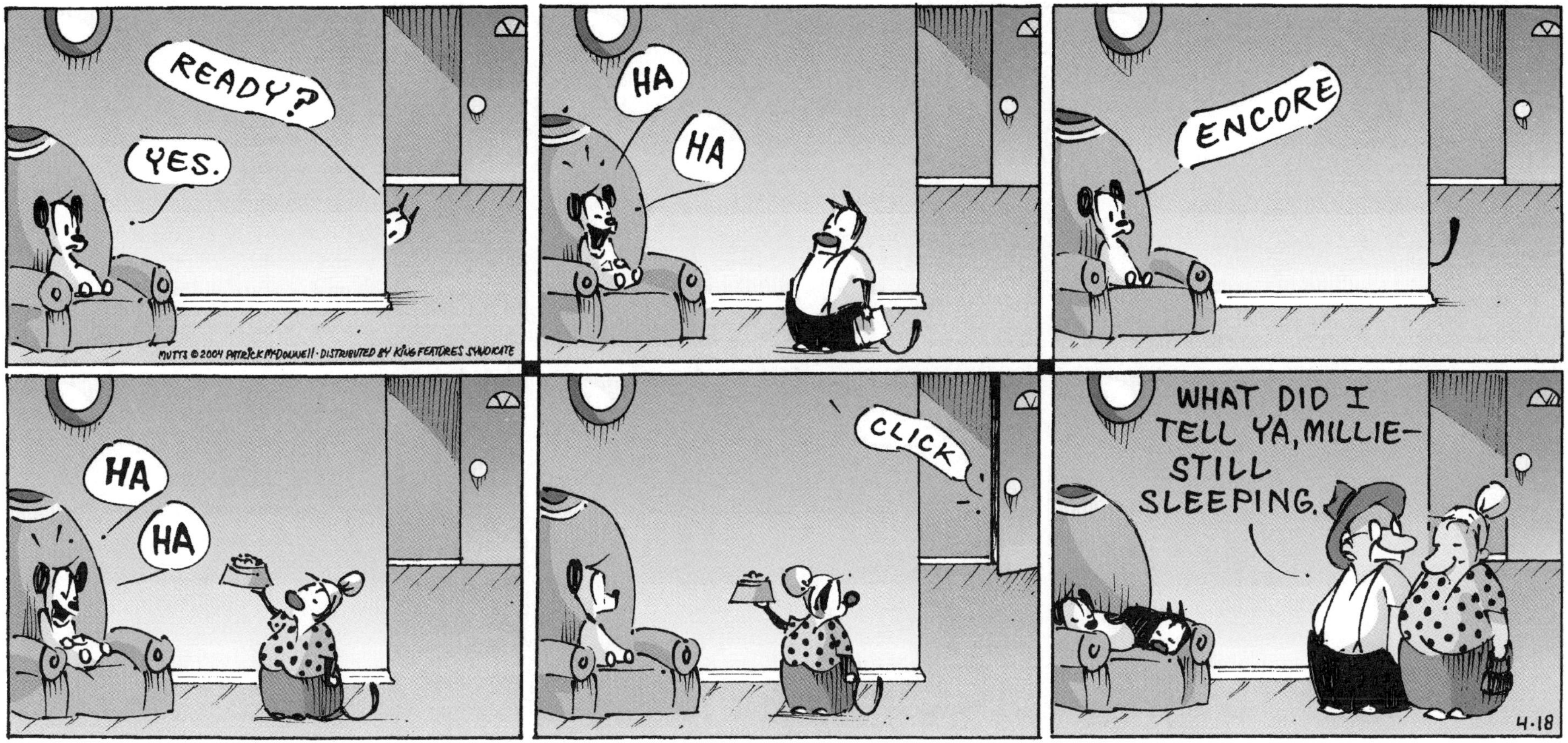
READY?
YES.
MUTTS © 2004 PATRICK McDONNELL · DISTRIBUTED BY KING FEATURES SYNDICATE
HA
HA
ENCORE
HA
HA
CLICK
WHAT DID I TELL YA, MILLIE- STILL SLEEPING.
4·18

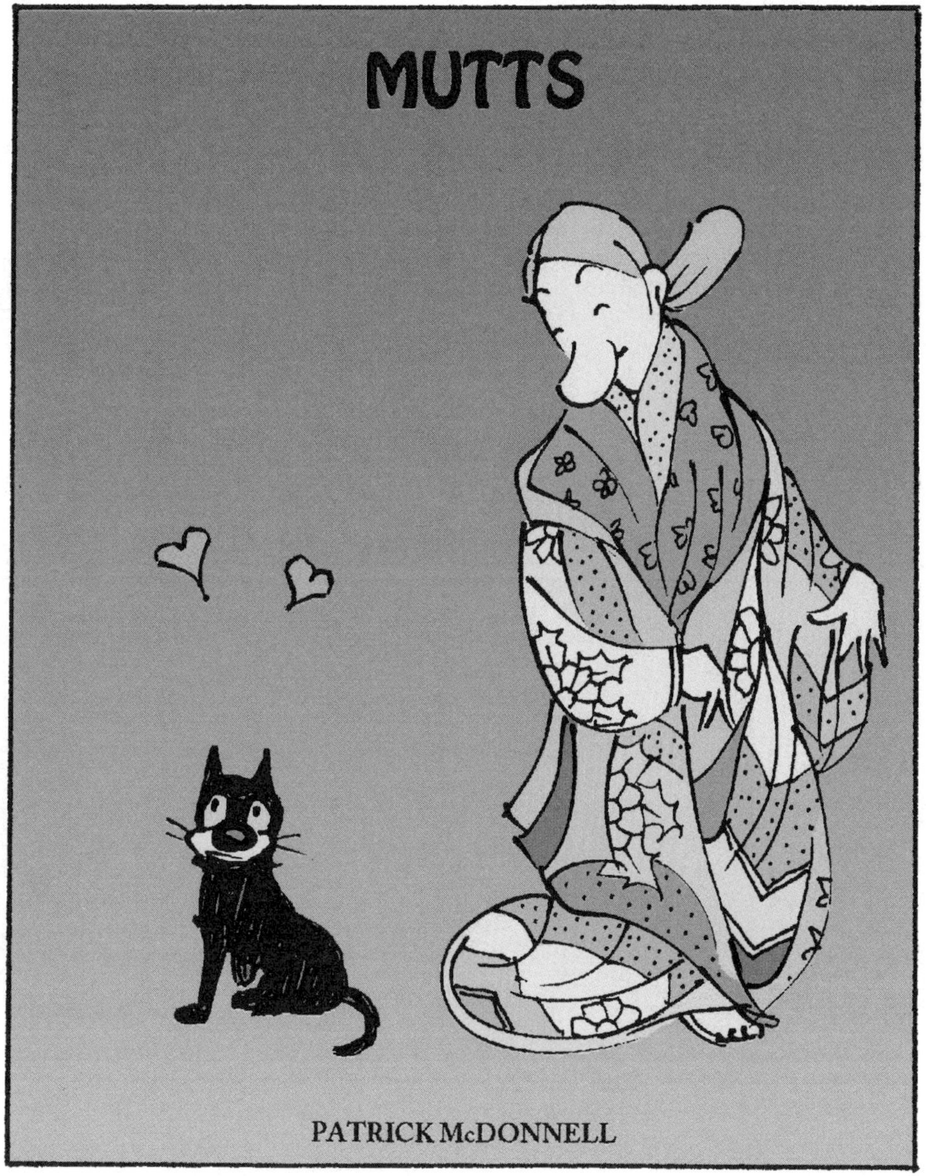
MUTTS
PATRICK McDONNELL

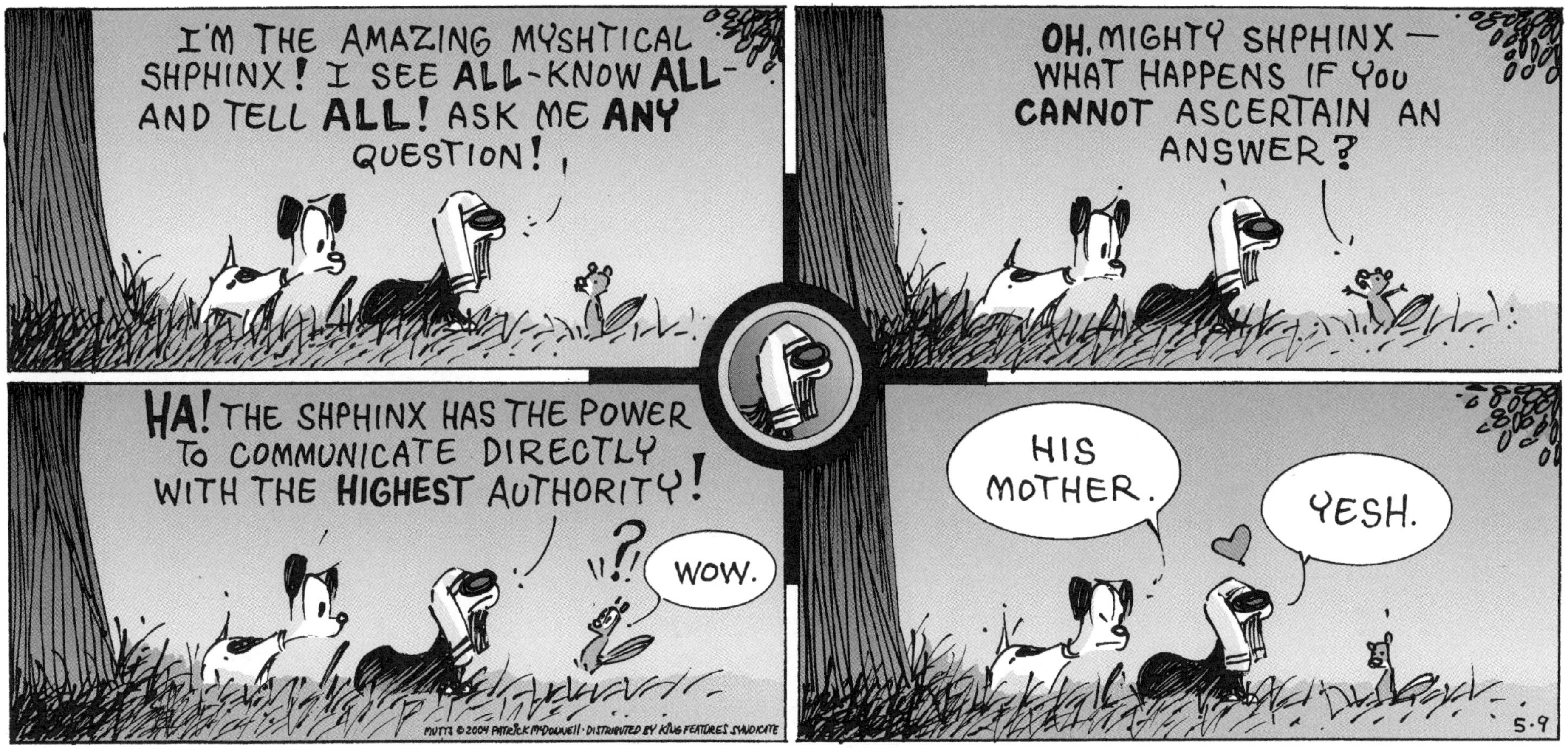
I'M THE AMAZING MYSHTICAL SHPHINX! I SEE ALL-KNOW ALL-AND TELL ALL! ASK ME ANY QUESTION!
OH, MIGHTY SHPHINX— WHAT HAPPENS IF YOU CANNOT ASCERTAIN AN ANSWER?
HA! THE SHPHINX HAS THE POWER TO COMMUNICATE DIRECTLY WITH THE HIGHEST AUTHORITY!
?
WOW.
MUTTS © 2004 PATRICK McDONNELL · DISTRIBUTED BY KING FEATURES SYNDICATE
HIS MOTHER.
YESH.
5·9

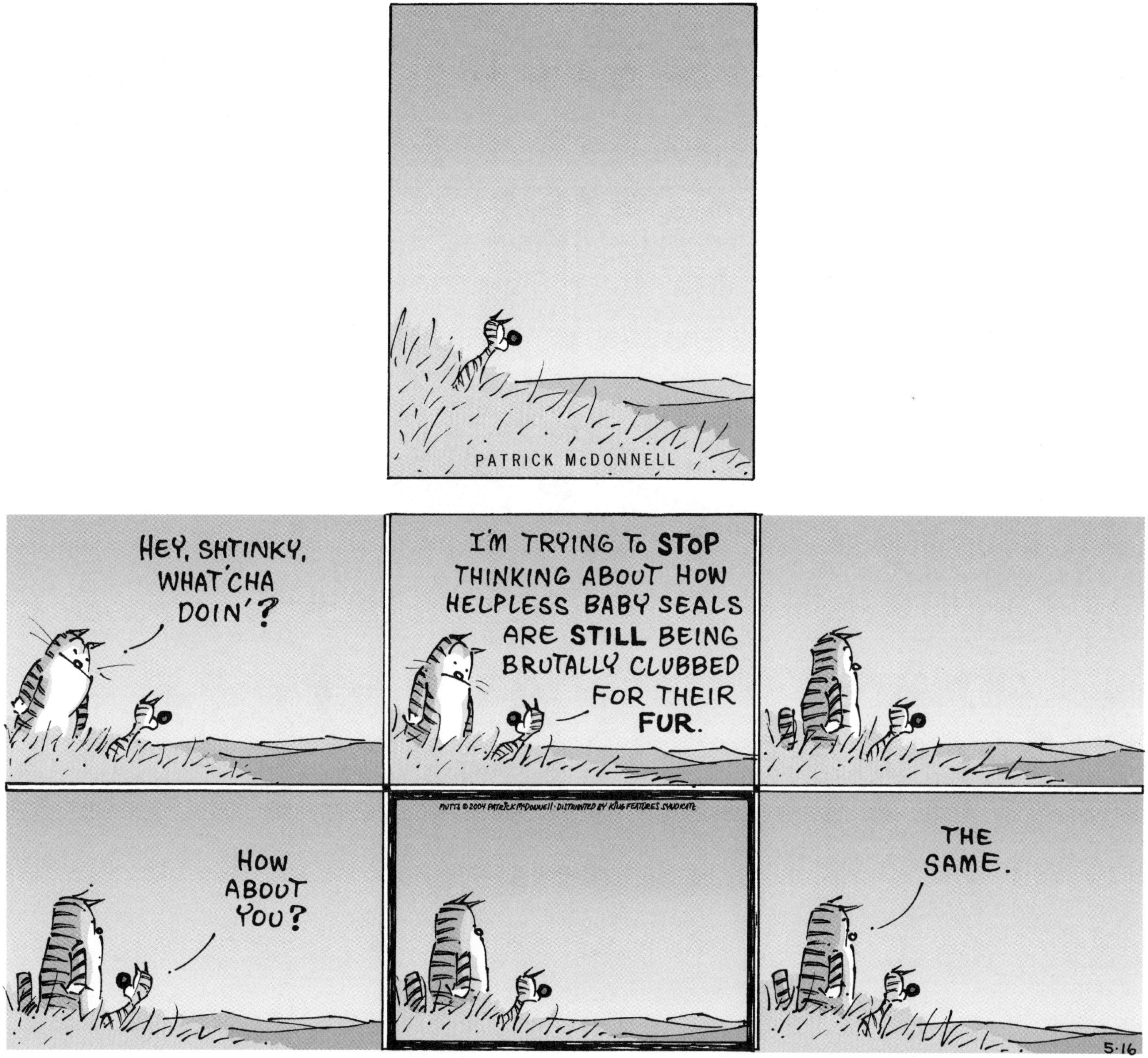
PATRICK McDONNELL
HEY, SHTINKY, WHAT'CHA DOIN'?
I'M TRYING TO STOP THINKING ABOUT HOW HELPLESS BABY SEALS ARE STILL BEING BRUTALLY CLUBBED FOR THEIR FUR.
HOW ABOUT YOU?
MUTTS © 2004 PATRICK McDONNELL · DISTRIBUTED BY KING FEATURES SYNDICATE
THE SAME.
5·16

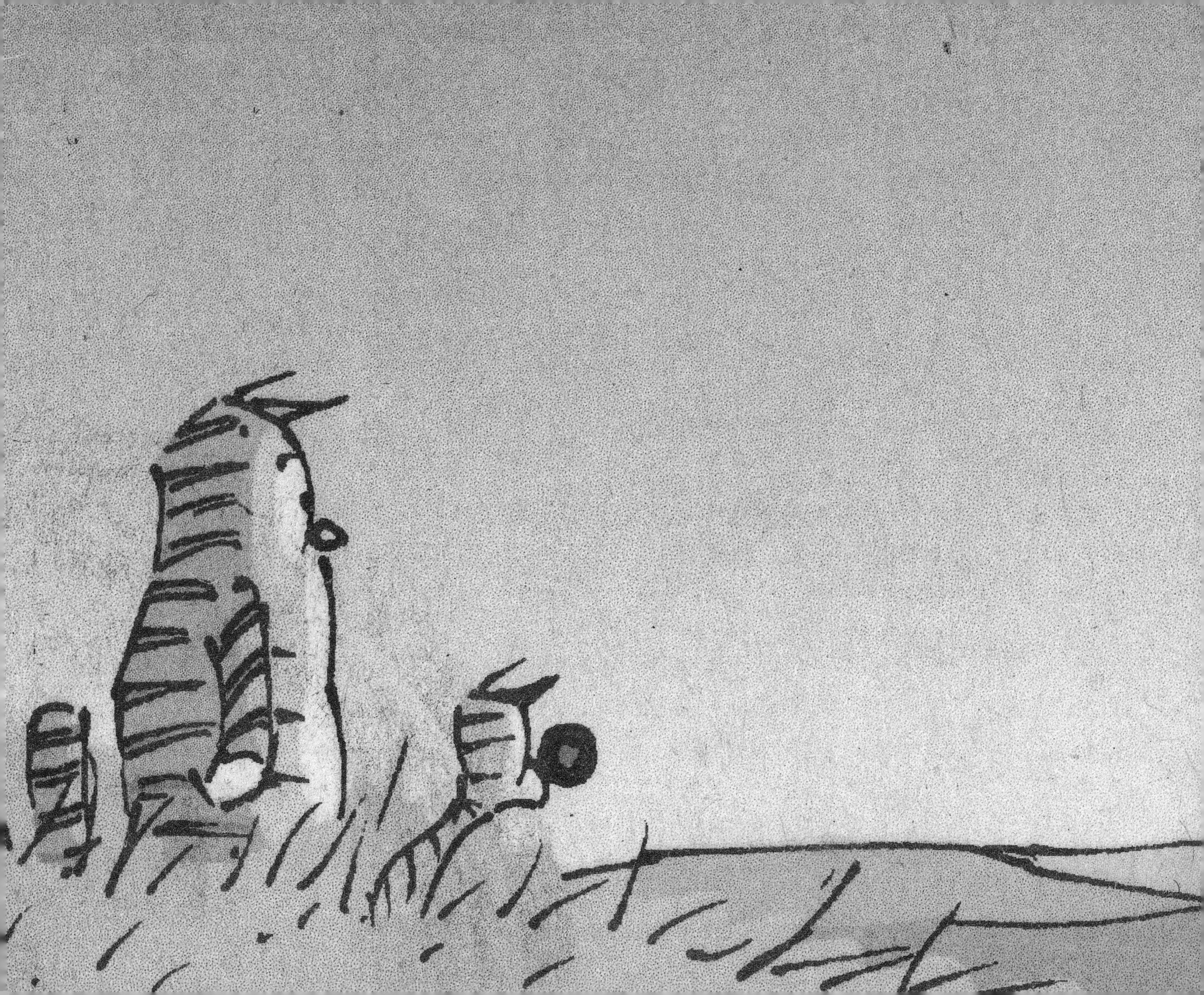

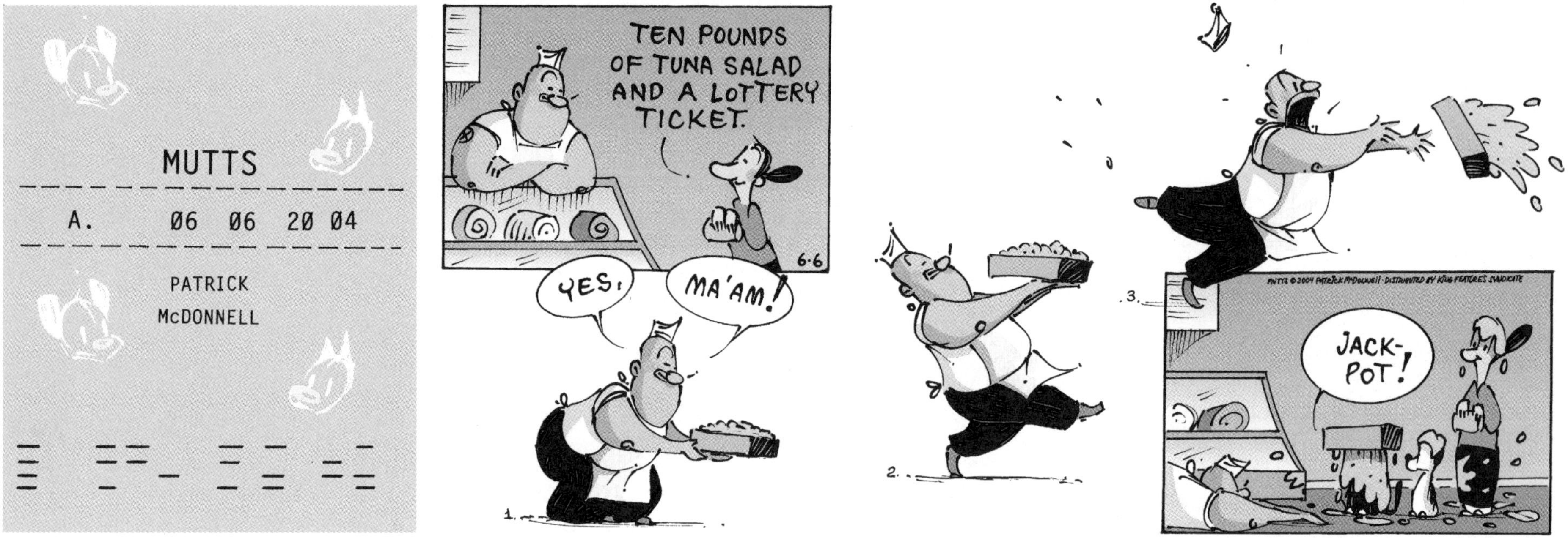
MUTTS
A. 06 06 20 04
PATRICK
McDONNELL
TEN POUNDS OF TUNA SALAD AND A LOTTERY TICKET.
6·6
YES,
MA'AM!
JACK-POT!
MUTTS © 2004 PATRICK McDONNELL · DISTRIBUTED BY KING FEATURES SYNDICATE

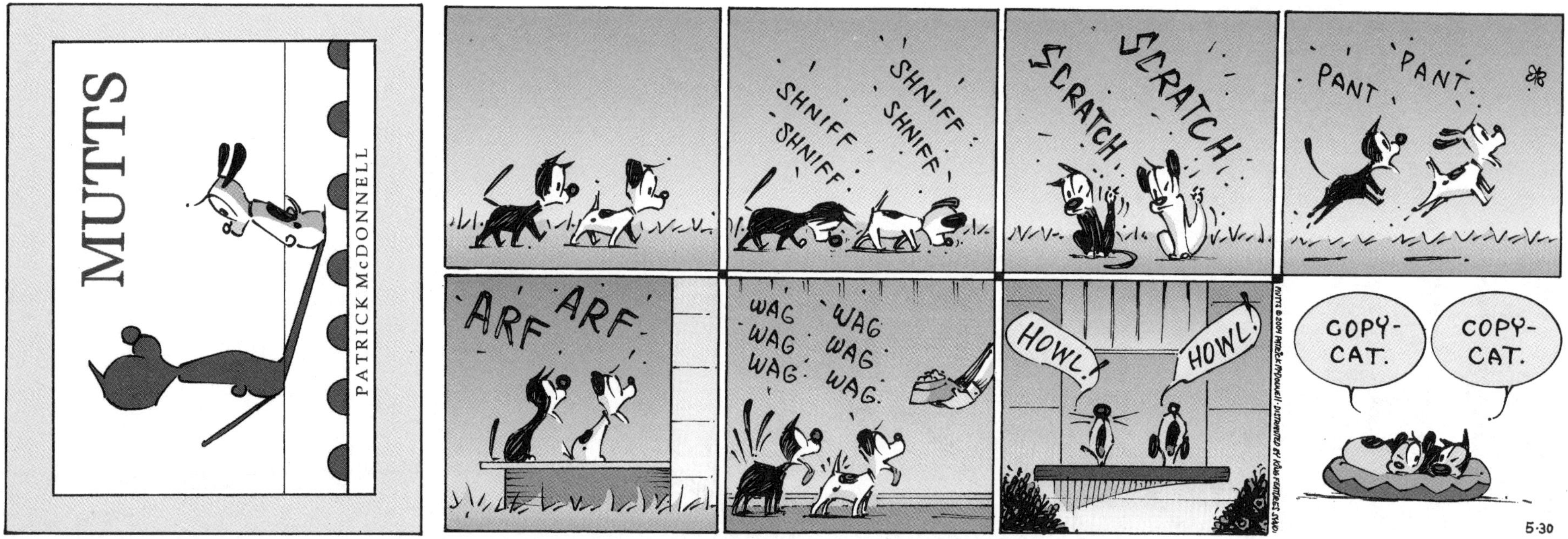
MUTTS
PATRICK McDONNELL
SHNIFF SHNIFF
SHNIFF SHNIFF
SCRATCH
SCRATCH
PANT
PANT
ARF
ARF
WAG WAG WAG
WAG WAG WAG
HOWL!
HOWL!
COPY-CAT.
COPY-CAT.
MUTTS © 2004 PATRICK McDONNELL · DISTRIBUTED BY KING FEATURES SYND.
5·30

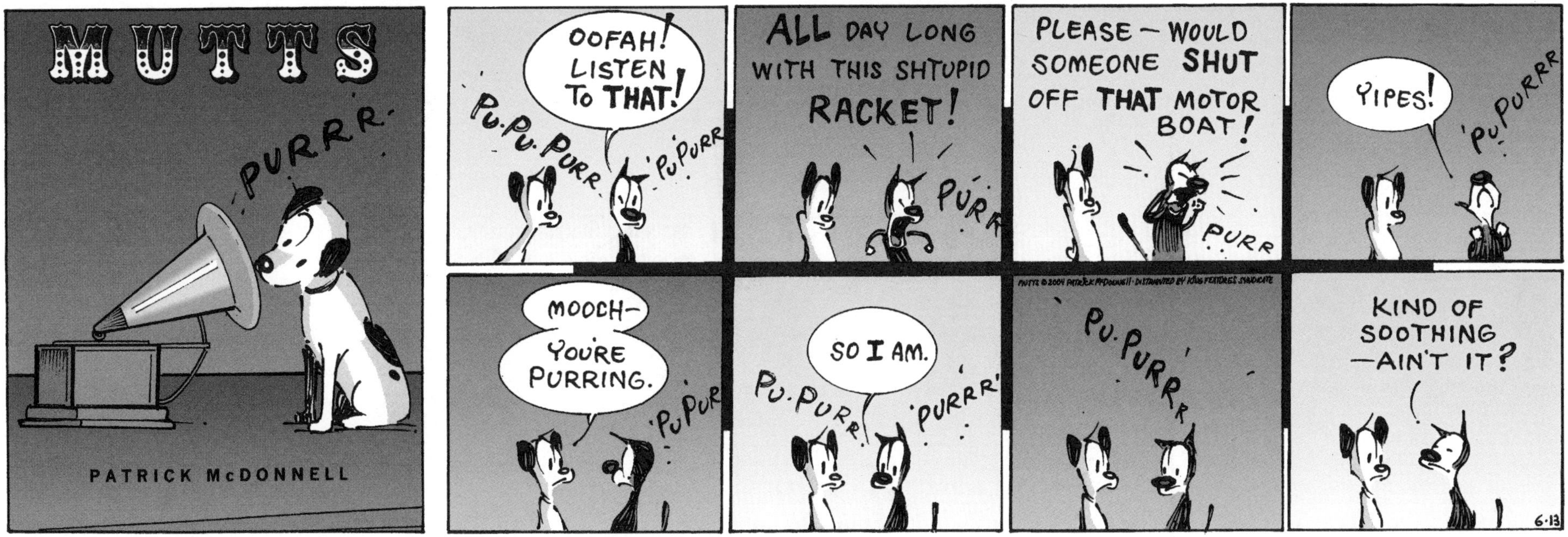
MUTTS
PURRR
PATRICK McDONNELL
PU-PU-PURR
OOFAH! LISTEN TO THAT!
PU PURR
ALL DAY LONG WITH THIS SHTUPID RACKET!
PURR
PLEASE — WOULD SOMEONE SHUT OFF THAT MOTOR BOAT!
PURR
YIPES!
PU PURRR
MOOCH—
YOU'RE PURRING.
PU PUR
PU-PURR
SO I AM.
PURRR
MUTTS © 2004 PATRICK McDONNELL · DISTRIBUTED BY KING FEATURES SYNDICATE
PU-PURRRR
KIND OF SOOTHING —AIN'T IT?
6·13

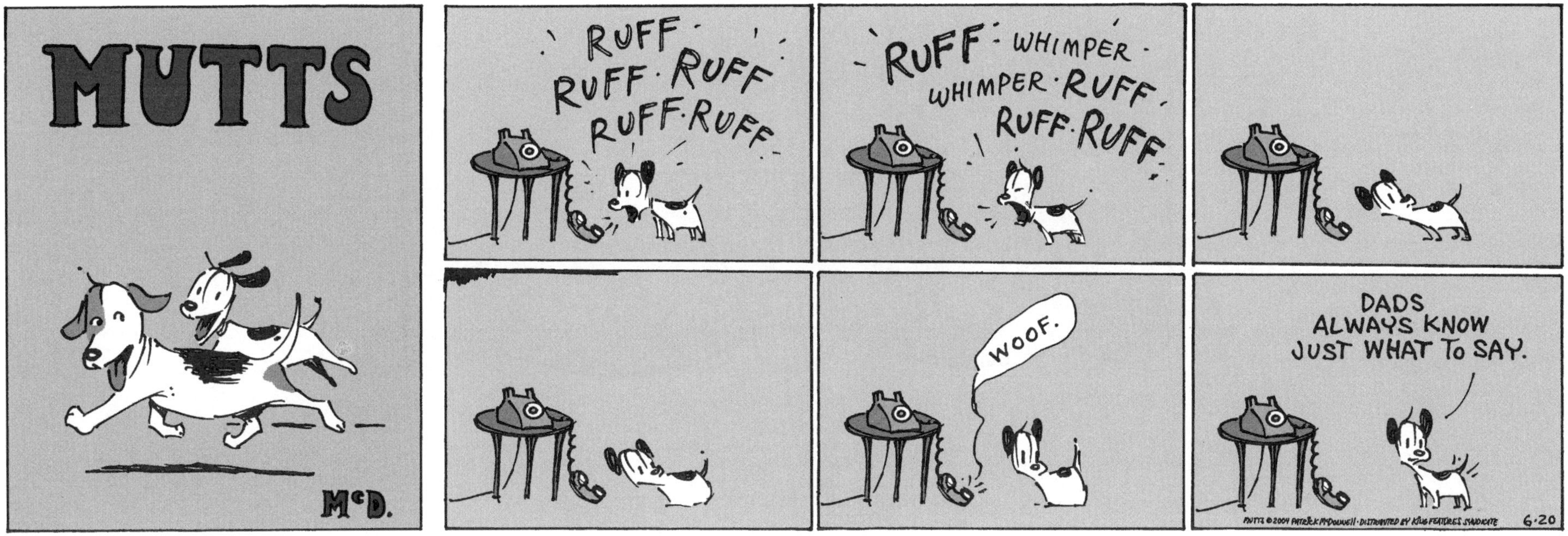
MUTTS
McD.
RUFF
RUFF · RUFF
RUFF · RUFF
RUFF · WHIMPER
WHIMPER · RUFF
RUFF · RUFF
WOOF.
DADS ALWAYS KNOW JUST WHAT TO SAY.
MUTTS © 2004 PATRICK McDONNELL · DISTRIBUTED BY KING FEATURES SYNDICATE
6·20

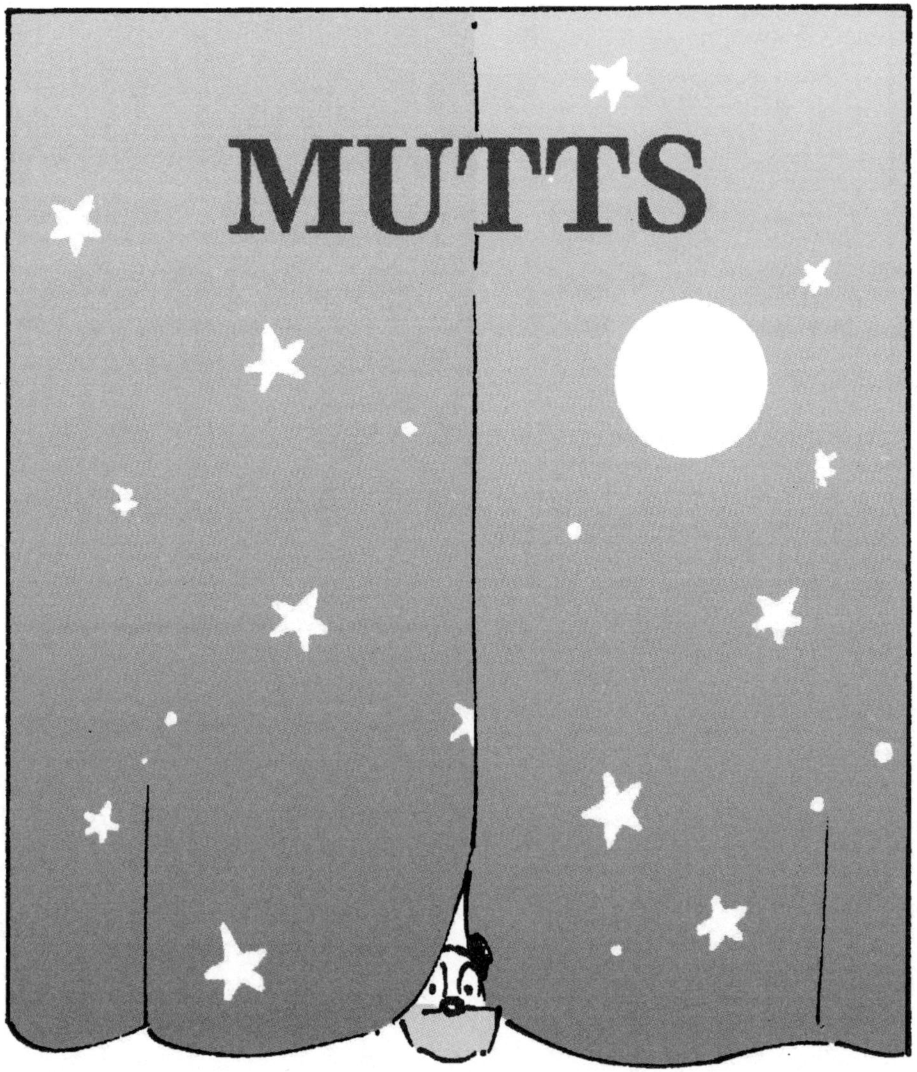
MUTTS

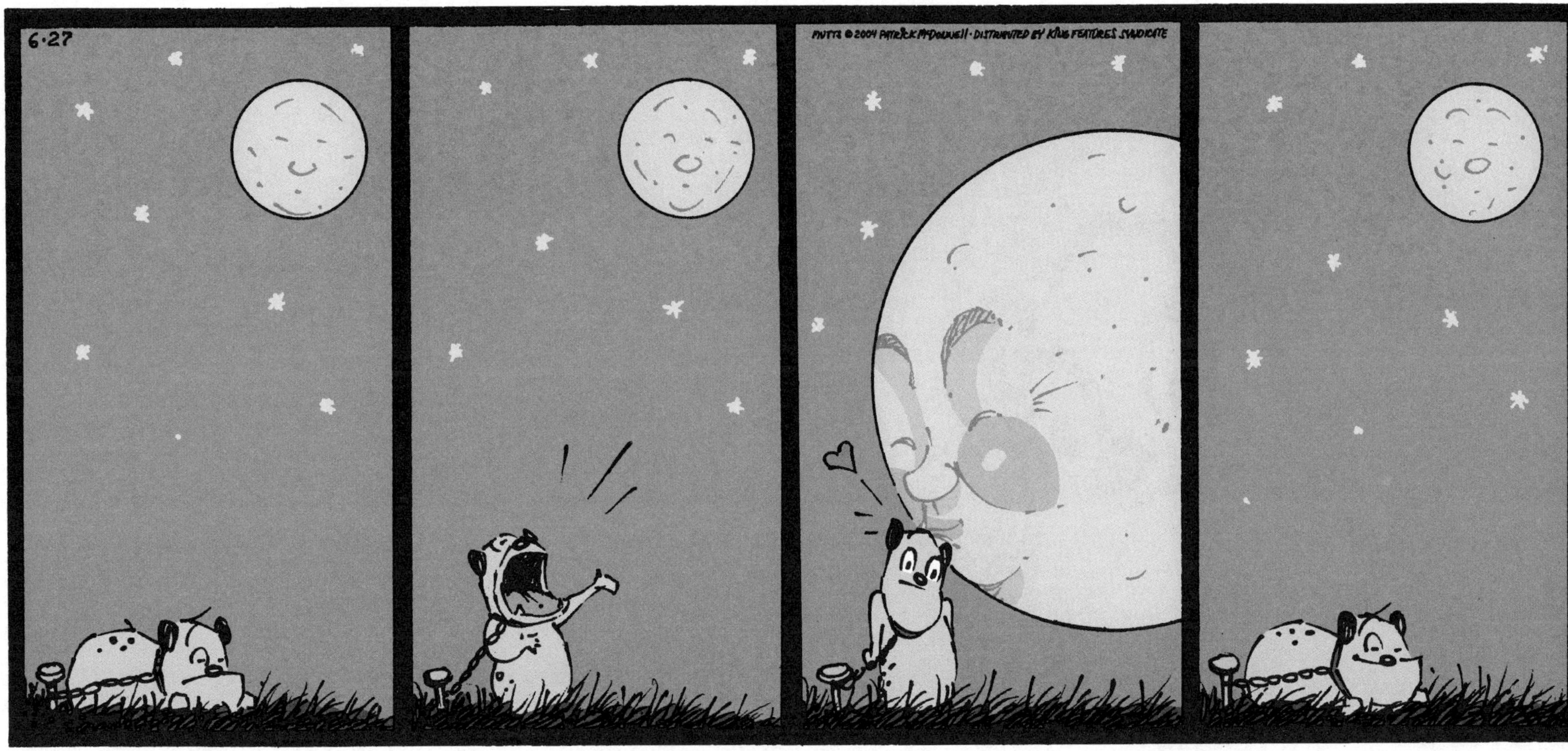
6·27
MUTTS © 2004 PATRICK McDONNELL · DISTRIBUTED BY KING FEATURES SYNDICATE

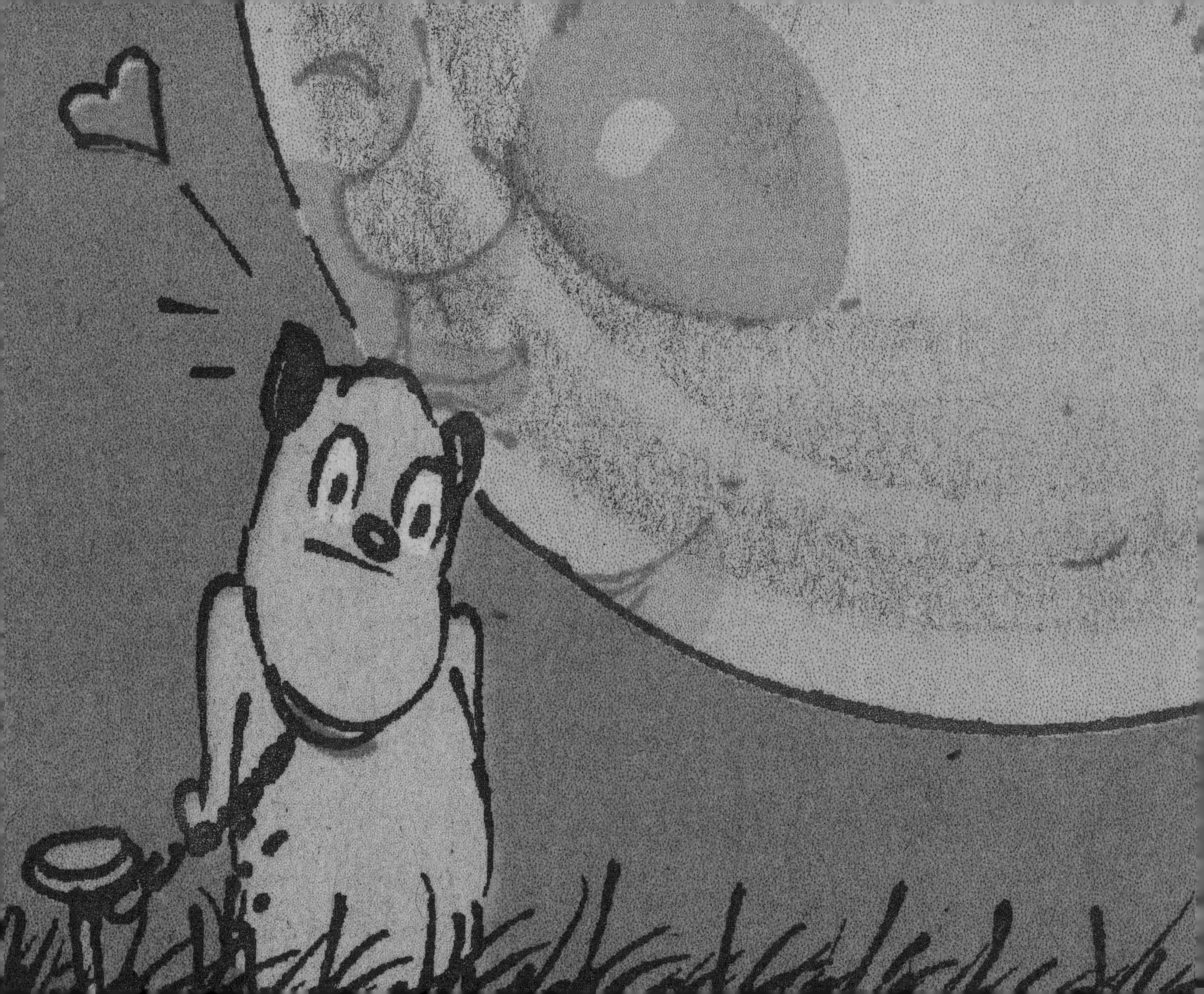

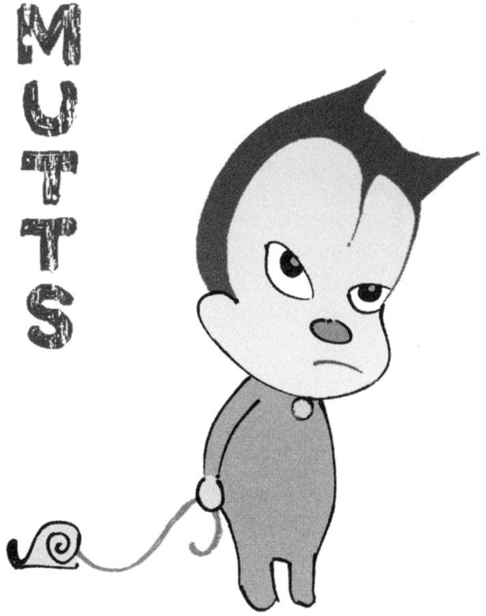
MUTTS

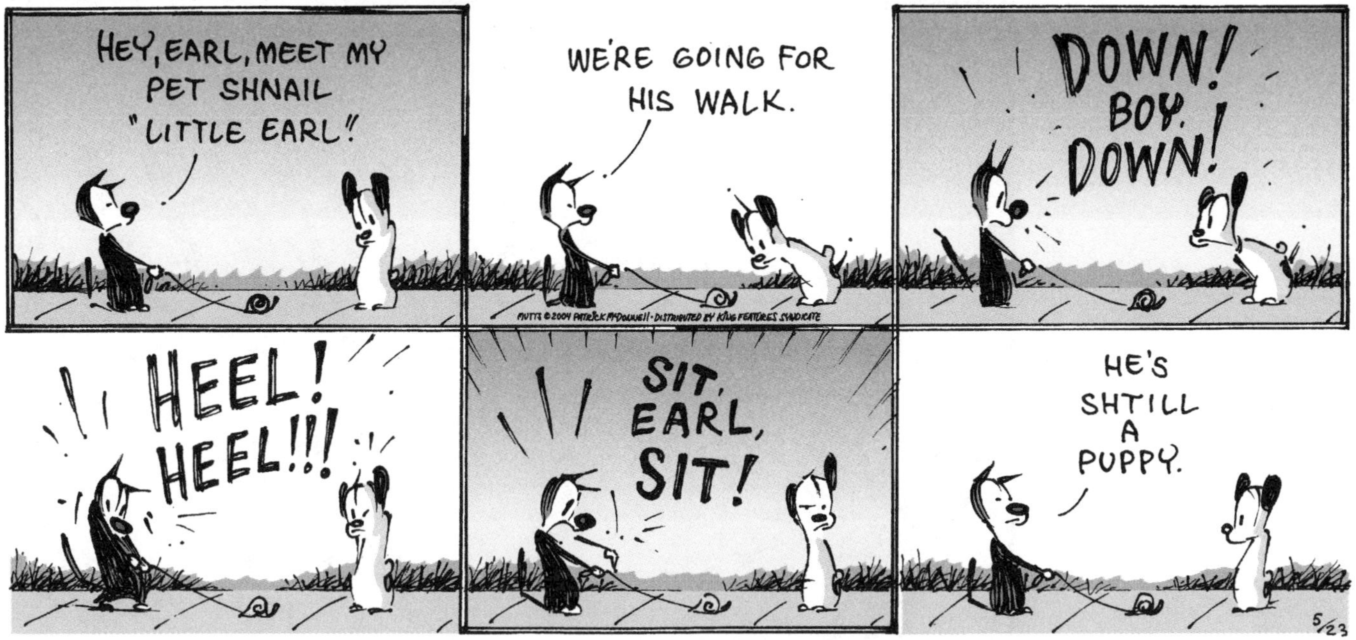
HEY, EARL, MEET MY PET SHNAIL "LITTLE EARL."
WE'RE GOING FOR HIS WALK.
DOWN! BOY. DOWN!
MUTTS © 2004 PATRICK McDONNELL · DISTRIBUTED BY KING FEATURES SYNDICATE
HEEL! HEEL!!!
SIT, EARL, SIT!
HE'S SHTILL A PUPPY.
5/23

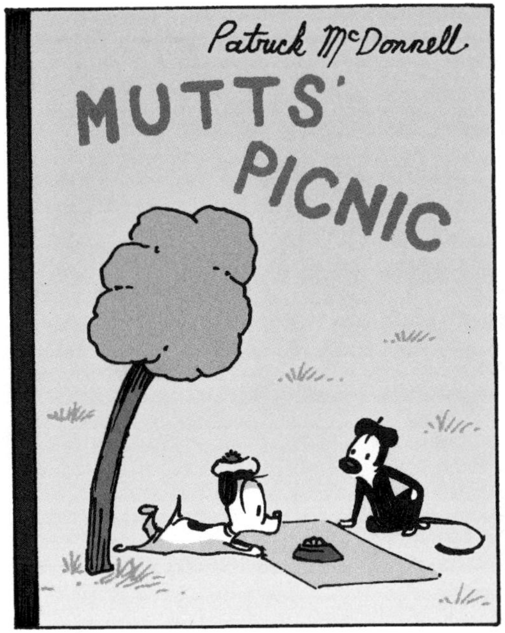
Patrick McDonnell
MUTTS' PICNIC

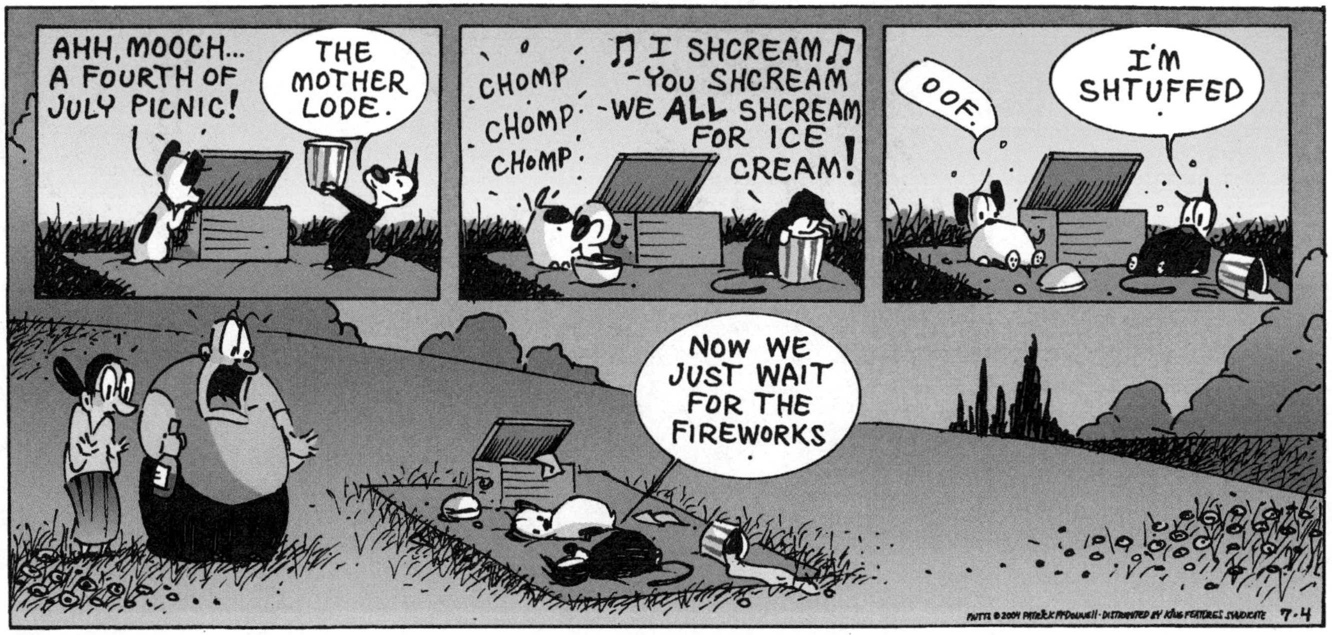
AHH, MOOCH... A FOURTH OF JULY PICNIC!
THE MOTHER LODE.
CHOMP CHOMP CHOMP
♫ I SHCREAM ♫ -YOU SHCREAM -WE ALL SHCREAM FOR ICE CREAM!
OOF.
I'M SHTUFFED
NOW WE JUST WAIT FOR THE FIREWORKS
MUTTS © 2004 PATRICK McDONNELL · DISTRIBUTED BY KING FEATURES SYNDICATE
7-4

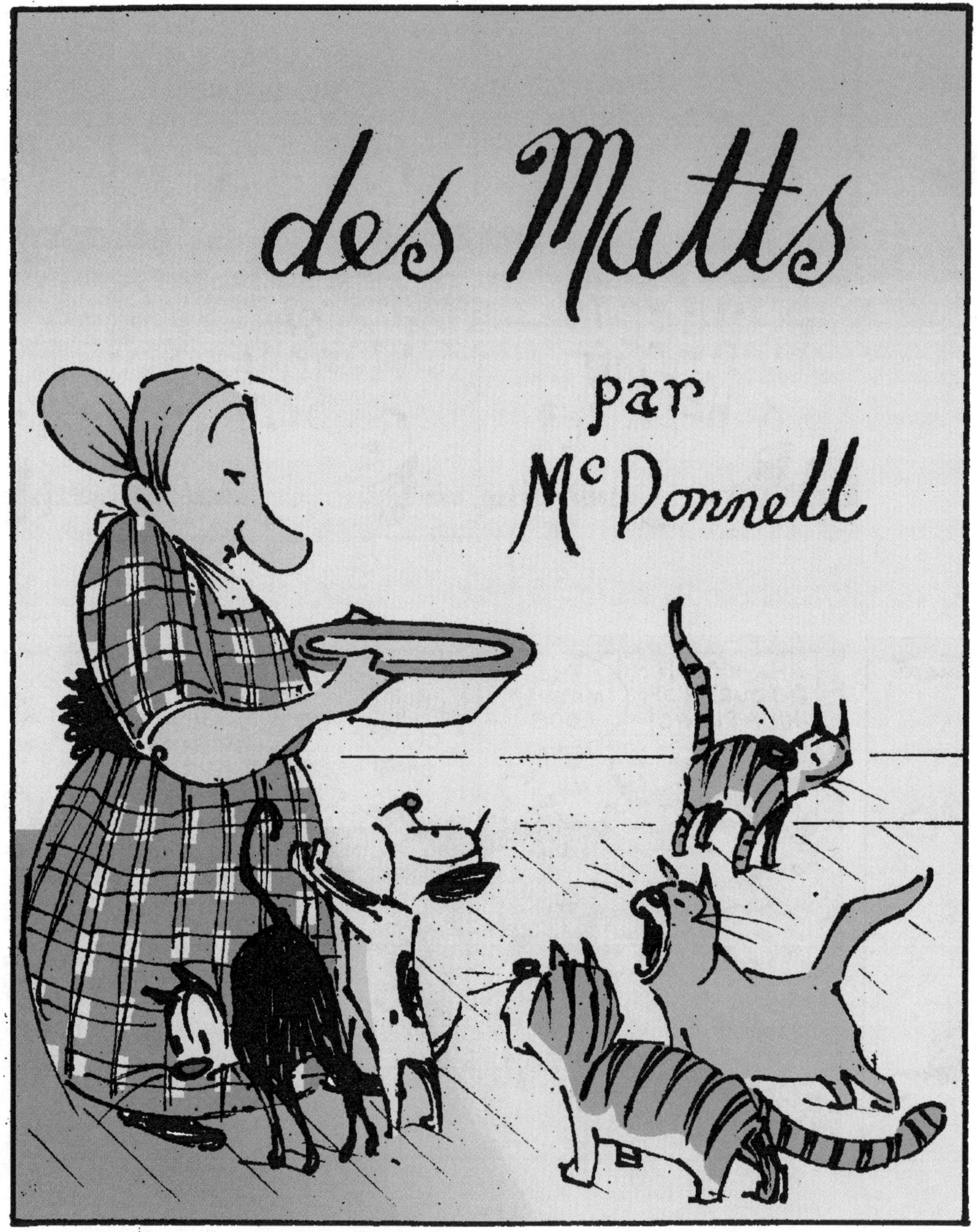
des Mutts
par
McDonnell

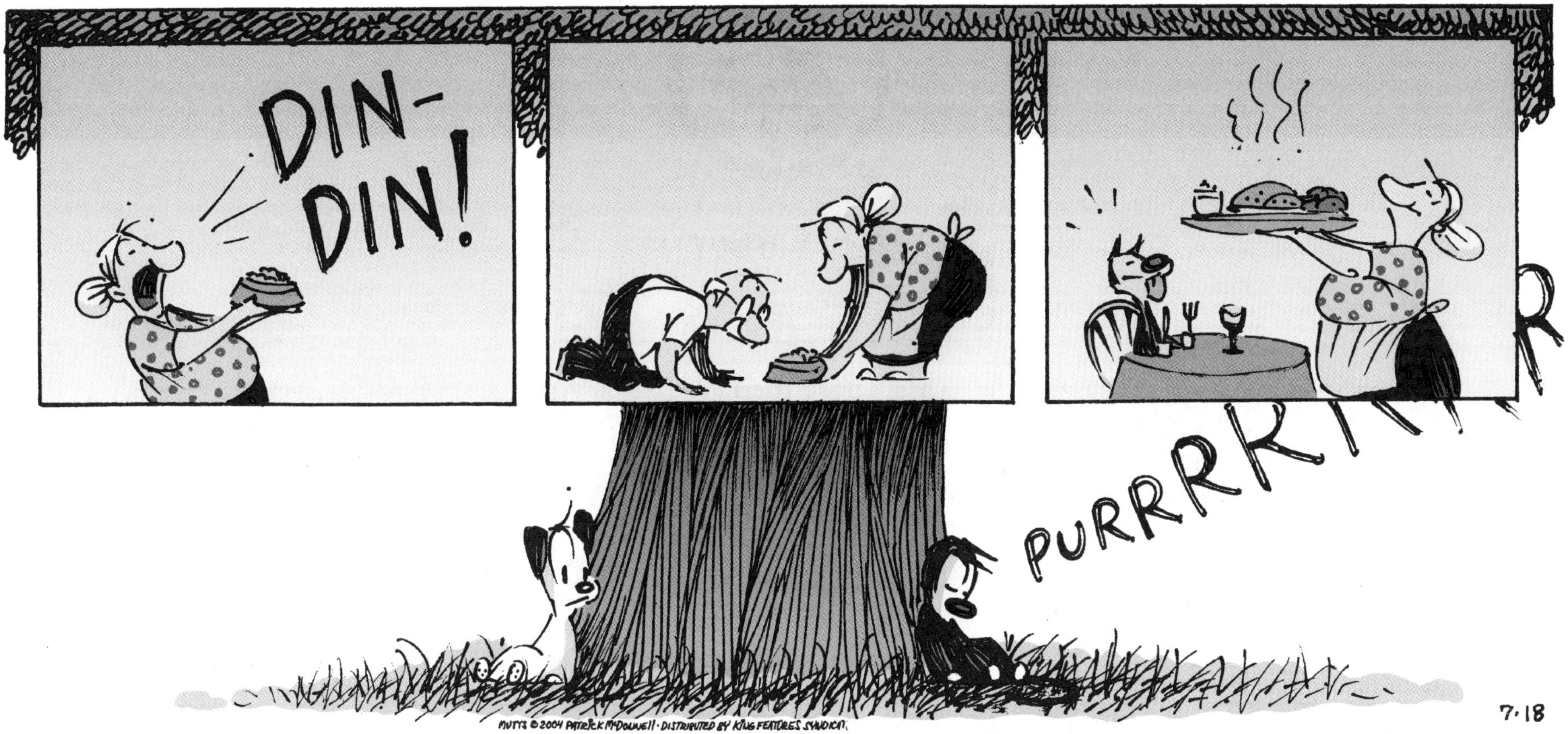
DIN-
DIN!
PURRRRRRRRR!
MUTTS © 2004 PATRICK McDONNELL · DISTRIBUTED BY KING FEATURES SYNDICATE
7·18

MUTTS
PATRICK McDONNELL

ACK! THE SUN IS TOO HOT!!! PHOOEY!
MUTTS © 2004 PATRICK McDONNELL · DISTRIBUTED BY KING FEATURES SYNDICATE
THE SAND IS ALL OVER AND THE OCEAN'S NOT BLUE ENOUGH! FAA!
AND THE PAPAYA AT BRUNCH WAS MUSHY! AUGH!
BLAH BLAH BLAH
KING CRAB
YOUR HIGHNESS!
YES?
I HAVE FOUND YOUR QUEEN.
7·11

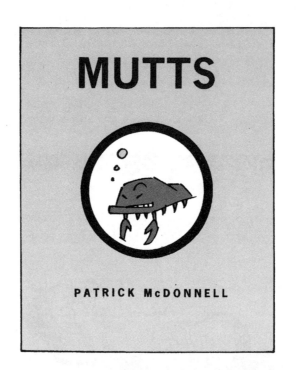

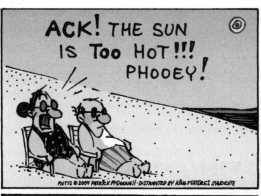

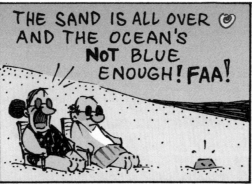

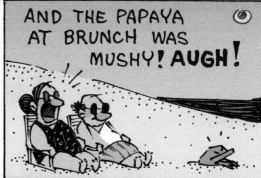

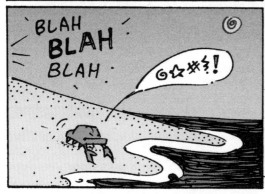

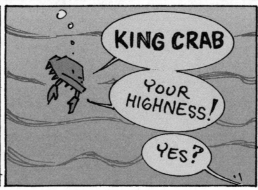

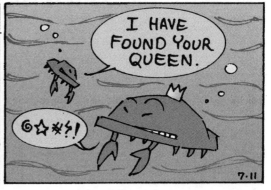

MUTTS
by
•PATRICK McDONNELL•
I TOLD YOU THE WATER'S TOO COLD.
7·25 MUTTS © 2004 PATRICK McDONNELL · DISTRIBUTED BY KING FEATURES SYNDICATE

MUTTS
STRANGE TALES.

I WAS IN STRANGE WATERS THIS WEEKEND, FELLAS.
IT WAS LIKE ANOTHER DIMENSION. ...UP WAS DOWN, DOWN WAS UP, NOTHING MADE SENSE...
ARG!
I FELT A HAZE COME OVER ME... TIME STOOD ABSOLUTELY @☆#$! STILL...
I WAS ADRIFT IN LIMBO— WITH NO WAY OUT...
OH, MY—YOU WERE STUCK AT THE BERMUDA TRIANGLE!?!
NO—
THE IN-LAWS'!
CRABBY!
MUTTS © 2004 PATRICK McDONNELL
DISTRIBUTED BY KING FEATURES SYNDICATE
8·1

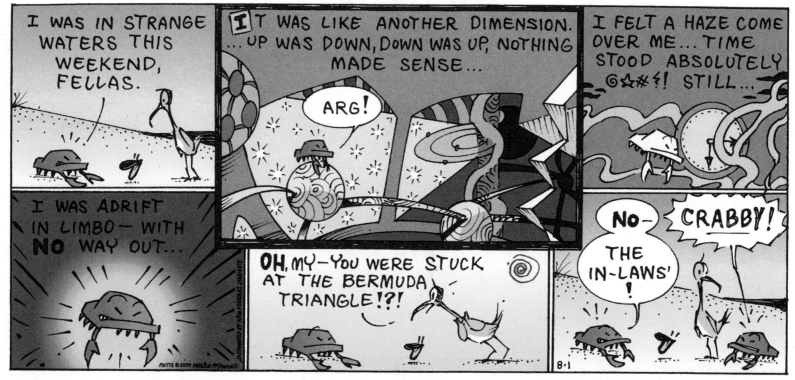

MUTTS
by
·PATRICK McDONNELL·
HEY! YOU'RE BLOCKING THE VIEW!
8·8

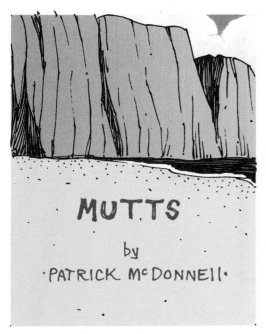

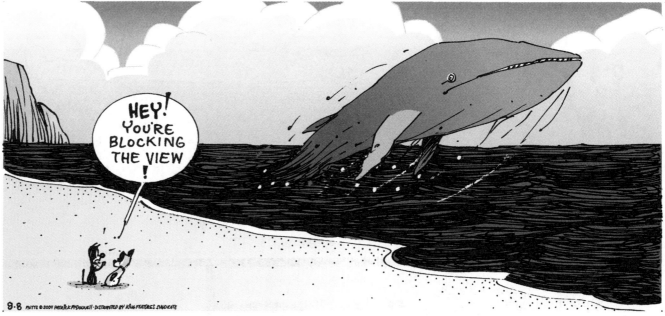

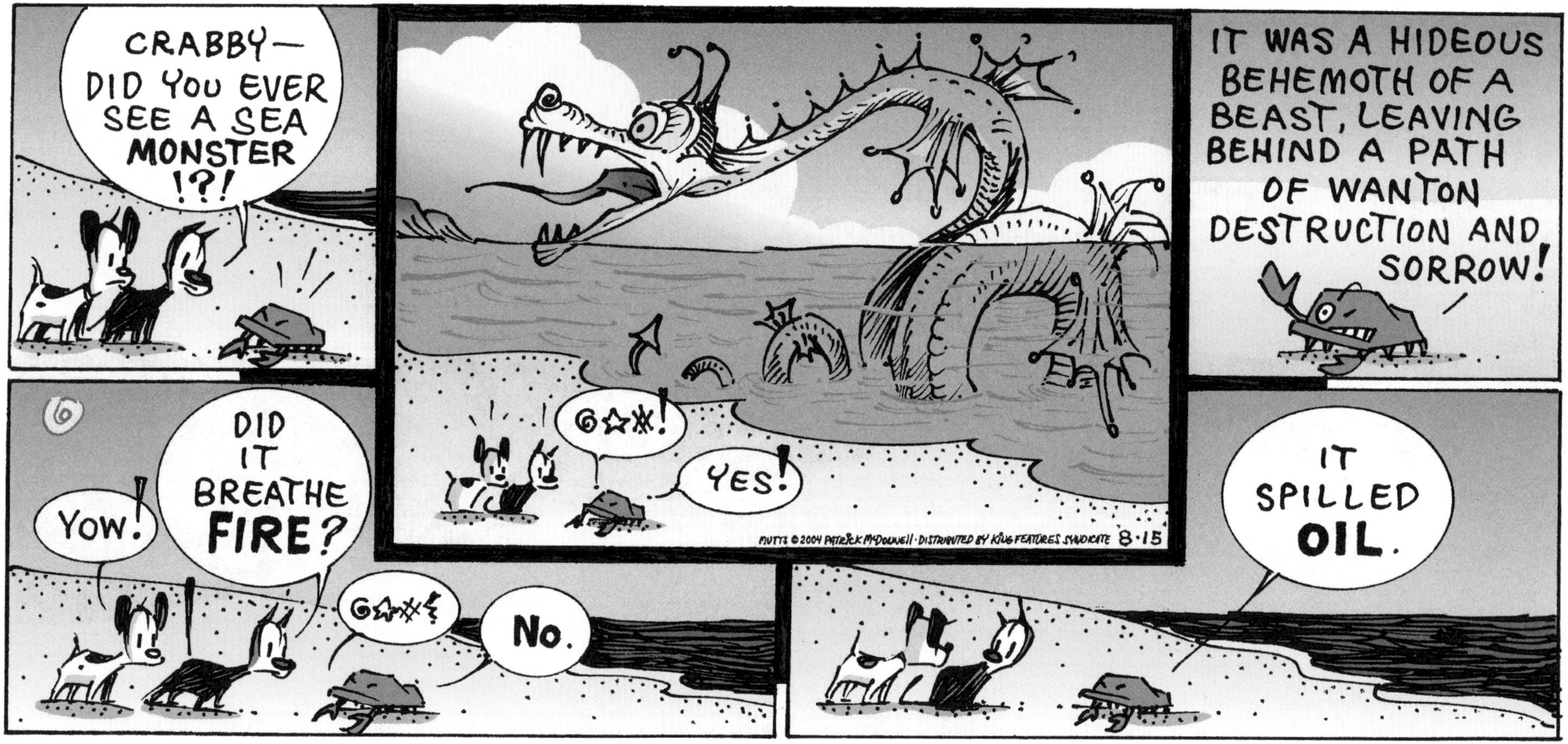
CRABBY— DID YOU EVER SEE A SEA MONSTER !?!
YES!
IT WAS A HIDEOUS BEHEMOTH OF A BEAST, LEAVING BEHIND A PATH OF WANTON DESTRUCTION AND SORROW!
YOW!
DID IT BREATHE FIRE?
No.
IT SPILLED OIL.
MUTTS © 2004 PATRICK McDONNELL · DISTRIBUTED BY KING FEATURES SYNDICATE 8·15

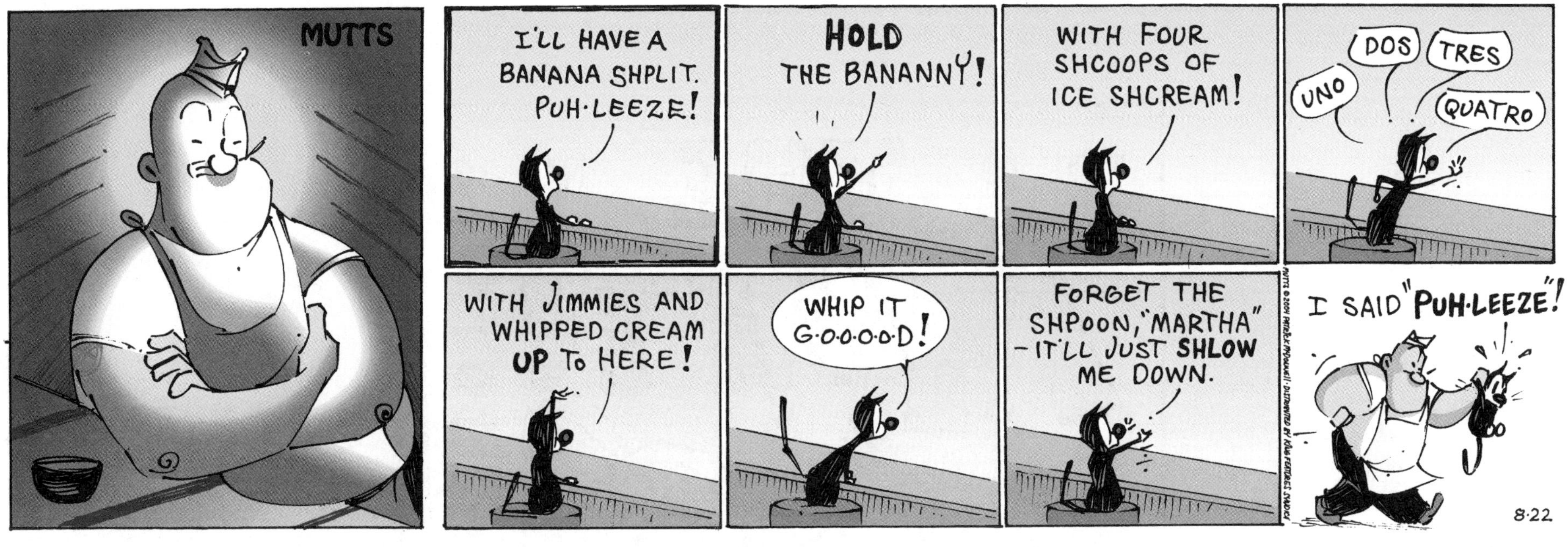
MUTTS
I'LL HAVE A BANANA SHPLIT. PUH·LEEZE!
HOLD THE BANANNY!
WITH FOUR SHCOOPS OF ICE SHCREAM!
UNO
DOS
TRES
QUATRO
WITH JIMMIES AND WHIPPED CREAM UP TO HERE!
WHIP IT G·O·O·O·O·D!
FORGET THE SHPOON, "MARTHA" - IT'LL JUST SHLOW ME DOWN.
I SAID "PUH·LEEZE"!
8·22

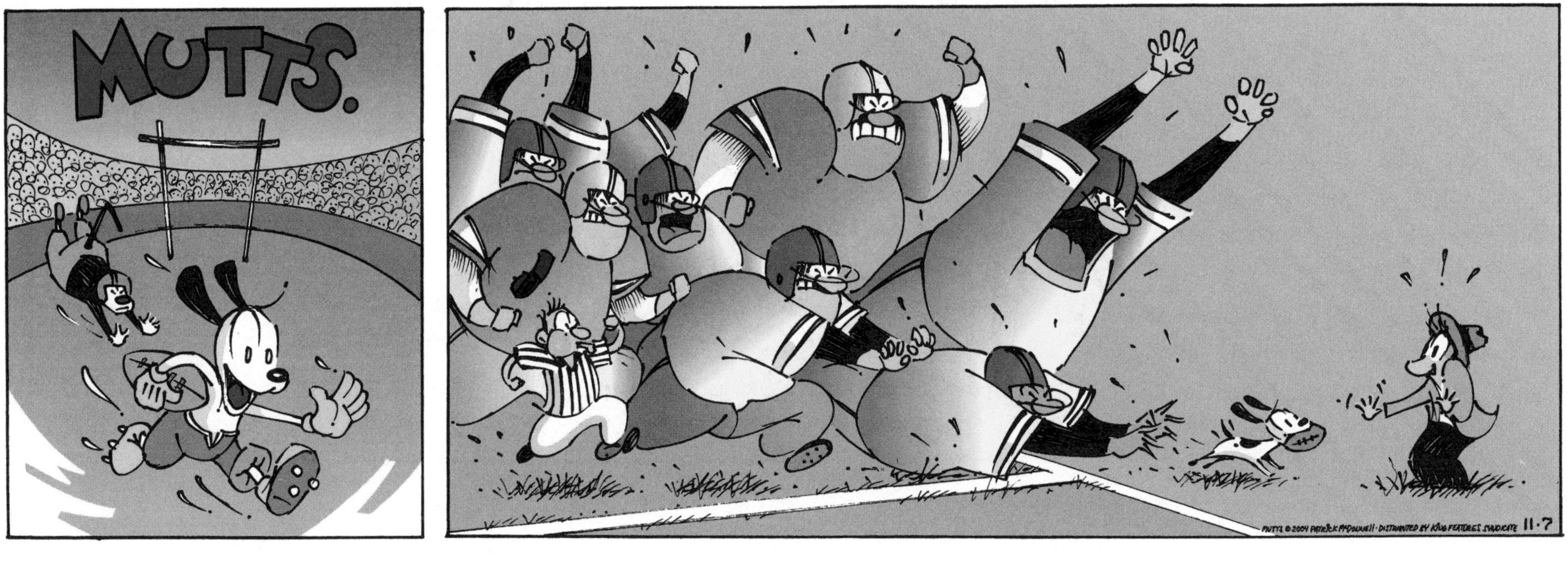
MUTTS.
MUTTS © 2004 PATRICK McDONNELL · DISTRIBUTED BY KING FEATURES SYNDICATE 11·7

VOL 10
THE MUTTS.
NO. 35
SAY IF YOU SEE IT IN MUTTS IT GOES SEE

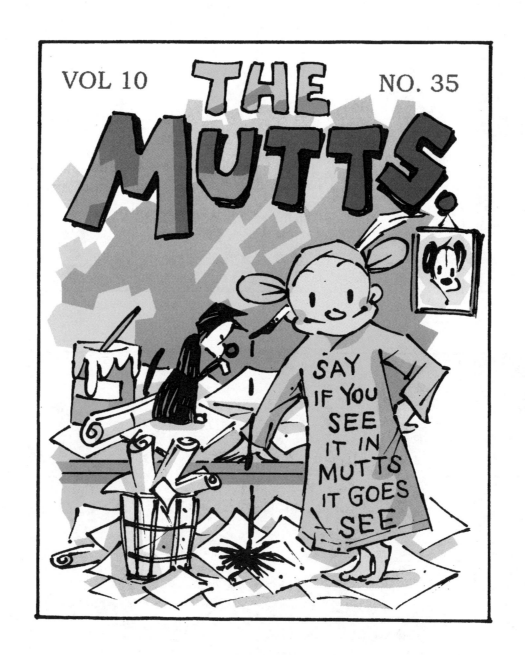

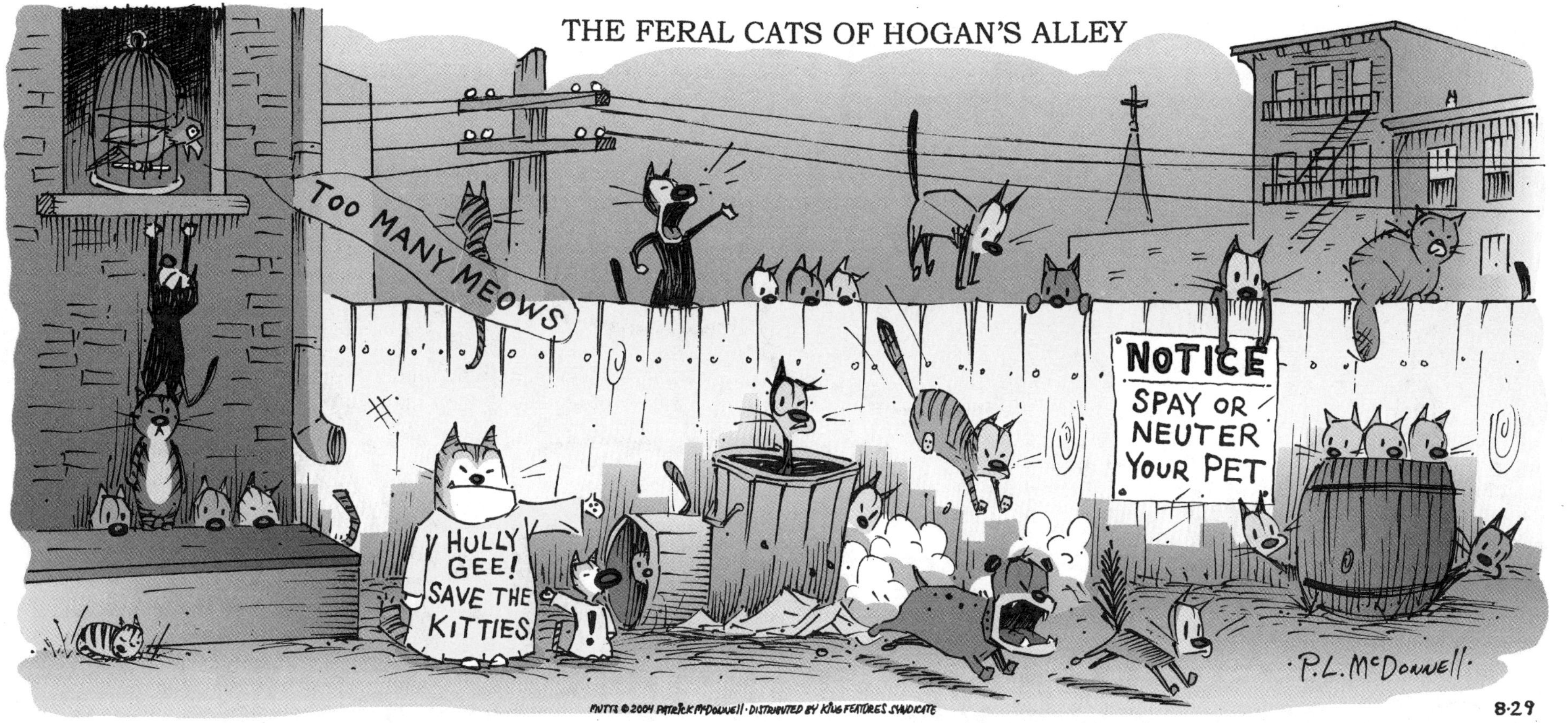
THE FERAL CATS OF HOGAN'S ALLEY
TOO MANY MEOWS
NOTICE
SPAY OR NEUTER YOUR PET
HULLY GEE! SAVE THE KITTIES
!
P.L. McDONNELL
MUTTS © 2004 PATRICK McDONNELL · DISTRIBUTED BY KING FEATURES SYNDICATE
8·29

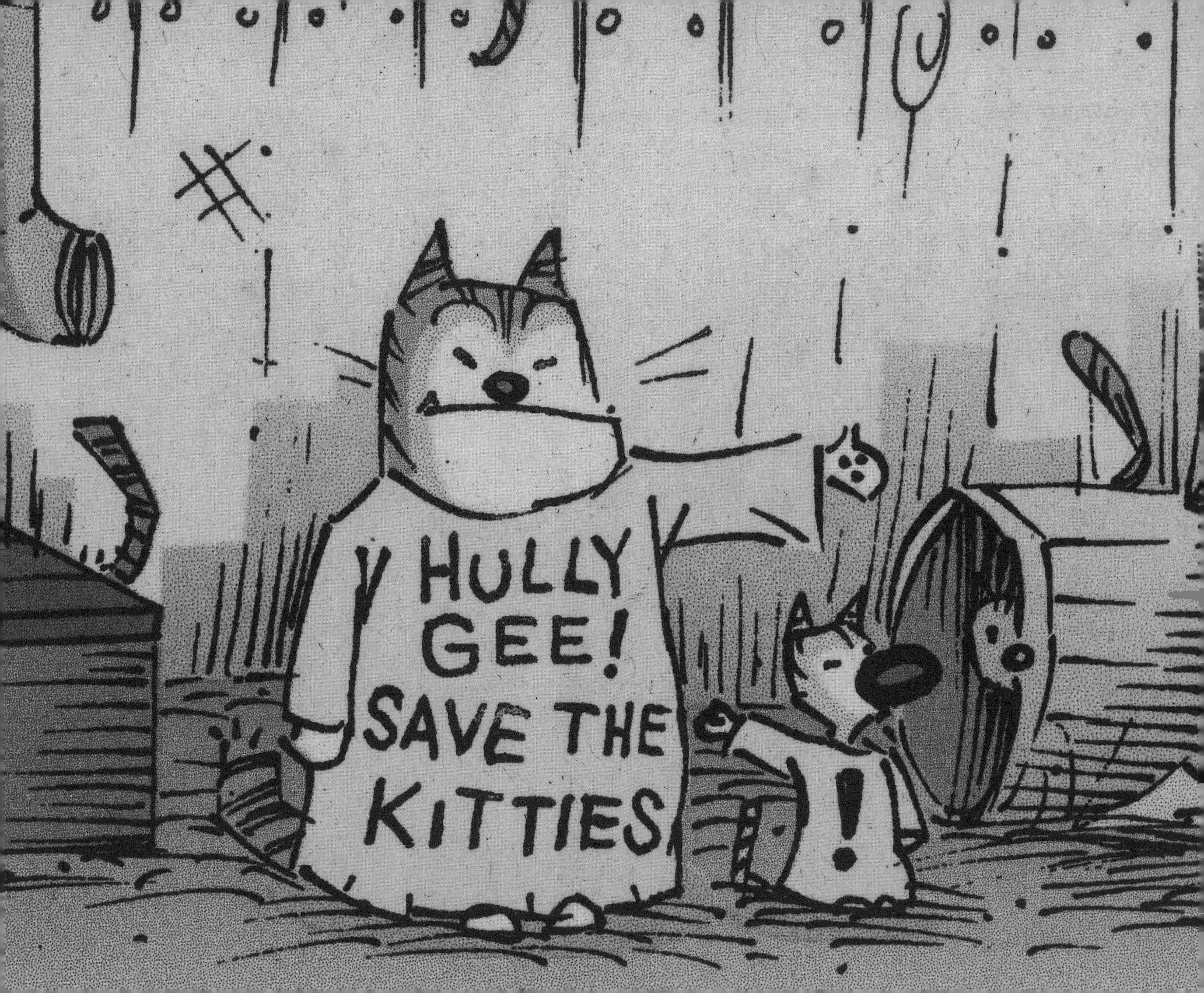
HULLY GEE! SAVE THE KITTIES

MUTTS.
by PATRICK McDONNELL
THE 400th TREAT
THE 2,500th WALK
THE 5,000th THROW
THE 8,000th BELLYRUB
THE 1,000,000th KISS
HAPPY ANNIVERSARY
94-04
9/5
MUTTS © 2004 PATRICK McDONNELL · DISTRIBUTED BY KING FEATURES SYNDICATE

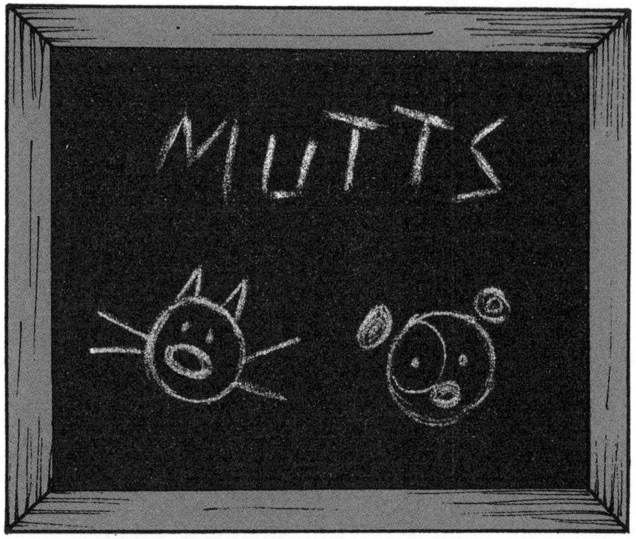
MUTTS

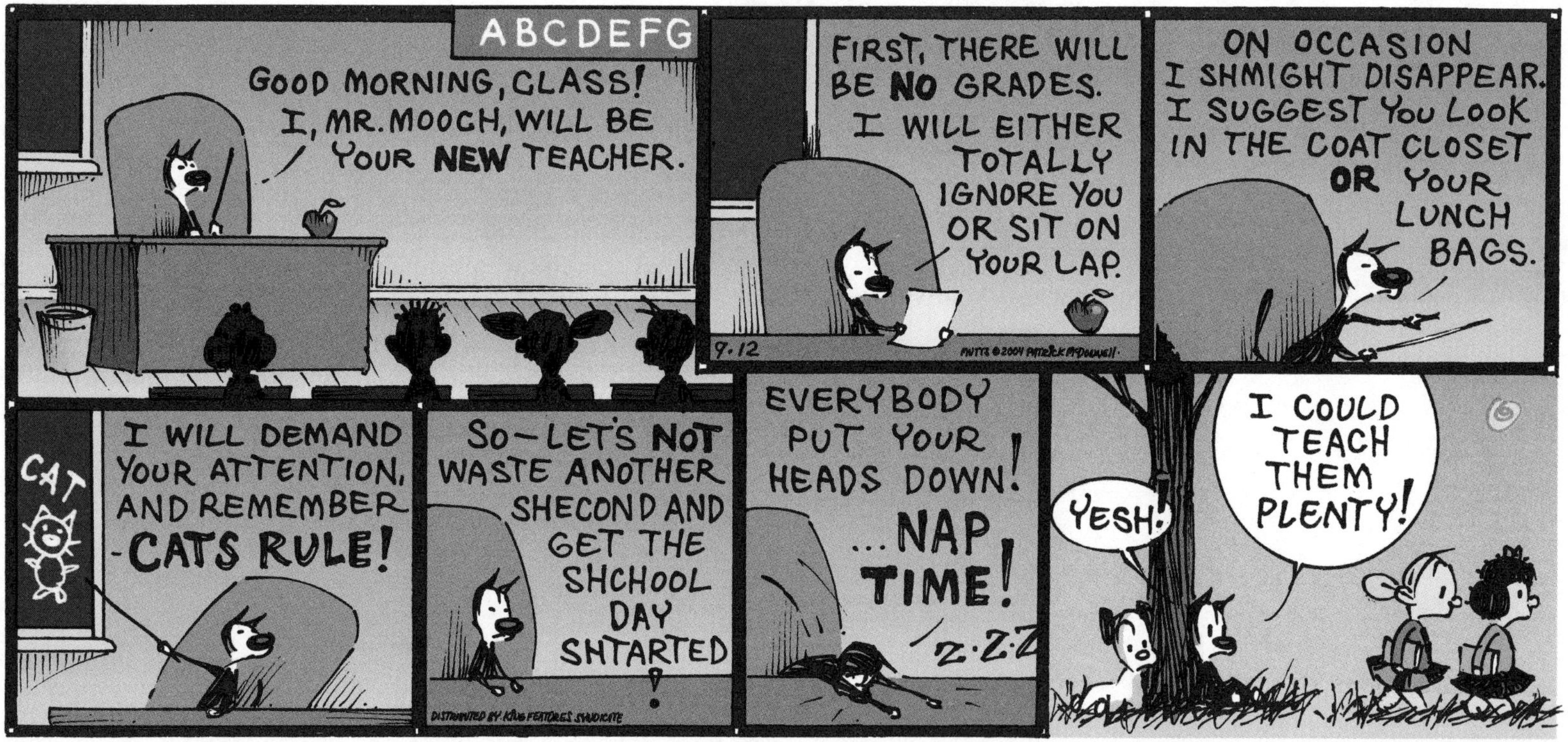
ABCDEFG
GOOD MORNING, CLASS! I, MR. MOOCH, WILL BE YOUR NEW TEACHER.
FIRST, THERE WILL BE NO GRADES.
I WILL EITHER TOTALLY IGNORE YOU OR SIT ON YOUR LAP.
9.12
ON OCCASION I SHMIGHT DISAPPEAR. I SUGGEST YOU LOOK IN THE COAT CLOSET OR YOUR LUNCH BAGS.
CAT
I WILL DEMAND YOUR ATTENTION, AND REMEMBER -CATS RULE!
SO— LET'S NOT WASTE ANOTHER SHECOND AND GET THE SHCHOOL DAY SHTARTED!
DISTRIBUTED BY KING FEATURES SYNDICATE
EVERYBODY PUT YOUR HEADS DOWN!
...NAP TIME!
Z·Z·Z
YESH!
I COULD TEACH THEM PLENTY!

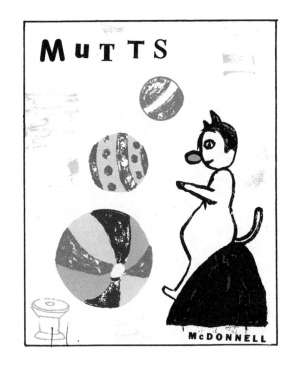

MUTTS
McDONNELL

C'MON KITTY
LET'S PLAY.
FWIP FWIP
FWIP
FWIP FWIP
FWIP
FWISH FWISH
FWISH
FWOP
OH... I GIVE UP!
I WIN!
MUTTS © 2004 PATRICK McDONNELL · DISTRIBUTED BY KING FEATURES SYNDICATE
9·19

MUTTS

TREE CLIMBING TIME...
BUT WHY, MOOCH, WHY?
WHY...
...BECAUSE IT'S THERE!
WHAT DOES THAT MEAN!?!
MUTTS © 2004 PATRICK McDONNELL · DISTRIBUTED BY KING FEATURES SYNDICATE
9.26

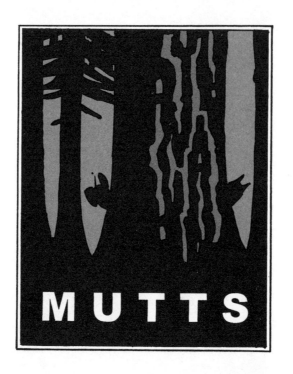

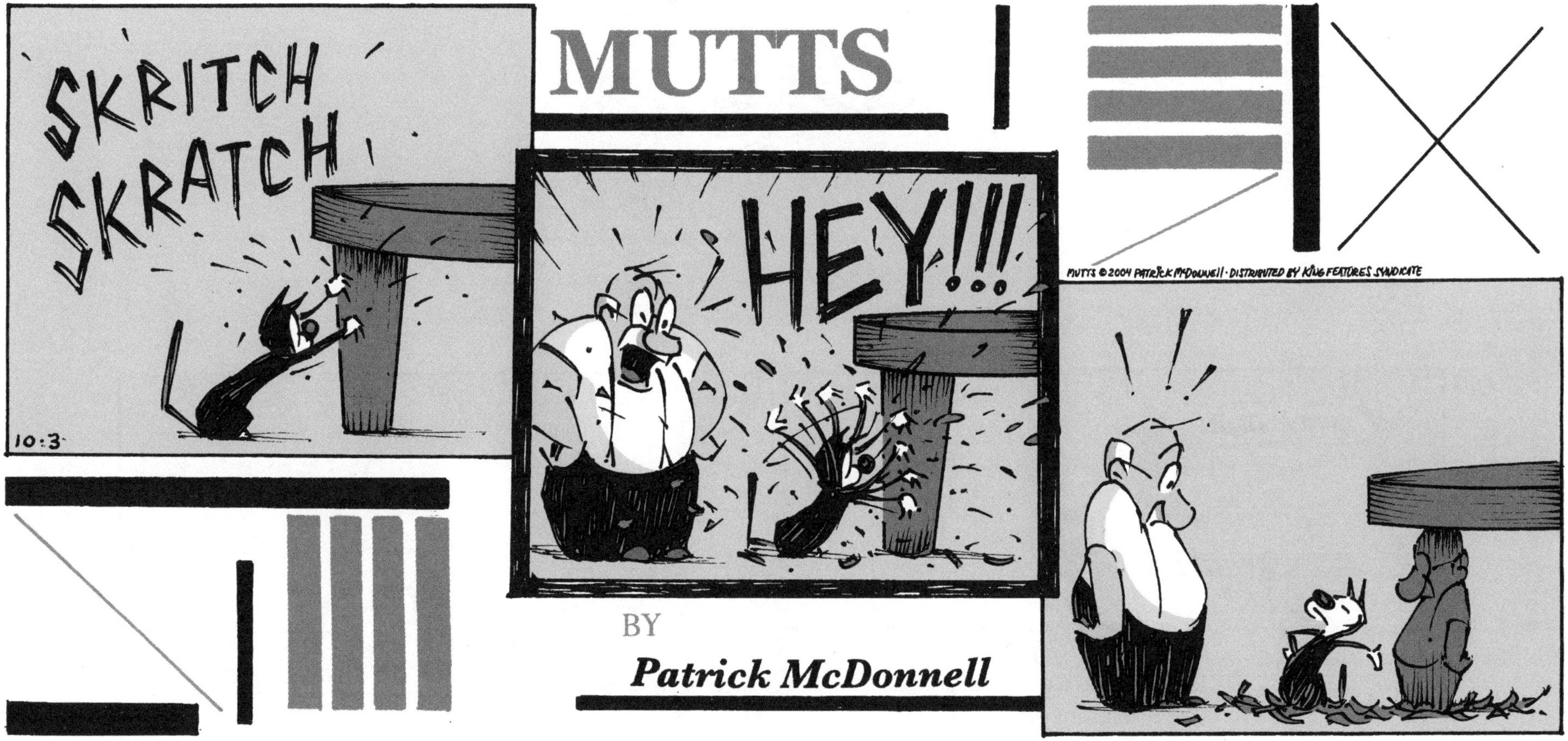
MUTTS
BY
Patrick McDonnell
SKRITCH
SKRATCH
10-3
HEY!!!
MUTTS © 2004 PATRICK McDONNELL · DISTRIBUTED BY KING FEATURES SYNDICATE

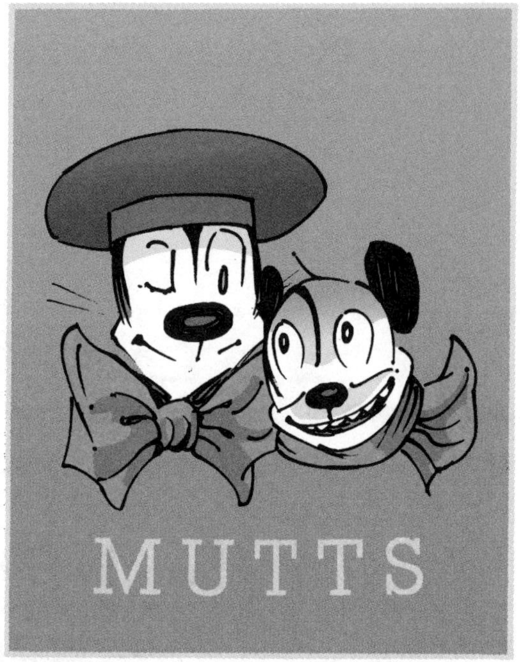
MUTTS

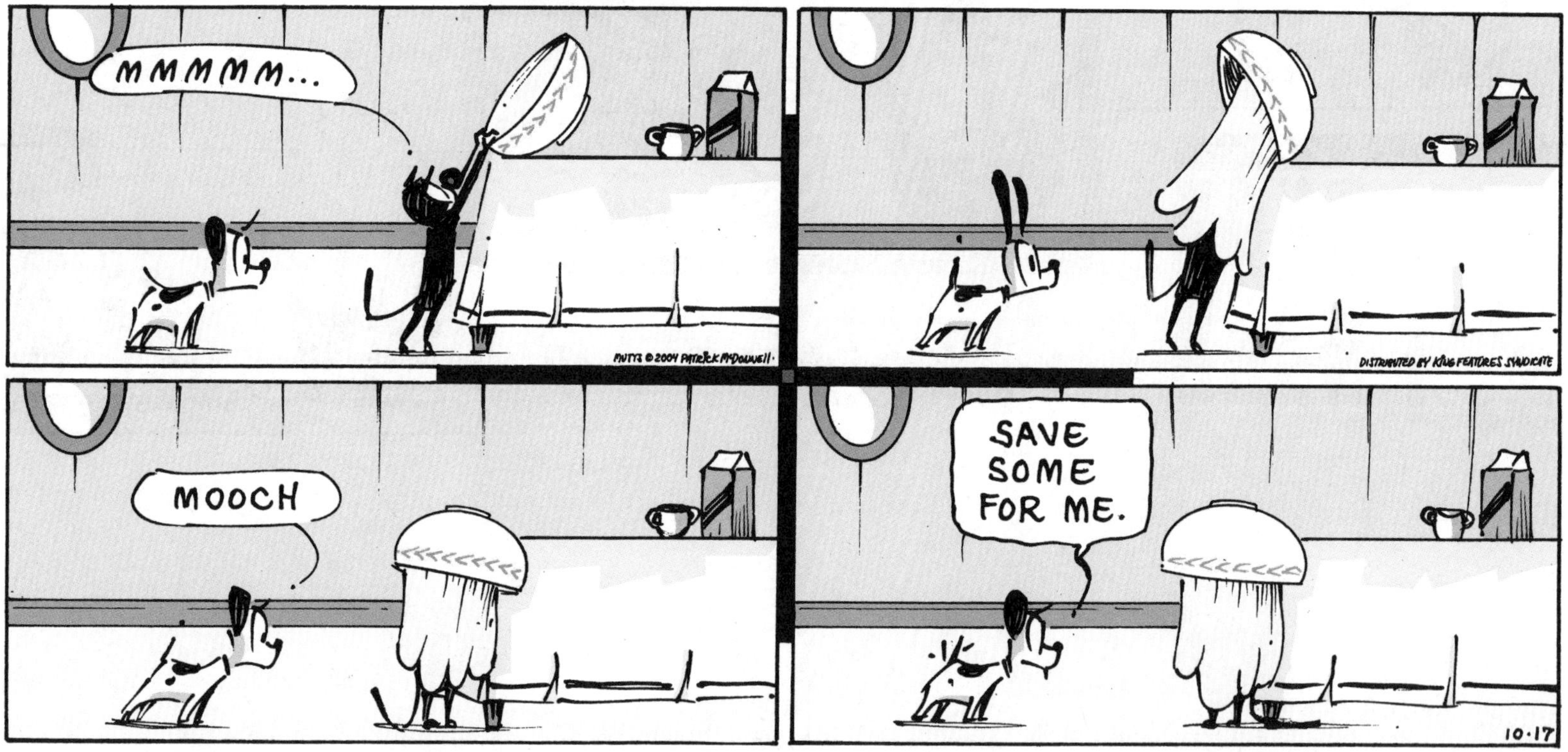
MMMMM...
MUTTS © 2004 PATRICK McDONNELL
DISTRIBUTED BY KING FEATURES SYNDICATE
MOOCH
SAVE SOME FOR ME.
10·17

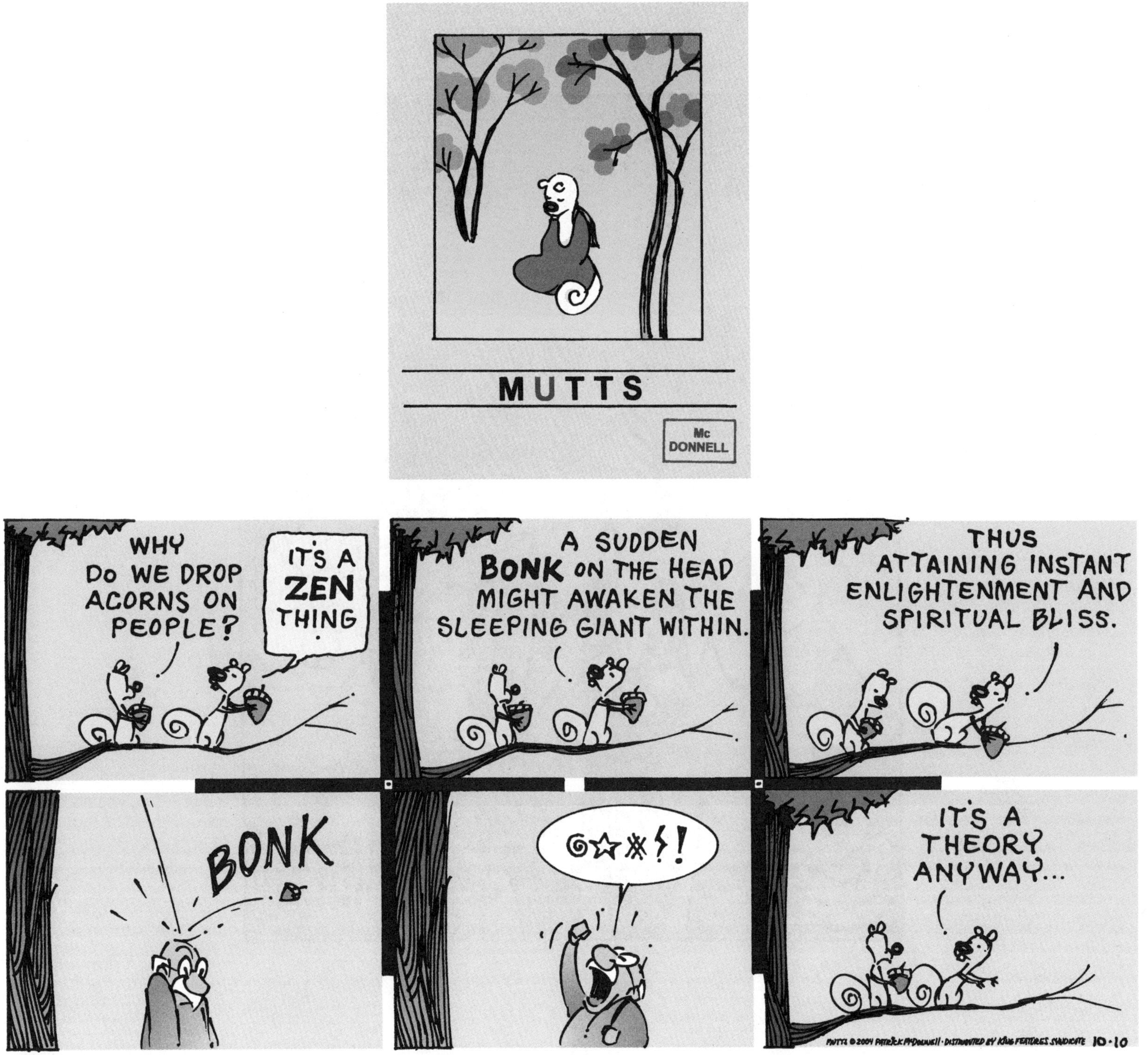
MUTTS
Mc DONNELL
WHY DO WE DROP ACORNS ON PEOPLE?
IT'S A ZEN THING.
A SUDDEN BONK ON THE HEAD MIGHT AWAKEN THE SLEEPING GIANT WITHIN.
THUS ATTAINING INSTANT ENLIGHTENMENT AND SPIRITUAL BLISS.
BONK
@☆#⚡!
IT'S A THEORY ANYWAY...
MUTTS © 2004 PATRICK McDONNELL · DISTRIBUTED BY KING FEATURES SYNDICATE 10·10

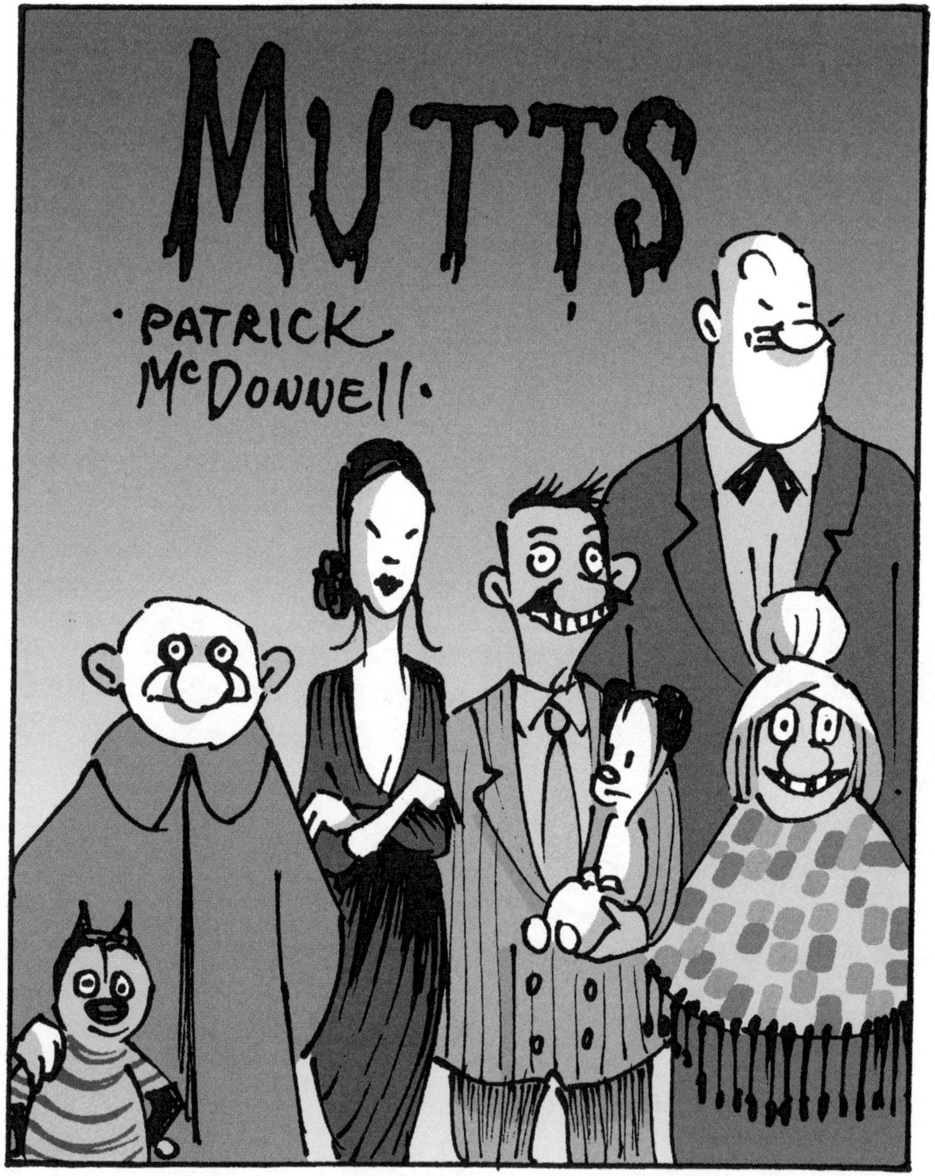
MUTTS
·PATRICK McDONNELL·

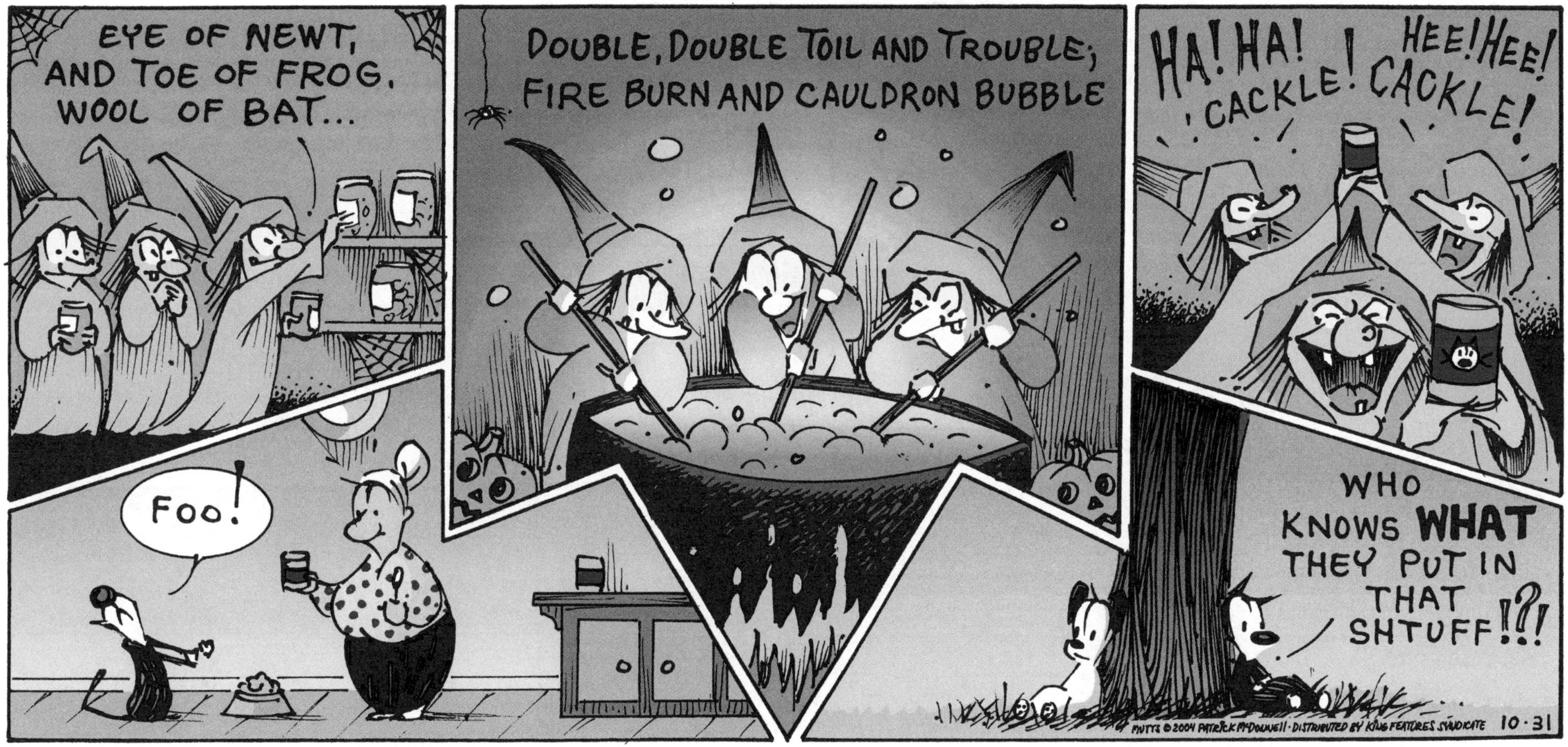
EYE OF NEWT, AND TOE OF FROG, WOOL OF BAT...
FOO!
DOUBLE, DOUBLE TOIL AND TROUBLE; FIRE BURN AND CAULDRON BUBBLE
HA! HA!
HEE! HEE!
CACKLE! CACKLE!
WHO KNOWS **WHAT** THEY PUT IN THAT SHTUFF!?!
MUTTS © 2004 PATRICK McDONNELL · DISTRIBUTED BY KING FEATURES SYNDICATE
10·31

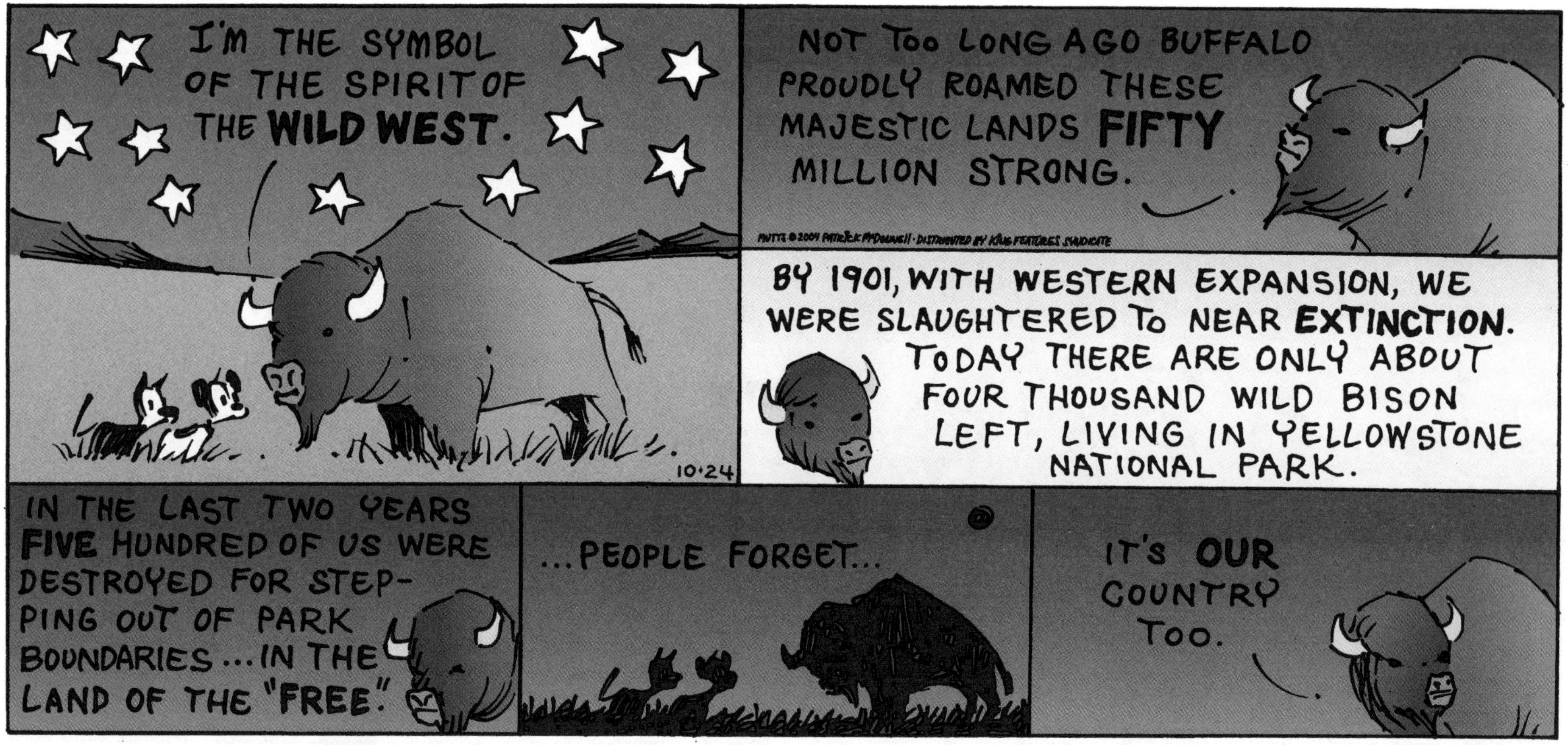
I'M THE SYMBOL OF THE SPIRIT OF THE **WILD WEST**.
10·24
NOT TOO LONG AGO BUFFALO PROUDLY ROAMED THESE MAJESTIC LANDS **FIFTY** MILLION STRONG.
MUTTS © 2004 PATRICK McDONNELL · DISTRIBUTED BY KING FEATURES SYNDICATE
BY 1901, WITH WESTERN EXPANSION, WE WERE SLAUGHTERED TO NEAR **EXTINCTION**.
TODAY THERE ARE ONLY ABOUT FOUR THOUSAND WILD BISON LEFT, LIVING IN YELLOWSTONE NATIONAL PARK.
IN THE LAST TWO YEARS **FIVE** HUNDRED OF US WERE DESTROYED FOR STEPPING OUT OF PARK BOUNDARIES ... IN THE LAND OF THE "**FREE**."
... PEOPLE FORGET...
IT'S **OUR** COUNTRY TOO.

MOOCH DU MUTTS
PATRICK McDONNELL

SLAM
CHEZ CHAZ
WE FORGOT TO FEED THE KITTY.
MUTTS © 2004 PATRICK McDONNELL
DISTRIBUTED BY KING FEATURES SYNDICATE
11.14

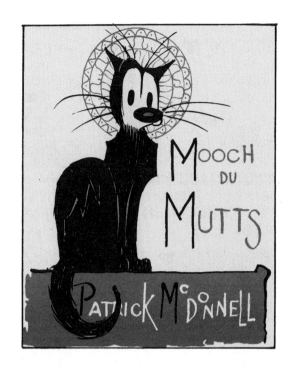

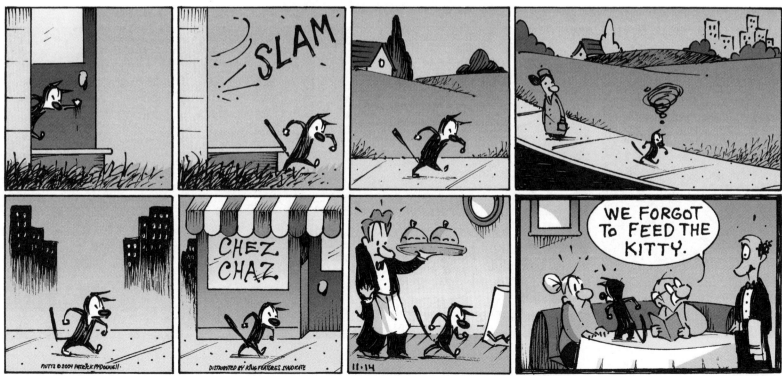

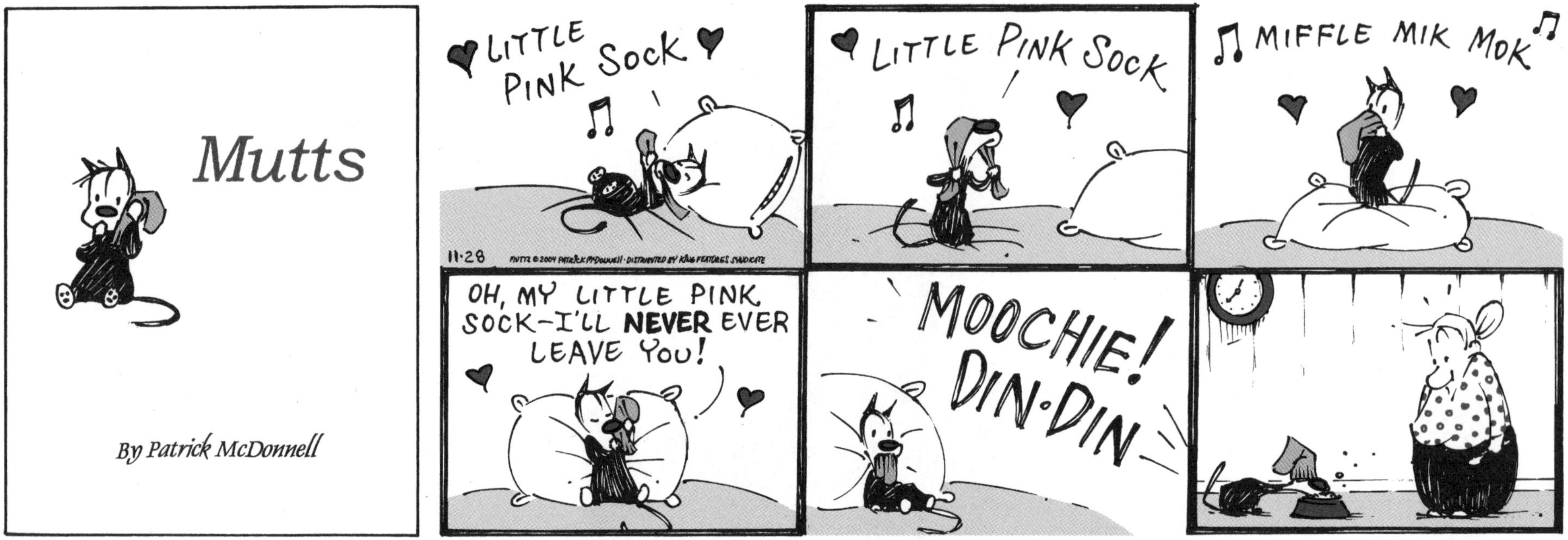
Mutts
By Patrick McDonnell
LITTLE PINK SOCK
11·28
LITTLE PINK SOCK
MIFFLE MIK MOK
OH, MY LITTLE PINK SOCK—I'LL **NEVER** EVER LEAVE YOU!
MOOCHIE! DIN·DIN

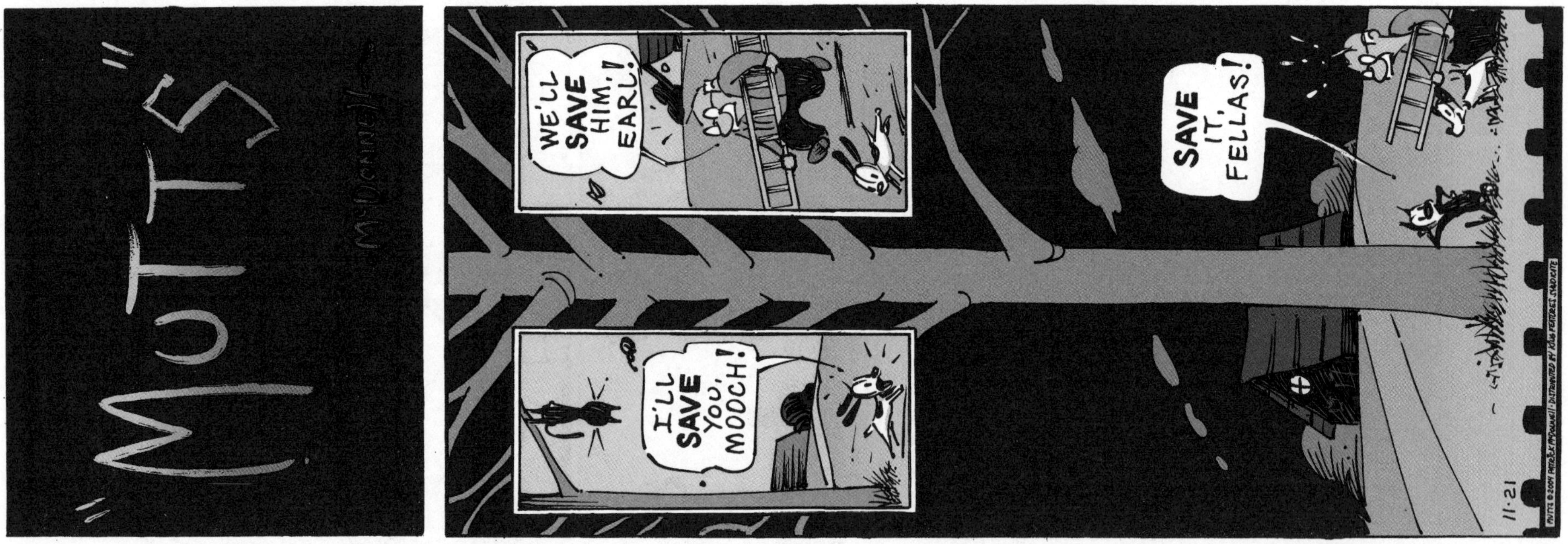
"MUTTS"
McDonnell
WE'LL **SAVE** HIM, EARL!
I'LL **SAVE** YOU, MOOCH!
SAVE IT, FELLAS!
11·21

Mutts
Patrick McDonnell

12·12
WELCOME!
MUTTS © 2004 PATRICK McDONNELL · DISTRIBUTED BY KING FEATURES SYNDICATE

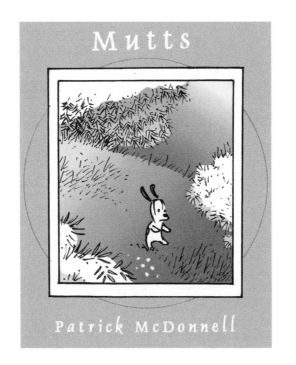

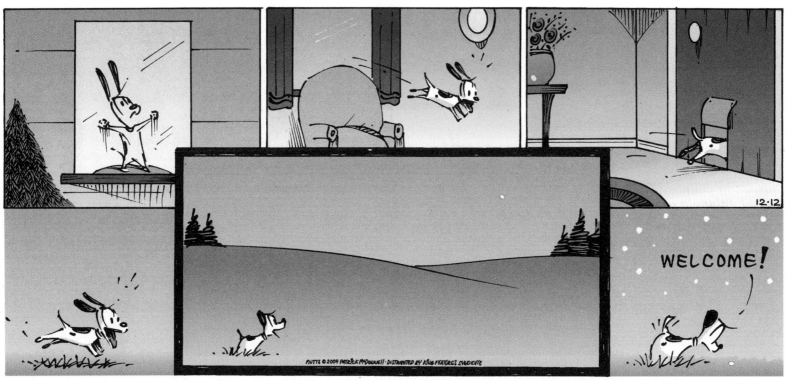

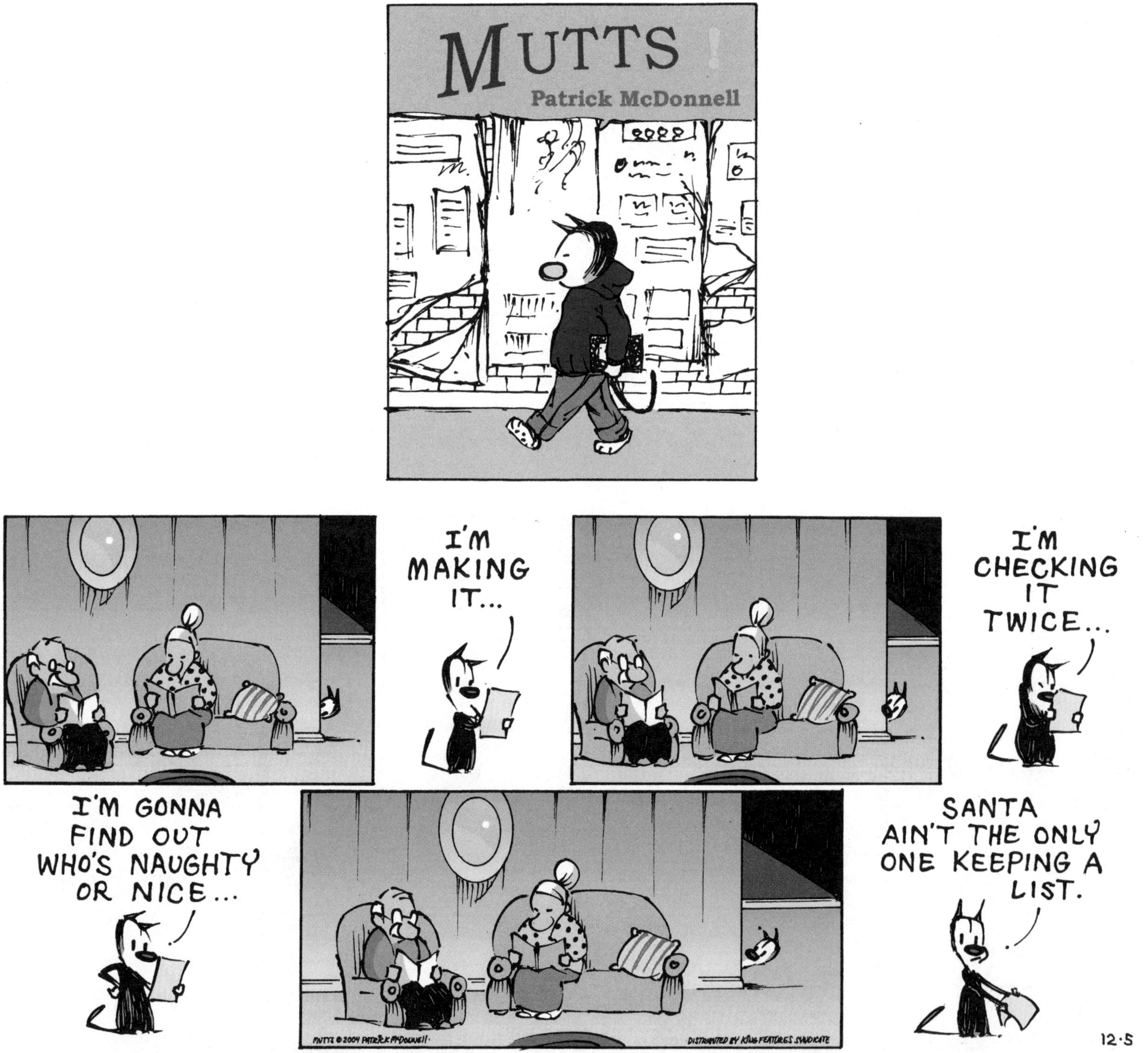
MUTTS
Patrick McDonnell
I'M MAKING IT...
I'M CHECKING IT TWICE...
I'M GONNA FIND OUT WHO'S NAUGHTY OR NICE...
SANTA AIN'T THE ONLY ONE KEEPING A LIST.
MUTTS © 2004 PATRICK McDONNELL
DISTRIBUTED BY KING FEATURES SYNDICATE
12·5

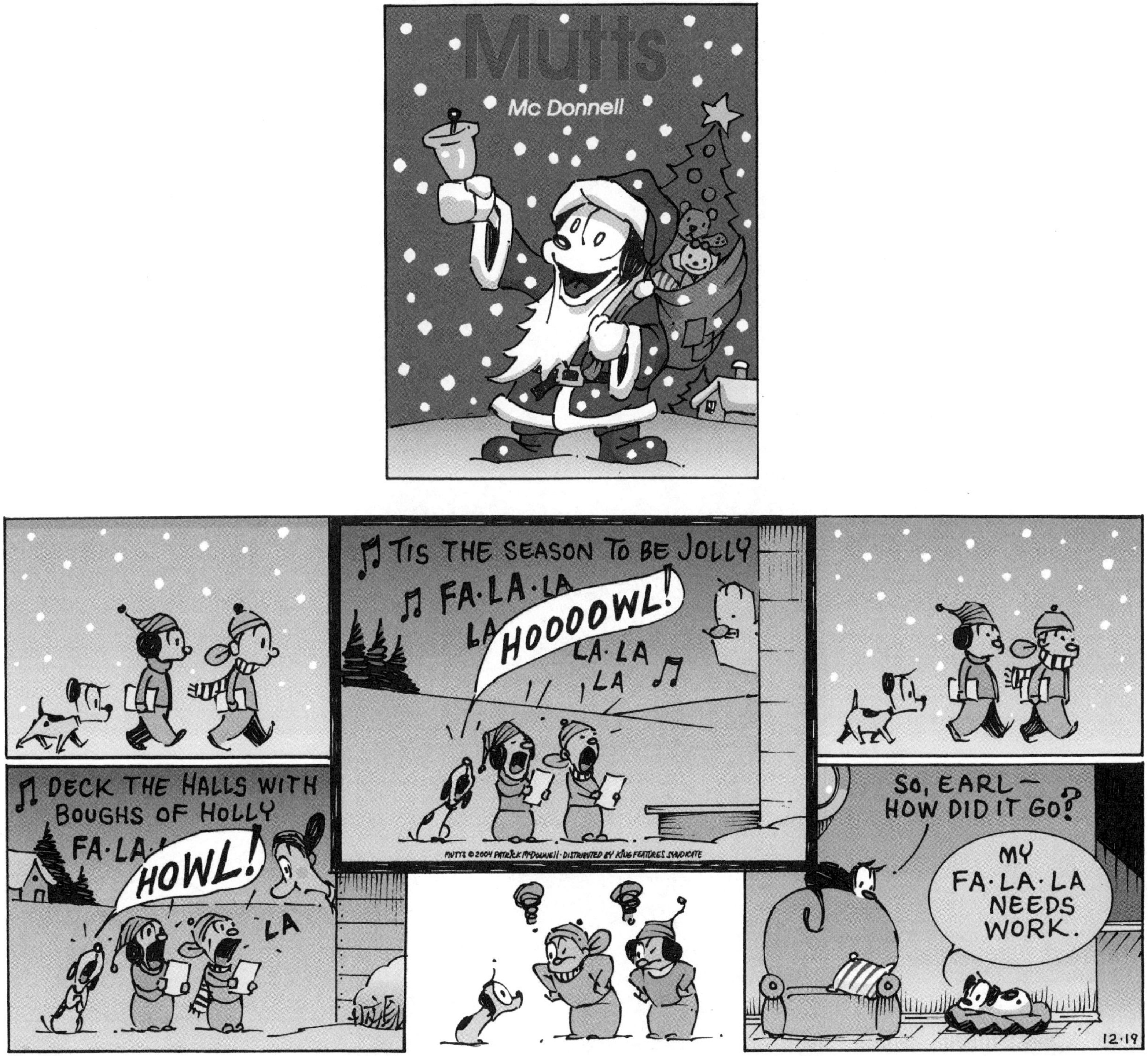
Mutts
Mc Donnell
♫ DECK THE HALLS WITH BOUGHS OF HOLLY
FA·LA·
HOWL!
LA
♫ TIS THE SEASON TO BE JOLLY
♫ FA·LA·LA
LA
HOOOOWL!
LA·LA
LA ♫
MUTTS © 2004 PATRICK McDONNELL · DISTRIBUTED BY KING FEATURES SYNDICATE
SO, EARL— HOW DID IT GO?
MY FA·LA·LA NEEDS WORK.
12·19

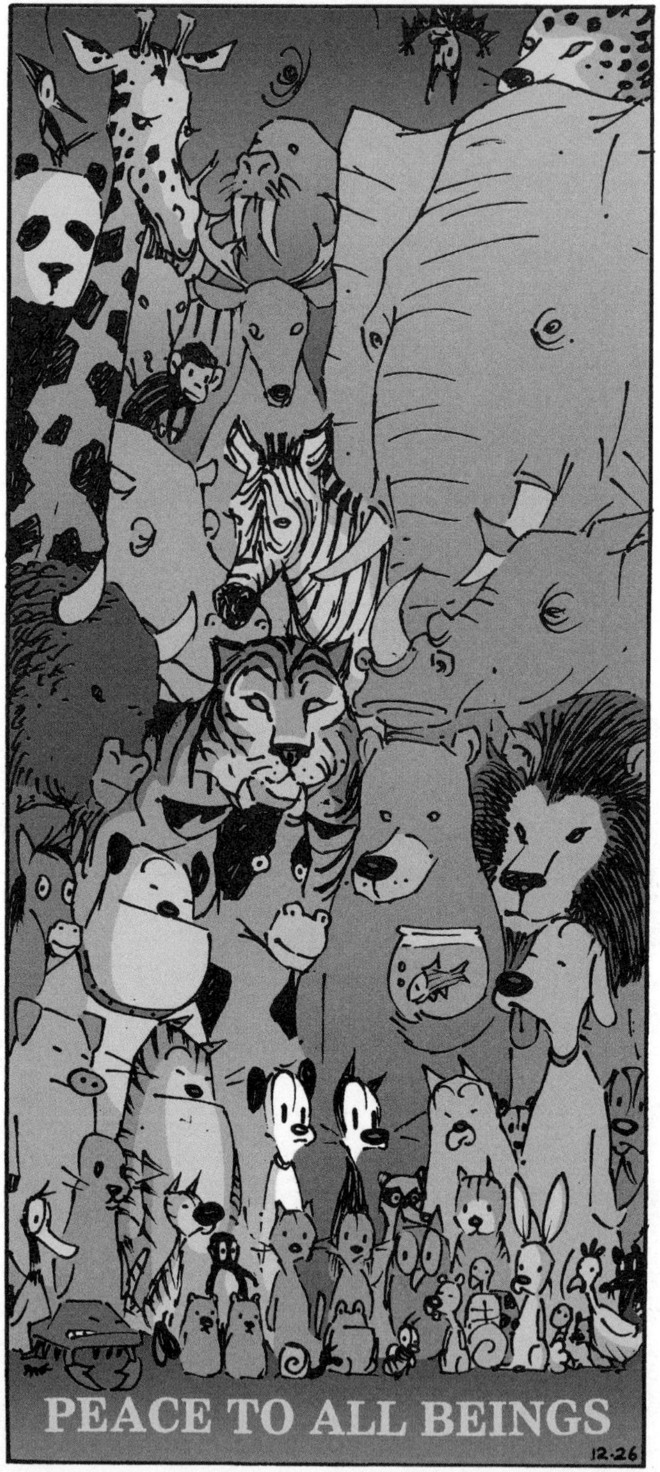
PEACE TO ALL BEINGS
12-26